D1083056

From Market-Places
to a
Market Economy

Winifred Barr Rothenberg

From Market-Places to a Market Economy

The Transformation of Rural Massachusetts, 1750–1850

The University of Chicago Press
Chicago and London

WINIFRED BARR ROTHENBERG is assistant professor of economics at Tufts University.

The University of Chicago Press, Chicago 60637
The University of Chicago Press, Ltd., London
© 1992 by The University of Chicago
All rights reserved. Published 1992
Printed in the United States of America

01 00 99 98 97 96 95 94 93 92   1 2 3 4 5 6

ISBN (cloth): 0-226-72953-2

Earlier versions of some chapters have been previously published—ch. 4: "The Market and Massachusetts Farmers, 1750–1855," in the *Journal of Economic History* (41, no. 2 [1981]: 283–314); ch. 5: "The Emergence of a Capital Market in Rural Massachusetts, 1730–1838," in the *Journal of Economic History* (45, no. 4 [1985]: 781–808); ch. 6: "The Emergence of Farm Labor Markets and the Transformation of the Rural Economy: Massachusetts, 1750–1855," in the *Journal of Economic History* (48, no. 3 [1988]: 537–66); and ch. 7: "Structural Change in the Farm Labor Force: Contract Labor in Massachusetts Agriculture, 1750–1865," in *Strategic Factors in Nineteenth Century American Economic History: A Volume to Honor Robert W. Fogel,* edited by Claudia Goldin and Hugh Rockoff (Chicago: University of Chicago Press, 1992). All are used with permission.
Credits for display illustrations appear on page 265.

Library of Congress Cataloging-in-Publication Data

Rothenberg, Winifred Barr.
    From market-places to a market economy : the transformation of rural Massachusetts, 1750–
    1850 / Winifred Barr Rothenberg.
        p.   cm.
    Includes bibliographical references and index.
    1. Capitalism—Massachusetts—History. 2. Massachusetts—Industries, Rural—History. 3.
    Markets—Massachusetts—History.
    4. Agriculture—Economic aspects—Massachusetts—History.
    I. Title.
    HC107.M4R67   1992
    330.9744′03—dc20   92-13535
                                                                        CIP

⊗The paper used in this publication meets the minimum requirements of the American National Standard for Information Sciences—Permanence of Paper for Printed Library Materials, ANSI Z39.48-1984.

This book is for my mother
whose memory I aspire with all my heart to honor.

Contents

Acknowledgments

Over the Many Years I Have Been Working on the Materials of this book, I have found extraordinary people who have sustained me in this enterprise. I am not sure one can do work like this without the intellectual stimulation, the generous encouragement, and the good cheer of what has proved to be a genuine community of scholars. Most indispensable of all—the burr under the saddle—has been the example their own work has set. I feel privileged to acknowledge with gratitude: first, and with a full heart, Jerome Rothenberg; then Joyce Appleby, Jeremy Atack, Paul A. David, Stanley Engerman, David Hackett Fischer, Robert W. Fogel, David Galenson, Robert E. Gallman, David Garman, Claudia Goldin, Oliver Hart, Morton Horwitz, Alice Hanson Jones, Julius Kirshner, Allan Kulikoff, Beth Lilienstein, Robert A. Margo, John J. McCusker, Sarah F. McMahon, Bettye Hobbs Pruitt, Ellen Rothenberg, Robert A. Rothenberg, Daniel Scott Smith, Kenneth Sokoloff, Richard Sylla, Peter Temin, Lorena Walsh, Gordon Wood, and Gavin Wright. That they made this book as good as it is in no way implicates them in its failure to be better.

I am grateful also to my "dear enemies," to Michael Merrill, James Henretta, Jonathan Prude, Steven Hahn, Christine Heyrman, Christopher Clark, and other "moral economists" whose lively opposition has given to the work of disagreeing with them an energy, a passion, a *frisson* it otherwise would not have had.

I had the support of a grant-in-aid from the Economic History Association, which is always worth more than its face value if it can be understood to be a validation by colleagues one greatly admires. The manuscript was completed with the support of a generous fellowship from the American Council of Learned Societies.

As everyone who does archival research knows, the librarians and their staffs are the Gatekeepers. I am indebted to David Proper, Florence Lathrop, Theresa Percy, Lorna Cobden, Kathy Majors, and Leo and Helen Flaherty, and their staffs, for access over many years to the treasures they have guarded at, respectively, Historic Deerfield, the Baker Library Archives, Old Sturbridge Village Library, the Society for the Preservation of New England Antiquities, the American Antiquarian Society, and the Massachusetts State Archives.

To Julie McCarthy, Editor at the University of Chicago Press, and to Joseph H. Brown, copyeditor, go my astonished thanks for their scrupulous efforts to make me look good.

Introduction

THIS WORK IS OFFERED AS A CONTRIBUTION TO A LONG-STANDING BUT vigorously ongoing debate about the pace, pattern, and genesis of growth in the early American economy. I say *long-standing* because interest in the performance of the economy can be traced back at least to the earliest years of independence, when documenting the growth of the "First New Nation" was indistinguishable from celebrating it, an act of fervent patriotism as well as a tool of public administration. Listing, measuring, weighing, enumerating, calculating—all were part of a growing obsession with counting that constituted what James Cassedy has called "the beginnings of the statistical mind."[1] Births, marriages, and deaths had to be recorded in civil registries (at least in those states that had voted to disestablish religion); population had to be counted to determine representation, taxation, the organization of wilderness into territories and of territories into states; ratable polls, acreage, and the values of real and personal, agricultural and commercial property had to be enumerated to determine the incidence of state and local taxation. Customhouse agents monitored the international traffic in dutiable commodities; naturalists catalogued indigenous plants and animals, took daily temperature readings, recorded climatic phenomena and related them to crop yields, mortality, and outbreaks of disease; farmers, artisans, traders, private bankers, and moneylenders recorded debts in account books and ledgers; surveyors calculated and almanacs published the longitude, latitude, and heights of hills ("eminences"), church steeples, and lighthouses; recruiting officers registered the height, birthplace, and residence of soldiers, sailors, and militiamen; clerks of courts of common pleas docketed actions for debt; ship manifests itemized the heights and weights of children carried in the domestic slave trade; almshouse hospitals recorded the weights of infants born to paupers; the Quartermaster Corps kept accounts of civilian wages and provisions prices paid at each fort; and probate courts in every county inventoried all the personal property (and, in the North, all the real property) owned by a large fraction of all decedents.

Because aggregate data were not collected before 1840, it is from sources such as these that economic historians have been attempting to reconstruct the performance of the American economy in its early dec-

1. Cassedy, *Demography in Early America.*

ades. The first modern estimate found the United States between 1800 and 1840 to have been an economy with falling per capita output, its rapid population growth outrunning the ability of a fairly rudimentary technology to generate a commensurate increase of real output.[2] This pessimistic view, however, has not prevailed. The westward movement to more fertile lands, the shift of resources from agriculture to higher-productivity sectors (commerce, construction, and manufacturing), and the increased productivity within agriculture itself all suggest that both per capita output and its rate of growth per annum rose between the Revolution and the Civil War,[3] and more recent research has yielded estimates tracking per capita output by decade.[4]

While no consensus on rates has yet emerged,[5] considerable importance attaches to the consensus that there *was* growth. In an overwhelmingly agricultural economy, as the United States was before 1840, a stagnant or declining agriculture would have canceled out the contributions of more vigorous sectors to the overall rate of growth. That resources were, instead, sufficiently mobilized to produce output ahead of prodigious population growth speaks to the dynamism of the farm sector in particular. But what were the sources of that dynamism? Was it due

2. Martin, *National Income in the United States.*

3. See, e.g., Kuznets, *Income and Wealth of the United States;* Parker and Whartenby, "The Growth of Output before 1840"; Seaman, *Essays on the Progress of Nations;* Taylor, "American Economic Growth before 1840"; Berry, *Estimated Annual Variations in Gross National Product;* David, "The Growth of Real Product"; Poulson, *Value Added in Manufacturing, Mining, and Agriculture;* Weiss, "U.S. Labor Force Estimates"; Gallman, "American Economic Growth before the Civil War"; Engerman and Gallman, "Economic Growth"; and Gallman, "The Pace and Pattern of American Economic Growth."

4. The following estimates of per annum growth rates are among those that have appeared in the literature. (*a*) Real GNP per capita grew at an annual rate of 1.4 percent between 1805 and 1809 and 1.1 percent between 1835–39 and 1855–59 (Berry, *Estimated Annual Variations in Gross National Product*). (*b*) Real GDP per capita grew at an annual rate of 0.25 percent between 1800 and 1820, 1.96 percent from 1820 to 1840, and 1.6 percent from 1840 to 1860 (David, "The Growth of Real Product"). (*c*) Real value added per capita grew at 0.4 percent per annum from 1809 to 1839 and 1.4 percent from 1835 to 1859 (Poulson, *Value Added in Manufacturing, Mining and Agriculture*). (*d*) Real GDP per capita grew at 1.51 percent per annum from 1793 to 1800, at 0.46 percent from 1800 to 1820, at 0.93 percent from 1820 to 1840, and at 1.44 percent from 1840 to 1860 (Weiss, "U.S. Labor Force Estimates," table 6 and p. 26). (*e*) Total factor inputs per capita grew at an annual rate of 0.12 percent from 1774 to 1800, 0.49 percent from 1800 to 1840, and 1.05 percent between 1860 and 1900 (Gallman, "American Economic Growth before the Civil War," table 8). (The values given in *a, b,* and *c* are adapted from Engerman and Gallman, "Economic Growth," table IV, p. 23.)

5. And what agreement may have been achieved must now come to terms with new estimates of the size of the labor force, the size of the capital stock, and the pattern of real wage growth (Weiss, "U.S. Labor Force Estimates"; Gallman, "American Economic Growth before the Civil War"; and Margo, "Wages and Prices during the Antebellum Period").

to an increase in the supply of inputs?[6] to an increase in the productivity of inputs? to improvements in the quality of inputs?[7] to more efficient organization of the production process?[8] Or was it the consequence of exogenous factors acting on the American export sector?[9] How should this multiplicity of growth factors be ranked?[10] It is in the context of these kinds of questions that this set of studies seeks to make a contribution.

This book had its beginnings in an attempt directly to measure the growth of an agricultural economy on the cutting edge of transforming change: rural Massachusetts between 1750 and 1850. The problem, as I initially formulated it, was to estimate for a sample of farms inventoried at probate a set of production functions, by which is meant the quantitative relations between farm outputs, on the one hand, and land, labor, and capital (working livestock and farm tools) inputs, on the other. Data problems proved to be serious, not the least of which was to construct an index with which to deflate probate values in order to avoid confounding real changes with fluctuations in the purchasing power of the currency.

It was in the course of constructing a deflator relevant to that economy—composed of the products raised by those farmers, constructed from farm-gate prices charged by those farmers, and weighted by the relative importance of each of those products to Massachusetts farmers—that two observations struck me as particularly significant: regional differentials in the price of corn appeared to narrow (converge) over time; and the farm price index, once constructed, appeared to ex-

6. Territorial expansion, farm making, and clearing expanded the land input, high rates of natural increase, the slave trade, and immigration expanded the labor input; capital imports, domestic savings, the natural increase of livestock, and, most of all, "the hard work of farm building" expanded the capital input (McCusker and Menard, *The Economy of British America*, 84).

7. The quality of cleared land is improved by fencing, rotation, fallowing, and manuring; the quality of labor by education, skills (including learning by doing), and health; and the quality of capital by technological change.

8. This includes increased specialization and division of labor on farms, in artisanal shops, and in factories; increasingly secure propertry rights; the improved articulation of markets; the proliferation of central places; improved transportation networks; and lowered transactions costs.

9. For example, the revolutionary war, the Embargo, the British industrial demand for cotton, West Indian plantation demand for foodstuffs, the Napoleonic Wars, Baltic grain harvests, American tariffs, and the decreased costs and increased productivity of ocean shipping.

10. "American growth before the nineteenth century flowed chiefly from an increase in the factors of production—land, labor, and capital." However, "almost half the gain in per capita product in the nineteenth century and roughly 80 percent in the twentieth century was due to the improvement in factor productivity" (Gallman, "The Pace and Pattern of American Economic Growth," 59).

hibit a pattern of cyclical fluctuations and sudden shocks synchronous with those observed in the Warren-Pearson index of New York City wholesale prices and the Bezanson index of Philadelphia wholesale prices.[11] Synchronicity *and* convergence in the behavior of prices is an acknowledged diagnostic of the role of market forces in their determination. In the light of the social historiography dominant in the last two decades, which would deny to market forces a hegemonic role in the preindustrial economy of New England,[12] I felt compelled to pursue a line of inquiry that, while closely related to productivity growth, is nonetheless different from it. When did the rural economy of Massachusetts become "market oriented"? How can we know? What role did market orientation play in the transformation of the rural economy; that is, what were its productivity consequences? In the end, the effort to document the emergence of a market economy would prove not to have been a digression at all but to have come around full circle not only to a measure of labor productivity growth but also to an explanation for it.

Thus, I attempt in this volume to address not one question but two. How does a market economy happen, and how does it provide the motive and the cue for transforming growth? Seventeen years ago, when this work was begun, it was an academic exercise, an antiquarian indulgence. Suddenly these have become among the most compelling questions of our time.

11. See my "A Price Index for Rural Massachusetts," esp. figs. 3 and 5, pp. 982 and 987.
12. For a full discussion of the role of the "moral economy" in what is now being called "the New England debate," see chap. 2.

1

From Market-Places to

a Market Economy

I

No More Compelling Issue Occupies Economic Historians of the modern world than understanding the process of modernization itself: the origins of that long and mysterious transformation in which the countryside[1] was propelled from a millennium of inertia to a violent and sudden clustering of technological changes;[2] from an economy of severely straitened possibilities and widespread poverty to one of "unheard-of material welfare";[3] from the perpetual specter of famine[4] to the expectation of a perpetual sufficiency; from zero or negative population growth to a "sudden" doubling of population;[5] from zero productivity growth to a doubling of labor productivity in agriculture;[6] from "the poor stockinger, the Luddite cropper, the 'obsolete' handloom weaver, the

1. "The decisive part in the transition from feudalism to capitalism is played out in the countryside. This is certainly one of the keys to the 'mystery' of the transition, though not readily perceived when one is obsessed by the commercial and industrial manifestations of nascent capitalism" (Bois, "Against the Neo-Malthusian Orthodoxy," 109, n. 7).

The eleventh century was also a transformational "moment" in which there was "a great moving of stagnant waters" (Ashley, *Introduction to English Economic History and Theory,* 1:130).

2. Mokyr, "Was There a British Industrial Evolution?" 4.

3. So acknowledged even by the transformation's severest critic, Karl Polanyi (*The Great Transformation,* 3).

4. According to Fernand Braudel, France suffered more than sixteen general famines as late as the eighteenth century and "hundreds and hundreds of local famines" (*The Structure of Everyday Life,* 74).

There seems to be a difference of opinion in the case of English famines. According to Andrew Appleby, England suffered its last famine in 1623 (see his "Grain Prices and Subsistence Crises in England and France," 867). But Robert Fogel, using Wrigley and Schofield's 1981 mortality data, finds a "lethal resurgence" of mortality crises during the late 1720s. In fact, argues Fogel, laissez-faire government policy repeatedly turned dearths into famines until the mid-nineteenth century (see his "The Conquest of High Mortality and Hunger in Europe and America" and "Second Thoughts on the European Escape from Hunger").

Markets play an ambiguous role in such crises, sometimes facilitating the flow of foodstuffs from regions of plenty to regions of dearth, sometimes depleting local grain supplies that might have buffered the effect of famine. Braudel reflects this ambiguity when he writes of the peasants of Tuscany that, on the one hand, they "could not have managed without" the merchants who supplied them with Sicilian grain, while, on the other hand, peasants elsewhere "in a state of dependency on merchants . . . had scarcely any reserves of their own" (Braudel, *The Structures of Everyday Life,* 74–75). In England, likewise, access to markets both encouraged diversification and periodically drained the countryside of food grains.

As the historiography of staple theory abundantly makes clear, access to markets, by itself, is a necessary but not sufficient condition for the welfare effects attributed to it.

5. The population of Europe was 84.5 million in 1340, 83.4 million in 1600, and 170 million in 1800 (Clark, *Population Growth and Land Use,* 64, table III.i).

6. English agricultural labor productivity, measured as the ratio of total population to agricultural population, was 1.32 in 1520, 1.43 in 1600, 1.82 in 1700, 2.19 in 1750, and 2.48 in 1801 (Wrigley, "Urban Growth and Agricultural Change," 720, cited in Allen, "The Growth of Labor Productivity in Early Modern English Agriculture," 119).

'utopian' artisan,"[7] to an industrial proletariat; from markets embedded within and constrained by values antithetical to them within the culture to the "disembedded" market whose values penetrated and reinvented that culture.[8]

Of course I overstate. Swinging history between "from" and "to," a common rhetorical device, tells us only the direction of change, nothing about the cause or process or rate or timing of change. What caused the transformation we call "modernization"? Was it indeed part of an inexorably ongoing historical process? Or was it a fortuitous accident, a "random walk"?[9] That is, can the change be plotted without, as it were, "lifting pencil off paper"?[10] Or was it precipitated by some sudden shift of exogenous parameters (a war, a plague, a pivotal technological breakthrough)? In either case—whether the change is understood as a continuous evolutionary process or as a discontinuity—how do we account for the absence of change, for "the layer of stagnant history"[11] that remains obstinately present within even the most rapidly modernizing societies? "From/to" dichotomies trick the mind into seeing historical change as deceptively simple. "The Day the Universe Changed" took centuries, and even so, much of it didn't.

The immense transformation that ushered in the modern world appears to have been an omnivorous process, ultimately (although not simultaneously) reshaping all institutions in its path—the locus of sovereignty, the prerogatives of kingship, the distribution of power within the political process, property rights, legal institutions, forms of land tenure, the level of technology and the pace of technological change, age at marriage, family size, patterns of authority and deference within the family, gender roles, the intensity of work effort, the age, gender, and skill composition of the labor force, labor/leisure trade-offs, the quantity, forms, and functions of money, the allocative efficiency of prices, the tenets of religious belief, the boundaries between public and private, sacred and secular, urban and rural—all linked by feedback loops to one another and to the great demographic surges and scourges of early mod-

7. Thompson, *The Making of the English Working Class,* 13.

8. *Disembedded* is Karl Polanyi's term for the hegemonic market cut loose from its social context to become an autonomous set of relations with laws, institutions, and motivations of its own. See also Crowley, *This Sheba, Self,* 111.

9. See Rostow, "No Random Walk."

10. Alexander Gerschenkron's definition of continuity in history in *Continuity in History and Other Essays.*

11. Braudel, *The Structures of Everyday Life,* 28. Elsewhere, Braudel describes "the stagnant layer" as "the lowest stratum of the non-economy, the soil into which . . . capitalism can never really penetrate" (*The Wheels of Commerce,* 229).

ern Europe.[12] Not least, in the process the market was reshaped into the principal agency of economic transformation.

In order for the market to become an agent of change, it had to be transformed from something acted upon to something acting. Understanding this process—the emergence of a self-equilibrating, self-regulating, hegemonic market economy out from under the constraints of the larger society—requires us to consider a host of questions.

How do we define a market economy or recognize it when we see it? From what did it evolve?[13] What environmental factors forced that evolution?[14]

Was its emergence a once-and-for-all event in the linear unfolding of western European history? If so, when, why then, and why there? Or has the so-called rise of the market been a recurring phenomenon, advancing, retreating, and advancing again on the rising and ebbing tides of civilizations?

Does a market economy have a threshold size? What role do scale factors play in the distinction between market-places and a market economy? Were the exchanges between medieval walled towns and their hinterlands, and the exchanges in the medieval cloth trade between Genoa and Novgorod, equally (even if not equal) market transactions?

In attempting to explain the emergence (or recurring emergences) of the market economy, are we sure we understand the direction of causation? Can we be confident that the usual "causes"—population pressure, technological change, an alteration in the nature and security of property rights—are not, in fact, consequences?

What relation does a functioning market economy bear to its *conceptualization* in classical economic theory as a free-standing, homeostatic feedback mechanism?

What relation does a market economy bear to the process of economic growth and transformation?

---

12. A controversy surrounds the question of the exogeny or endogeny of demographic factors in the development of agrarian capitalism in England. That controversy is central to the whole so-called Brenner debate.

13. Joyce Appleby writes, "The development of the free market was one of the true social novelties in history" ("The Social Origins of American Revolutionary Ideology," 939). To speak of the free market as "developing" suggests a process evolving incrementally in historical time. But to speak of the free market as a "novelty" suggests its emergence out of a nonmarket process, discontinuously, even suddenly, as a fortuitous adaptation unlike anything that had gone before.

14. As formerly socialist economies attempt to legislate this transformation, the question is no longer a mere academic exercise but a matter of the utmost urgency. See, e.g., Feige, "Perestroika and Socialist Privatization," and "Socialist Privatization."

II

If in the hegemony of the market economy lies the genesis of the modern world, then we shall need first to distinguish it from its look-alike, market-place economies the existence of which can be traced back so far in human history that "the tendency to truck and barter" was long thought to be "innate."

There is a growing body of archaeological evidence that "English kings instituted a network of marketing centers during the 9th and 10th centuries,"[15] and studies in shire tax rolls suggest the existence of "a dense network" of local and regional peasant markets in the early medieval period.[16] One scholar discerns market forces at work in England as early as 1297 in the determination of debt, migration, rents, wages, and specialization in animal husbandry.[17] The Statute of Labourers (1349), which compelled employment at fixed wages under pain of imprisonment and mutilation, is usually portrayed as the very antithesis of a market process. But requiring unemployed farm workers to stand for hire in open markets "with the tools of their trade in hand" made human labor a commodity five centuries before the capitalist "commodification" of labor.[18] The monks of Battle Abbey were farming the manor lands at Marley entirely with wage workers (i.e., with a labor force alienated from its ascriptive rights to the land) by 1350, and in raising livestock for the beef and hide markets these monks anticipated by perhaps four hundred years the market-oriented husbandry we call the Agricultural Revolution.[19] At the same time, peasant lands were changing hands so rapidly that a "virtually free market in peasant holdings . . . had come into being" by the late fourteenth century.[20]

15. Biddick, "Medieval English Peasants and Market Involvement," 823.

16. Biddick, "Missing Links," 279.

17. Biddick, "Medieval English Peasants and Market Involvement," 824.

18. On the Statute of Labourers, see Clark, "Medieval Labor Law and English Local Courts," 333. For Polanyi, the repeal of the Speenhamland Plan (the Old Poor Law) in 1834 marked the creation of a capitalist labor market and hence of a market economy: "Not until 1834 was a competitive labor market established in England; hence industrial capitalism as a social system cannot be said to have existed before that date" (*The Great Transformation*, 83).

19. Searle, *Lordship and Community*, 304.

20. Faith, "Peasant Families and Inheritance Customs in Medieval England," 92. But was there a free market in peasant land? Were peasant lands privately owned and fully negotiable? To these questions Joel Mokyr has introduced a cautionary note. "Yes and no," he writes. "Ordinary peasant land was privately owned, but not by peasants. The Fee Simple that dominates American landowning today barely existed, and certainly not among the peasantry. Tenants holding land in

But the history of markets goes back much further, to the very earliest times when commercial caravans plied the major trade routes between Egypt and Mesopotamia. Ships of ancient Greece have been re-
covered from the bottom of the sea equipped with bins to carry grain
and with amphorae to carry oil and wine in the Mediterranean trade,
and in the surviving written record have been found contracts "between
the merchant, the ship owner and, in some cases, the banker who put
up the money for a trading voyage (and, through a clause cancelling the
debt if the ships were lost at sea, provided the ancient equivalent of
shipping insurance)."[21]

One could make the case that the wrath of the Biblical prophets
against commercial values testifies a fortiori to the dominant role that
commerce must have played in Israelite life in the eighth and seventh
centuries B.C.E. Indeed, one would be hard pressed to find in any of
today's decline-and-fall literature a depiction of the downfall of a great
mercantile power as vivid as Ezekiel 27, written, in all likelihood, at the
end of the sixth century B.C.E.

Documents of the fourteenth century B.C.E., found at Ugarit, mention a trade in cedars from Lebanon, textiles from Acco, Ashdod, and
Ashkelon, iron, copper, and gold from the land of Punt, salt from the
Dead Sea, perfumes, and the royal purple dye called "phoenix."[22] Further back still, there was in all likelihood a market within the walls of
Jericho, the oldest city in the world, dating from the seventieth century
B.C.E.: "Modern research has affirmed that ancient Western Asia knew
money (in the generic sense of a medium of exchange), market places,
wage labor, profit-oriented businessmen and firms, and supply-demand-
determined market prices."[23]

There is even evidence that suggests to some paleoanthropologists
that the transition from hunting-gathering to settled agriculture in the
Neolithic may have had its origins in the specialized cultivation of

---

villain socage had certain 'rights' in land, the right to use arable land, that sometimes included and
sometimes excluded the right to use the commons or stock-grazing. These rights, to be sure, were
bought and sold but precisely because they were often vague and in dispute, based on custom and
witnesses, this market in rights to land must have been fraught with transactions costs, disputes,
fraud, and legal fees. Just imagine what a title search and a deed to home ownership would look
like if owning your house included the right to use your neighbour's kitchen for Thanksgiving night
while he could use your swimming pool every second Monday in August." Joel Mokyr, "Comments" [on Donald N. McCloskey, "New Findings on Open Fields"], p. 3.

21. Landels, *Engineering in the Ancient World*, 164.
22. Aharoni and Avi-Yonah, *The Macmillan Bible Atlas*, 16–20.
23. Silver, *Prophets and Markets*, 253.

crops—such as grains and sugarcane for fermented beverages; flax, wool, and cotton for textiles; and sisal, jute, and hemp for baskets, ropes, nets, and fish lines—the "industrial" uses of which gave them high value in trade.[24]

There is, then, abundant documentation of a long history of market-place economies. But market-place economies are not market economies. While undoubtedly contributing to the economic *growth* of Europe, market-place economies did not forge its transformation. As governor of the exchange relations in an economy, the market is something more than, and other than, the sum of market-places. Identifying the difference between a market-place economy and a market economy and locating the "moment" in time when a market economy can be said to have emerged will occupy us for much of the balance of this book.

III

I begin with four "revolutions" that have been credited with having had a major impact on the development of a market economy in early modern Europe: in the sixteenth century, the Protestant Reformation, the so-called Price Revolution, and the rise of mass demand for consumer goods; in the seventeenth, the securing of private property rights as a consequence of the century-long struggle between Parliament and the Stuart kings.

Merely to mention the Reformation in this context calls up Max Weber's magisterial thesis linking the spirit of capitalism to the Protestant ethic.[25] It is not my intention to walk that ground again. The point I raise here is limited to an area Weber underemphasized: the attack by

24. A conference of anthropologists, prehistorians, and skeletal biologists held in 1982 resulted in the publication of a conference volume entitled *Paleopathology at the Origins of Agriculture,* edited by Mark Nathan Cohen and George J. Armelagos. "Noted at the conference was the suggestion that the *industrial* value of the agricultural product may have been the primary stimulus for the development of agriculture," according to a private communication from Arthur C. Aufderheide of the Department of Pathology and Laboratory Medicine at the University of Minnesota–Duluth. This line of inquiry derives from the discovery in skeletal remains that the shift from hunting-gathering to a diet based on cultivated grains in Neolithic Mesopotamia—and whenever and wherever the shift to sedentary agriculture has taken place—had deleterious consequences for human health.

25. Despite the chain of causal links that Weber forged between the Protestant (in particular, Calvinist) Reformation and the spirit of capitalism, Benjamin Nelson charges that only "careless critics" could accuse Weber of ignoring the medieval (i.e., Catholic) origins of capitalism and of "imagining that the capitalist economy was an emanation of the capitalist spirit" (*The Idea of Usury,* 74, n. 3).

the Reformation's leading theologians on Catholic usury laws.[26] Freeing interest from the odor of sin to become a genuine price of money and of time allowed the emergence of a free market for money.[27]

Catholic usury laws rested on the church's reinterpretation of Deuteronomy 23:21: "Unto a foreigner thou mayest lend upon interest; but unto thy brother thou shalt not lend upon interest; that the Lord thy God may bless thee in all that thou puttest thy hand unto, in the land whither thou goest in to possess it." To accommodate Mosaic law to canon law, church fathers had only to redraw the boundaries of the brotherhood, thrusting outside the pale the tribe for whom the law had been written, and bringing within its embrace the outsider, in a new brotherhood of believers in Christ.

First enunciated by Saint Augustine in the fourth century as part of the just price doctrine, usury laws were incorporated into the canon law in the eleventh century in a move to check the revival and northward spread of Roman law. While under Roman law profit taking and interest taking were justified as natural right, the church interpreted the injunction, "Do as thou would be done by," as categorically denying that there is a natural right to exploit asymmetries in exchange relations.

But despite church doctrine, the charging of interest was in fact tolerated in Catholic Europe throughout much of the medieval period. "The practice of lending money at interest was recorded in the south of France as early as the tenth century"[28] and continued thereafter, disguised as vif-gages, as discounts, as penalties for late payment, or as double indemnity for defaults. But the policies of Catholic regimes to-

26. "Had Weber had the opportunity to pursue the insights of his last lectures, he might well have hit upon the fact that Calvin's view of usury was one of the first monuments of the Universal Otherhood, whose characteristics he had so well envisaged. For reasons too complex to recall here, it was not until the end of his life that he detected the fruitfulness of taking the usury question as a point of departure for the history of the capitalist spirit" (ibid.).

27. For Polanyi, the creation of a market for money is as necessary to a market economy as the creation of a market for land and labor, and as ominous. For "labor, land, and money are obviously *not* commodities; the postulate that anything that is bought and sold must have been produced for sale is emphatically untrue in regard to them. . . . Labor is only another name for a human activity which goes with life itself. . . . Land is only another name for nature, which is not produced by man; actual money, finally, is merely a token of purchasing power which, as a rule, is not produced at all. . . . None of them is produced for sale. The commodity description of labor, land, and money is entirely fictitious" (*The Great Transformation,* 72).

28. Reyerson, *Business, Banking and Finance in Medieval Montpellier,* 61. Reyerson does, however, point out that "the loan evidence from the Montpellier contracts does not permit the calculation of interest levels" (p. 83).

According to W. J. Ashley, canon law on usury was not formulated until the late eleventh century, in which case tenth-century practice cannot be judged to have been in violation of canon law (see his *Introduction to English Economic History and Theory,* 1:133ff.).

ward interest vacillated. It was condemned in the late twelfth century and tolerated in the early thirteenth century. Saint Louis (Louis IX) vigorously opposed it in the mid-thirteenth century, but rates as high as 15–20 percent were recorded in the early fourteenth century in Montpellier, under the very noses of the Avignon popes.[29] The public debt of fourteenth- and fifteenth-century Florence was held by private wealthholders in a variety of interest-bearing, negotiable instruments, one of which paid 7 percent annually. That this so-called Seven Percent Fund is described as "a good option for investors preferring peace of mind to higher yielding, but riskier, short-term commercial loans" suggests that there were higher-yielding, but riskier, short-term alternatives.[30]

Eventually, canon law itself came to justify the charging of interest "to make the creditor whole."[31] Until the change in canon law, however, the prohibition of interest, whether vigorously enforced or not, constituted one of the most important constraints placed by church and state on economic activity.

But how much of a constraint could the usury laws have been if, despite doctrinal prohibitions against it, interest taking was, intermittently, common during much of the medieval period? And if, in the medieval period, usury laws were honored more in the breach than in the observance, then what role remains for the Reformation to have played in their demise? For Luther, Melanchthon, Zwingli, and Calvin this issue took on a special urgency. The first three utterly repudiated Deuteronomy 23:21—that is, they denounced the efforts of evangelicals to do away with interest—because they dreaded the bloody social revolution that a thoroughgoing leveling in the name of universal brotherhood would loose upon Europe. But Calvin, a far subtler mind, repudiated Deuteronomy 23:21 because, "from the standpoint of the capitalist spirit, the crying need was to transcend, rather than to buttress,

---

29. Reyerson, *Business, Banking and Finance in Medieval Montpellier,* 83–84. However, it was the first of the Avignon popes, Clement V, who issued a decretal in 1312 according to which merchants', bankers', and moneylenders' account books could be subpoenaed and searched for evidence of usury—which was defined as any accrual, large or small, above the principal. It is not surprising, therefore, that interest, if it appeared at all, was disguised in medieval account books as "yield," "cost," "gain," "gift," "gratuity," or "reward" or was obtained in advance (discounting) (see de Roover, *Business, Banking and Economic Thought in Late Medieval and Early Modern Europe,* chap. 3).

30. Kirshner and Klerman, "The Seven Percent Fund of Renaissance Florence," 327.

31. Canon law made a distinction between two kinds of loss creditors were at risk of sustaining: the loss of principal (*damnum emergens*) and the forgoing of gain (*lucrum cessans*) (see Ashley, *Introduction to English Economic History and Theory,* 1:148–63, 195–204).

the double-edged rule."[32] To do this he used a double-edged argument: he appealed to the Christian brotherhood to expunge the discrimination against the foreigner while using the discrimination against the foreigner to expunge the prohibition of interest.[33] "In modern capitalism, all are 'brothers' in being equally 'others.' "[34]

By the mid-seventeenth century, especially in England, the traditionalist forces had been thoroughly routed. The word *usury* virtually disappeared after 1640 and especially after 1660.[35] The argument henceforth would be about the level of interest rates and not about the taking of interest.

The long inflation of the sixteenth century was often attributed by contemporaries to usurious rates of interest, but Earl Hamilton's pathbreaking study,[36] supported as it was by the quantity theory of money and prices,[37] persuaded a generation of historians that the principal cause of the inflation was the flood of silver that had poured into Spain from her South American colonies and was spread throughout Europe and Asia by the persistent balance of trade deficits that Spain ran as a consequence of her inflated domestic price level.

Recent work on the Price Revolution of the sixteenth century has focused on the timing of the alleged cause and its effect, and doubts have been raised: if the mines of Potosi did not begin flooding Spain with silver until 1560, then the long price inflation that began in 1525 must be blamed, not on the influx of American silver, but rather on other, "real" factors.[38] Revisionist historians have drawn attention to variables other than the stock of specie in the quantity theory equation: to

---

32. Nelson, *The Idea of Usury,* 68.

33. I am here paraphrasing Benjamin Nelson (ibid., xxiv).

34. Ibid., xxv.

35. Letwin, *The Origins of Scientific Economics,* 82.

36. Hamilton, *American Treasure and the Price Revolution in Spain.*

37. The quantity theory identifies four macroeconomic variables: the stock of money, M (specie, paper money, and bank deposits); the velocity of circulation of money, V; the general price level, P; and Q, the quantity of goods and services produced in the economy (measured as real GNP). Then $MV = PQ$. If V is assumed to have been approximately constant over time and Q is assumed to be at full employment, then P moves directly and proportionally with changes in M.

38. For 1560 as the date that Potosi "produced silver in prodigious quantities," see Kindleberger, *Spenders and Hoarders,* 2. According to Kindleberger, "The rise in prices preceded the silver arrivals by several decades, and was much more pronounced in food than in prices in general, suggesting that it was caused more by real than by monetary factors, and especially by the faster comeback of population than of agriculture after the Black Death of the fourteenth century" (p. 3). For a differing view—that 1525 is indeed the date of both the onset of the inflation and "the most rapid inflow of New World specie"—see Fisher, "The Price Revolution," 883.

the behavior of *relative* prices (including wages); the influence of population growth and population density (urbanization) on velocity; the pervasive debasement of currencies throughout Europe at the time; and the effect of sectoral inelasticities of supply on the size of real output and hence on the level of prices.[39]

Here detailed case studies have been useful. Richard Goldthwaite notes, for example, that, "with its commerce closely tied to Spain and a balance of payments very much in its favor, Florence was one of the first to feel the repercussions of the silver imports from the New World."[40] But the repercussions were felt in prices, not in wages. Goldthwaite's compilation of three hundred years of Florentine wages and wheat prices reveals that laborers' nominal wages, which had remained virtually constant for nearly two hundred years, began to rise sluggishly after 1525, at a rate of about 1 percent per annum, but were easily overtaken by the rapid rise in wheat prices. Consequently, workers' living standards at the end of the inflationary sixteenth century fell "as low as they had been on the eve of the Black Death," 250 years earlier.[41] Real wages (wages in wheat) had lost 80 percent of their purchasing power from their peak in 1440.

E. H. Phelps Brown and Sheila V. Hopkins tell much the same story of a "catastrophic" loss of 60 percent of the real value of laborers' wages in England, France, and Alsace between 1510 and the 1630s.[42] And again it is due to a more than sixfold increase in food, fuel, and cloth prices between 1500 and 1600 while nominal wage rates, having remained constant from 1400 to 1550, rose no more than 2 percent per

---

39. See Miskimin, "Agenda for Early Modern Economic History," 172–83.

40. Goldthwaite, *The Building of Renaissance Florence,* 335.

41. Ibid., 334; see also the graph on pp. 318–19. In terms of our inquiry into the origins and integration of markets, the fact that nominal wages in Florence remained virtually constant from 1350 to 1530 deserves our attention. If the sensitivity of wages to relative changes in demand and supply is a necessary condition for the existence of a labor market, then how do we interpret nearly two hundred years of wage stability in Florence? Goldthwaite finds no evidence that wages were fixed either by guilds or by government policy; rather, the stability of wages was a result of a general equilibrium of demand and supply: "The loss of population in the fourteenth century and the slowness of its recovery kept supply tight, while the increased activity in construction in the fifteenth century stimulated demand" (p. 329). But these upward pressures on wage rates were buffered by a reserve pool of underemployed labor, on the one hand, and, on the other, the willingness of patrons of major construction projects to stop work on them rather than raise wages. In addition, broad acceptance of the notion of a customary wage for a day's work acted to stabilize fluctuations about the equilibrium wage.

42. Phelps Brown and Hopkins, "Seven Centuries of Building Wages," "Seven Centuries of the Prices of Consumables," and "Wage Rates and Prices."

annum in the last half of the sixteenth century. Phelps Brown and Hopkins believe that this asymmetry in the behavior of prices and wages
suggests that the inflation of the sixteenth century played only a limited
role in the transformation of early modern Europe, while population
pressure played a major role. The population of England and Wales may
have doubled between 1500 and 1700,[43] which, in the face of technological constraints on agricultural output, would explain both the sharp rise
of food prices (even without American silver) and the downward pressure on the wages of the laboring classes.

Steadily declining real wages was only one index of the deteriorat-
ing position of the laboring classes in sixteenth-century England. Another dimension of that deterioration was the rapidly increasing proportion of the rural population who were without real property, without
livestock, excluded from rights in and access to the arable, and totally
dependent for food, for textiles, and for the services of milling, baking,
malting, weaving, dyeing, sewing, and shoemaking on what could be
bought with their wages. In a recent study, Carole Shammas puts that
proportion at 20–33 percent in 1524, increasing to 65 percent by 1688,[44]
and suggests that the growing incidence of wage dependency alone
would have accounted for "the transformation of peasants from producers to consumers"[45] and the rise of mass demand for consumer
goods.

Of course, in the face of the catastrophic fall in real wages, the
growing wage dependency of the poor must have led not only to the
creation of a consumer class but also, alas, to increasingly widespread
pauperization. Even if "being poor and being a consumer . . . were not
mutually exclusive conditions" in principle,[46] they must frequently have
been mutually exclusive conditions in fact. Nevertheless, a rise in the
number and diffusion of store-bought commodities, such as tobacco,
sugar, coffee, tea, pewter, textiles, pottery, glass, apparel, housewares,

43. Sir John Clapham, *A Concise Economic History of Britain* (1949), cited in Phelps Brown
and Hopkins, "Wage Rates and Prices," 295. This estimate is not wildly inconsistent with Wrigley
and Schofield's estimates of 2,773,851 in 1541, and 5,057,790 in 1701 (*The Population History of
England,* table A3.1, p. 528).

44. Shammas, *The Pre-Industrial Consumer in England and America.* Shammas's estimate
of the size of the wage-dependent classes at the beginning of her period is confirmed by Phelps
Brown and Hopkins: "It is generally reckoned that in the first half of the sixteenth century about
one-third of the occupied population in England were wage earners" ("Wage Rates and Prices,"
299).

45. Shammas, *The Pre-Industrial Consumer in England and America,* 3.

46. Ibid., 1.

and furnishings, can be confirmed from probate inventories between 1550 and 1730[47] and from the expansion of market towns, retail shops, and peddlers through which consumption goods were made available to village households: "Virtually every [small market] town had a shop by 1700."[48]

To make use of Shammas's important work for our purposes, the case would have to be made that the expansion of demand worked on *production,* not consumption—on supply, not demand—to generate economic growth.[49] It is the way in which extending the market removes limitations on the degree of specialization and division of labor that generates economic growth. It is the way in which a peasant agriculture is disciplined by the market to mesh outputs and the movement of capital and labor with urban demands, to specialize, to diversify, to seek scale economies, to husband livestock, and intensively to cultivate marketable surpluses that transforms the household economy of peasant farmers and the larger economy surrounding it.[50]

Holland is frequently cited as a case in point. Dutch peasants, having avoided seigneurial feudalism almost completely[51] and "blessed with poor soil," had turned, as early as the Carolingian period, from grain agriculture to livestock herding, to by-employments in the nonagricultural sector, and to the regular use of money, all of which generated rural-urban complementarities and contributed to the development of "capitalist" relations in the countryside.[52] By the early seventeenth century Holland's prosperous agriculture, vigorous middle class, worldwide mercantile trade, low interest rates, far-flung colonial outposts, and republican institutions had generated an "embarrassment of

47. Shammas may have underemphasized the role of intergenerational transfers in the accumulation of consumer goods. Bequests may account for much of the buildup of durables in household inventories over time, and to that extent the value of consumer durables held by decedents becomes a less accurate proxy for household expenditures on consumer durables. The wealth bias in probate inventories is widely acknowledged. In England, estates valued at less than £5 were not probated (ibid., 19).

48. Ibid., 248.

49. See the exhaustive and closely reasoned argument that demand cannot have been an input (or a factor) in the growth of output during the Industrial Revolution in Mokyr, "Demand vs. Supply in the Industrial Revolution" (reprinted in Mokyr, ed., *The Economics of the Industrial Revolution*).

50. DeVries, *The Dutch Rural Economy in the Golden Age,* 10. "Implicit in this study is the belief that some relationship exists between the structure of an *agrarian* economy and the prospects for growth in the total economy" (p. xiii; emphasis added).

51. DeVries, "On the Modernity of the Dutch Republic."

52. DeVries, *The Dutch Rural Economy in the Golden Age,* 55.

riches"[53] that was the envy of all Europe and, for a time, a galling rebuke to the Stuart kings of Great Britain.

IV

The mention of Holland's republican institutions serves to introduce the fourth revolution, arguably of far greater significance to the development of a market economy than any (or indeed all) of the other three. I refer, of course, to the British Parliament's struggle through most of the seventeenth century to define the property rights of private citizens and to design the institutions to secure them against royal usurpation: "The development of free markets must be accompanied by some credible restrictions on the state's ability to manipulate economic rules to the advantage of itself and its constituents. Successful economic performance must be accompanied by institutions that limit economic intervention and allow private rights and markets to prevail in large segments of the economy."[54]

The issue was joined in the decade of the 1640s, when a crisis of legitimacy befell virtually every institution that had claimed to exercise power under the authority of the ancient British constitution. Parliament emerged triumphant, having beheaded the king, executed his closest advisers, abolished his Star Chamber, denounced his church, executed his archbishop, seized command of his armed forces, sealed its authority over the taxing and spending powers, and arrogated to itself the governance of the realm and the locus of sovereignty. By mid-century, the Dutch republic and the English commonwealth had arrived from very different medieval pasts at similar parametric institutions: a free peasantry, closed fields, a measure of private control over land, and redress against arbitrary taxation.

The epic struggle between the four Stuart kings and Parliament created new coalitions that cut across the traditional class lines of an agrarian society in favor of new commercial, entrepreneurial, and mercantile elites. From the point of view of the growth of a market economy, by far the most significant of the institutional innovations designed by and for these new elites was the securing of property rights favoring the creation of a modern capital market. According to Douglass North and Barry Weingast, these innovations were set not in the 1640s, when Parliament extinguished the monarchy, but in 1688, when, having deposed

53. I refer here to the title of Simon Schama's recent *Embarrassment of Riches*.
54. North and Weingast, "Constitutions and Commitment," 808.

two sovereigns (Charles I and James II) and elected a third (William III), Parliament came to terms with the reconstituted monarchy in a "glorious" settlement that institutionalized a system of checks—"an explicit set of multiple veto points"[55]—on the absolutism of both sides, the crown's and its own. Among the "veto points" was the guarantee of an independent judiciary with the authority to defend private undertakings against regulation, confiscation, expropriation, encroachment, and violations of commitments by the state. "Increasing the number of veto players implied that a larger set of constituencies could protect themselves against political assault, thus markedly reducing the circumstances under which opportunistic behavior by the government could take place."[56]

V

While the consequences for economic actors of such a change in the institutional environment are obvious, I will argue that the hegemonic and autonomous market emerged in England in the seventeenth century as a consequence not only of the political settlement but also of a profound "paradigm shift"—an intellectual revolution with resonances and ramifications throughout the entire society—that privatized economic decision making, put the *individual* at the center of the society, and wrenched ("disembedded") the expanding economy from the dominance of state, crown, and church.

That the market system appeared in England contemporaneously with the apotheosis of Puritanism, with republican political theory, with empirical science, and with the first stirrings of deistical religion and skeptical epistemology is, I suggest, of immense significance. In terms of their intellectual lineage they are all elaborations of a single idea: one that Daniel Bell has called "the fundamental assumption of modernity, the thread that has run through Western civilization since the sixteenth century, . . . that the social unit of society is not the group, the guild, the tribe, or the city, but the person."[57] Polanyi to the contrary notwithstanding, the "disembedded" market in western capitalist economies does not reside outside the culture and in opposition to its values. Quite the contrary, the market (for better or worse) objectifies some of the culture's most cherished values, ratifying a theory of distributive justice

55. Ibid., 829.
56. Ibid.
57. Bell, *The Cultural Contradictions of Capitalism*, 16.

based on the sovereignty of the individual that has been at the core of British religious and political culture since the sixteenth century.

From Calvin to Adam Smith, the individual, in this intellectual tradition, is seen as ultimately singular in society, ultimately alone in worship, ultimately the sole perceiver of reality, alone in judgment, alone in action. The process of individuation had its origins in Puritanism, a theology riven through from its sixteenth-century beginnings with the terrible contradiction of personal Grace within a congregational covenant, of the elect who "walk by such a rule as cannot stand with the peace of any state."[58]

Exiled to Massachusetts by the English church and to the wilderness by Massachusetts churches, the "irrepressible I" found a congenial host in English secular philosophy. Although deistical skepticism was an eighteenth-century phenomenon, it had its origins in the mid-seventeenth century, in Descartes, whose first principle—"Je pense, donc je suis"—forced him to rely on his own mind to test the validity of all first principles, including the existence of his own mind.[59] Thereafter, in an almost straight line from Locke to Berkeley to Hume, the truth of causation, of reality itself, no less than of God, begins and ends with the sensory perceptions of the individual perceiver.

British liberal political theory, built on this skeptical epistemology, begins with the solitary individual delegating, withholding, contracting, but always poised, conditionally, on the outer rim of the society of others. The tenets of classical liberalism can be inferred from two fundamental propositions that define the axiomatic position of the individual: (1) A can take care of himself (by which is meant, make decisions respecting his well-being) better than he can take care of B; and (2) B can take care of himself better than A can take care of him.[60] Several things follow from these fundamental propositions. (*a*) There is, in a manner of speaking, a space or arena surrounding both A and B, and defined by the notion of rights, within which each is to be left free, not only of each other, but of all others. (*b*) The coercive apparatus of the state is expressly excluded from penetrating that arena. That is, the state can legislate only with respect to those matters over which *all* citizens have a right equal to B's to make decisions respecting him. (*c*) Over those

58. Statement of Governor Winthrop at the civil trial of Anne Hutchinson in Boston, 1637; quoted in Battis, *Saints and Sectaries*, 286.

59. "The freed intellect begins by proving assumptions hitherto taken for granted" (Stephen, *History of English Thought in the Eighteenth Century*, 1:22).

60. Cropsey, *Polity and Economy*, 28.

areas where the state does have the right to legislate for B, it would appear to follow that all citizens, having a right equal to that of B to decide, have equally the right to vote. (*d*) "Where a man cannot call his Tongue his own he can scarce call any Thing else his own."[61] Freedom of speech is not so much another right as it is an application of the right to property in one's self that defines the arena of individual sovereignty.

That the individual, autonomous and sovereign, emerges in England in the seventeenth and eighteenth centuries as the unit of decision making in secular philosophy, Puritan theology, liberal political theory, and economic theory suggests the strength of the logical and methodological links between them. The market is the elaboration of the economic consequences of individual sovereignty; liberalism is the elaboration of the political consequences of individual sovereignty. Both institutions can be understood as arguments in a perpetual dialectic around the pivotal concept of individual sovereignty.

VI

By the opening of the seventeenth century the pattern of world trade had changed as well. When its center of gravity shifted from the Mediterranean to the Atlantic, England moved from the periphery to challenge the Spanish, the Dutch, and the French for the center. The changing conformations of world trade, a severe depression in the woolen trades, the debasement of silver coinage throughout Europe, and the attempts to plant English colonies in the New World provoked in England, in 1620, an important debate on depreciation, foreign exchange rates, and international trade policy.[62] The debate appears to have played a role in

61. Trenchard and Gordon ("Cato"), "Of Freedom of Speech, That the Same is Inseparable from Publick Liberty" (4 February 1720), in Jacobson, ed., *The English Libertarian Heritage*, 38–39.

62. The debate—which has been called the first important economic controversy in England—was among Thomas Mun, Gerard de Malynes, and Edward Misselden. Mun's attack on bullionism in that debate was published in 1621 as "A Discourse of Trade, from England unto the East-Indies; answering to diverse Objections which are usually made against the same."

According to C. H. Wilson, "The controversies of the 1620s would have no particular claim to record if they had turned merely on abstract principles: but they did not. The outcome was in effect a victory for . . . the doctrine that no amount of monetary manipulation—prohibitions on bullion export, enhancing or debasing of moneys, compulsory regulations governing the proceeds of exports, the 'admirable feats of bankers'—could affect the national welfare: it was "The Ballance of our Fforraign Trade' that was 'the Rule of our Treasure'. And these beliefs guided, or at any rate coincided with, an increasing volume of legislation . . . which all aimed at enlarging exports" ("Trade, Society and the State," in Rich and Wilson, eds., *The Cambridge Economic History of Europe*, 4:504).

redirecting British trade policy away from its sixteenth-century obsession with the accumulation of "treasure" for its own sake and toward the vigorous encouragement of international commodity trade.[63]

But more important for our purposes, the century and a half of controversy over bullionism, mercantilism, protectionism, and laissez-faire—from Thomas Mun in 1620 to Adam Smith in 1776—forced the *conceptualization* of an autonomous economic system, abstracted from other systems and understood as functioning in accordance with the laws of a new science.

Historians of economic thought disagree over who should be credited with having been the first "economic theorist." For Joyce Appleby that honor goes to Thomas Mun, not because he imagined an economy independent of political intervention—he was, after all, a mercantilist—but because he differentiated things economic from their social context: "We can say that Mun created a paradigm. He abstracted England's trade relations from their real context and built in that place an intellectual model."[64]

While Barry Supple considers Mun's theories on the balance of trade to be "the most influential economic doctrine before Adam Smith," Mun's willingness, like that of his contemporaries, to accept government regulation of economic affairs rather than rely on the free play of market forces constitutes "one of the major theoretical flaws in his system[;] . . . he did not acknowledge the ultimate tendency to equilibrium."[65] If Supple is right, then Mun cannot be said to have conceptualized a homeostatic economic system, which must, to be freestanding, be self-regulating.

T. W. Hutchinson also acknowledges Mun's contribution, but it pales, he writes, beside Sir William Petty's (1662): "A profoundly significant change in intellectual quality must be noticed between the works of Mun and his contemporaries and those of Petty. . . . The vital difference is to be found in the fact that such theories as could be said to underlie Mun's policy conclusions were almost completely inchoate and

63. "Let the meer Exchanger do his worst; Let Princes oppress, Lawyers extort, Usurers bite, Prodigals wast . . . so much Treasure only will be brought in or carried out of a Commonwealth, as the Forraign Trade doth over or under ballance in value. And this must come to pass by a Necessity beyond all resistance" (Mun, *England's Treasure by Forraign Trade*, 218–19 [Abbott, ed., *Masterworks of Economics*, 1:26]).

64. Appleby, *Economic Thought and Ideology in Seventeenth Century England*, 41. For a discussion of Appleby's view that the Mun-Malynes-Misselden debate was a highly significant event in the conceptualization of an abstract, homeostatic market, see her chap. 2, pp. 24–51.

65. Supple, *Commercial Crisis and Change in England*, 213, 217.

inexplicit [while Petty's were based on] explicit methodological and theoretical foundations."[66]

William Letwin, who casts his vote for Sir Dudley North (1691), dismisses Mun, whose "books were to economic theory as an engineer's manual is to theoretical mechanics." North's *Discourses upon Trade*, had it not dropped out of sight soon after being published, says Letwin, "should have marked the birth date of economic theory": "North's is the first full equilibrium analysis in the history of economic theory; or, more exactly, North was the first economic writer to construct a cogent analysis founded on a few, broad, general principles of axiomatic simplicity, which enable him to provide a mechanistic explanation of an economic process, and to reach policy conclusions which are deducible strictly from the premises."[67]

The most interesting of these commentators, I find, is not a historian of economic thought at all but an engineer and historian of technology. Otto Mayr has sought to establish causal, analogical, even metaphorical links between the ways in which a culture chooses its government, designs its machines, and conceptualizes its economic system, links rooted deep within the values of that culture. He confesses, after two books, to being unable to prove his hunch, yet it has such power that it lives on vividly in the imagination.[68] For the conceptualization of a homeostatic market that governs the economy by equilibrating supply and demand, the arrangement of interests that governs the state by means of checks and balances, and the invention of machinery governed by automatic feedback controls (i.e., automatically self-regulating) are all expressions of (or analogies to or metaphors for) the preference of the English for liberty and equilibrium.[69]

66. Hutchinson, *Before Adam Smith*, 6–7.

67. Letwin, *The Origins of Scientific Economics*, 183, 204, 198. Letwin reminds us that the concept of an economic system as a *self-equilibrating machine* appears to be politically neutral—merely a metaphor transferred from mechanics—but is in fact politically charged: "A guillotine blade is in equilibrium once it has come to rest at the bottom of the guides; whether that equilibrium is desirable or not depends on whose head has rolled. Machines that tend toward equilibrium will be given full scope only by those men who believe that the position at equilibrium is in some degree desirable" (p. 199).

68. See Mayr, *The Origins of Feedback Control*, and *Authority, Liberty and Automatic Machinery in Early Modern Europe*.

69. For Mayr, David Hume (1750) was the first "economic theorist" fully to model a homeostatic economic system.

I repeat the word *govern* or *governor* deliberately. According to Mayr, the word comes from the Greek *kubernetes*, meaning "steersman," and was used for the first widely known feedback mechanism, the centrifugal "governor" on James Watt's steam engine. The neologism *cybernetics*, from the same root, was invented by Norbert Wiener for the science of feedback mechanisms of control and communication.

On this inconclusive but, I think, resonant note, I turn my attention, finally, to describing more concretely what this abstraction, a market economy, is and how it is to be distinguished from an economy with markets, or a market-place economy.

VII

Fernand Braudel has suggested that a market economy exists "when prices in the markets of a given area fluctuate in unison."[70] But this synchronicity could be observed throughout Europe as early as the twelfth century, far too early to be a diagnostic of the transition from a market-place economy to a market economy. Parallel price movements, while necessary, are in fact not a sufficient condition for an integrated market system. Prices in medieval Europe moved in rough synchronicity because—and only to the extent that—the economies of Europe were "rocked by the same ground-swells":[71] the same severe climatic episodes, morbidity and mortality crises, technological constraints, wars, crusades, periodic infusions of silver and gold, movements of population onto and off of marginal lands, waves of town and cathedral building, and so forth. That exogenous shocks drove prices in many European markets to move congruently is evidence of the ubiquity of those shocks, but it does not establish the articulation *between* market-places that defines an integrated market economy.

Marc Bloch had a less operational formulation of the elusive transition from market-place to market system. "The society [of the feudal age]," he wrote, "was certainly not unacquainted with either buying or selling. But it did not, like our own, *live by* buying and selling."[72] This distinction sounds intuitively right—"market involvement without market orientation"[73]—but on reflection it raises more problems than it lays to rest: not least the problem of dating and verifying the transition from one to the other. It is not clear, in other words, how "living by buying and selling" would show up differently in the empirical evidence from "buying and selling." And is it really so obvious that we live by buying and selling in a way that, say, the Guatemalan Indian—"in the context of [whose] culture . . . selling the produce (rather than harvesting it) is the real culmination of the cycle of agriculture, just as buying . . . is

70. Braudel, *The Wheels of Commerce,* 227.
71. Day, *The Medieval Market Economy,* 90.
72. Bloch, *The Growth of Ties of Dependence,* 67 (emphasis added).
73. Hoffman, "Medieval Origins of the Common Fields," 28.

the beginning of social living"[74]—does not? Or in a way that the bailiff of Battle Abbey, who over six hundred years ago hired and managed a large force of wage laborers, amassed lands, collected rents, consolidated the demesne, rationalized the ley farming, and marketed the outputs of grain and livestock, did not? Does "living by buying and selling," then, refer solely to a new *mentalité*, a new conformation of attitudes? If so, was Bloch making the most far-reaching transformation of the modern world a mere "epiphenomenon," as one critic put it, "of the mentalités of those who willed it"?[75]

Alfred Marshall defined a market as a "region" in space and time over which prices for the same good (net of transport costs) tend toward uniformity.[76] Marshall's definition rests on the *convergence* rather than the synchronicity of prices. The convergence process works like this. The price differentials obtaining between isolated markets present an opportunity to buyers, sellers, and owners of resources to profit by moving between markets from lower to higher returns. But buying in cheap markets and selling in dear markets—"arbitrage"—narrows the very price differentials that invited it, integrating markets formerly isolated in space, and widening the market over which a uniform price prevails. And as arbitrage and price convergence extend the market in space, it becomes possible to realize those Smithian processes of output growth, achieved through specialization and division of labor, which in turn are limited by the extent of the market.

The movement of buyers, sellers, and resources, which acts as the arbitrageur between market-places, can be inhibited, indeed severely obstructed, by high transactions costs—an umbrella term for all impediments to mobility, from the cost of transportation to the cost of transferring property rights. Some transactions costs are embedded in institutions that are slow to change. Some are attitudinal and are slow to change. Some, like inadequate transportation, must wait upon new techniques and the emergence of a capital market and are slow to change.

74. Tax, *Penny Capitalism*, 88.

75. "The whole conception of mentalités as inherited from Febvre stresses the absence or impossibility of certain concepts and attitudes existing in given periods. In so doing, it tends to create a uniformity which hides or denies the capacity of individuals and societies to hold contradictory and incompatible ideas and ideals simultaneously. It also implies that change must come as some total mental and psychological transformation—which LeRoy Ladurie locates in the Enlightenment, with peasants becoming political and religious nonconformists after 1760. One may still wonder how agricultural progress and rises in productivity were possible in Flanders, Lodigiano, Catalonia or Brescia before any transmutation of mentalités" (Cooper, "In Search of Agrarian Capitalism," 140–41).

76. Marshall, *Principles of Economics*, 324.

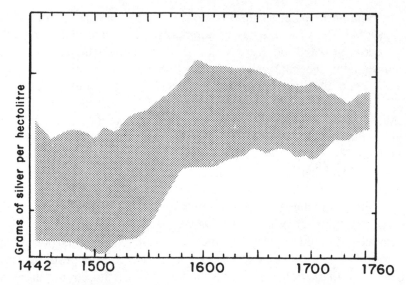

Fig. 1 European wheat prices in grams of silver per hectolitre: ten-year averages, 1450–1750. (The shaded portion shows the range between the maximum and the minimum prices.)

Source: Adapted from Braudel and Spooner, "Prices in Europe from 1450–1750," fig. 19, pp. 470–71.

Note: Based on price observations from Holland, England, France, Italy, Poland, Germany, Spain.

What emerges from our idiosyncratic survey of early modern Europe is that the sixteenth and seventeenth centuries, for a host of reasons, appear to have been a time in which changes in institutions, attitudes, techniques, and capital markets were coming at an accelerating pace, lowering transactions costs, releasing constraints on mobility, and permitting the arbitraging of price differentials that integrated marketplaces into a market economy.

Figure 1 presents evidence of the convergence of wheat prices throughout Europe in the sixteenth and seventeenth centuries.[77] It is in the narrowing over time of the spread between the minimum and the maximum prices that we see the emergence of a single, integrated European wheat market. Tracking over time a similar pattern of price convergence for all traded commodities would identify a market economy, date its emergence, and set the geographical boundaries of its hegemony.

77. Braudel and Spooner, "Prices in Europe from 1450 to 1750," 470–71.

VIII

Price convergence is an observable, empirically verifiable, operationally meaningful diagnostic of a market system. But can its naked abstraction contain the immense weight of social and cultural baggage conveyed by the term *capitalist transformation?* It was mentioned above that Marc Bloch has been criticized for relying on a mere epiphenomenon—a shift in *mentalité* from "buying and selling" to "living by buying and selling"—to make the momentous distinction between the feudal economy and the modern. But can that distinction be made entirely *without* taking account of the shift in *mentalité?* These kinds of questions lie at the heart of the debate over the so-called moral economy.

The identification of moral economies—of communities *in* but not *of* the modern world, clinging to "traditional" values in standing rebuke of "capitalist" values—has centered on New England, where their tenacious resistance is alleged to have acted as a brake on the spread of the market. Acknowledging the power of this argument while at the same time evaluating its substance are the tasks of chapter 2.

2

The Moral Economy Model and
the New England Debate

THE "MORAL ECONOMY" IS AS MUCH A MODEL OF AN ECONOMY AS OF a community and has therefore to be evaluated in terms of the rural New England village economy it purports to model. This chapter will present the model and thereafter will be concerned with a range of empirical problems that, in my view, compromise its verifiability, stand in the way of its operationalization, and undermine its relevance. But I begin by placing the debate that the moral economy model has aroused within its historiographic context.[1]

I. The Historiography of the Debate

Inspired by the improving spirit of Jethro Tull and Arthur Young and by the revolution in English agriculture they brought to pass, much attention was focused in the late 1740s on the state of American agriculture. The Reverend Jared Eliot in 1749, and a host of writers thereafter,[2] observed in New England a slovenly and predatory husbandry for which they placed the blame in part on the poor quality of the soil but more pointedly on the ignorance, risk aversion, and hidebound conservatism of the farmers.[3] More sophisticated observers were less judgmental. Neglectful farming was a natural consequence of America's low labor/land ratio: "The aim of the farmers in this country (if they can be called farmers) is, not to make the most from the land, which is or has been cheap, but the most of the labour, which is dear: the consequence of which has been, much ground has been scratched over, and none cultivated or improved as it ought to have been."[4]

With Percy Bidwell, in 1916, the critique moved beyond the hortatory literature of agricultural improvement societies to a genuine understanding of rural economic processes. Scarce and expensive labor, poor

---

1. For a superb treatment of the debate, with emphasis on its intellectual content and with more sympathy for the moral economy argument than I have, see Kulikoff, "The Transition to Capitalism in Rural America."

2. Carman and Tugwell, eds., *Jared Eliot's Essays.* See also, e.g., Chickering, *A Statistical View of the Population of Massachusetts;* Strickland, *Observations on the Agriculture of the United States of America;* Dwight, *Travels in New England and New York;* Deane, *The New England Farmer;* Blodget, *Economica;* the *Papers* of the Massachusetts Society for Promoting Agriculture; the *Massachusetts Agricultural Repository and Journal;* Morse, *The American Gazeteer,* and *The American Universal Geography;* and Weld, *Travels through the States of North America.*

3. According to Timothy Dwight, what was attributed to the poverty of the soil ought really to have been ascribed to the inferiority of the husbandry (Dwight, *Travels in New England and New York,* 1:72).

4. George Washington to Arthur Young, 5 December 1791, cited in Blodget, *Economica,* 91.

soils, and lack of initiative—alone or in combination—are insufficient
to explain the pockets of careless agriculture in New England. It was the
lack of local markets for farm output, wrote Bidwell, that trapped
eighteenth- and early nineteenth-century inland farmers in poor husbandry. It was the lack of access to southern and West Indian markets
that isolated a chronically low-yield, subsistence agriculture from the
growth that was being generated in the commercial sectors of the Massachusetts economy:

> If the farmers of the inland towns had had an opportunity to exchange
> for the products of the outside world their grain, meat and dairy prod-
> ucts, they would have seized upon every scrap of information regard-
> ing the means by which their fields and live stock could be made more
> productive; their adherence to traditional methods would have been
> weakened, and they would have applied to the conduct of agriculture
> the same adventurous and ingenious spirit which they displayed in the
> field of mechanical invention and in that of commercial enterprise.[5]

Bidwell's paradigm of a rural economy stunted by lack of access to
markets dominated New England studies for a very long time indeed,
but by 1952 (the heyday of consensus historiography), the story was
being told another way based on evidence that—contrary to Bidwell—
trade, exchange, and commerce in the eighteenth century had in fact
been ubiquitous. Bidwell's argument for the lack of a market, said Rodney Loehr,[6] was inadequately supported and heavily deductive: the nar-
rowness of the market had only been deduced from the small size of the
nonfarm sector; low productivity had only been deduced from the high
level of out-migration; lack of specialization had only been deduced
from the premise—likewise deduced—of self-sufficiency. Loehr, on the
other hand, had examined contemporaneous travelers' diaries and found
evidence there of abundant exchange activity.

This perspective was then elaborated by others, using a variety of
sources and measurable proxies and boring back further and further in
time. The pedigree of these ideas is by now well known. Charles S.
Grant and James T. Lemon found ways to estimate the capacity of rural
economies to produce farm surpluses and inferred from the existence of
these surpluses the existence of markets for agricultural output in the
eighteenth century.[7] Grant went beyond the inference of market *behav-*

5. Bidwell, "Rural Economy," 352. See also his "The Agricultural Revolution in New England"; and Bidwell and Falconer, *History of Agriculture in the Northern United States.*
6. Loehr, "Self-Sufficiency on the Farm."
7. Grant, *Democracy in Kent;* Lemon, "Household Consumption in the Eighteenth Century."

ior to discern a market *mentalité,* attributing to eighteenth-century settlers an acquisitive yearning for speculative profits not unlike, he said,
"perhaps the embryo John D. Rockefeller."[8] Richard Bushman found
Connecticut farmers producing surpluses for a market as early as the
mid-seventeenth century and by 1690 tearing that "peaceable kingdom"
asunder in fierce struggles over land speculation, paper money, and the
political representation of economic interests.[9] J. Emery Battis's remarkable study of the antinomian controversy pushed back even further,
to 1637, the date when the market began to color values and attitudes
otherwise alien to it.[10] That the "core support" for Anne Hutchinson
came overwhelmingly from the commercial and mercantile interests in
Boston confirmed the curious symbiosis between predestinarian Calvin-
ism and emergent capitalism, between free grace and free trade.[11] From
the earliest years of settlement, wrote Louis Hartz, virtually everyone
"had the mentality of an independent entrepreneur."[12]

What Lemon, Grant, Bushman, Battis, and Hartz were describing
was a mind-set, a market *mentalité,* an attitude, a set of values and ideas
that, it would appear, existed—and, they insisted, had always existed—
like noumena, independent of the material relations of production yet
predetermining its direction.[13] The rural economy of colonial Massachusetts must have been linked to markets, they seemed to be saying, because people thought in market terms. Was this, then, the "ineluctable
singularity" of America: that it was, and always had been, "a democracy
in cupidity"?[14]

Of course, in building this historiographic consensus, one skein of
Bidwell's braided argument had, unaccountably, been allowed to drop.
Impeded access to markets had been his explanation for the low productivity of New England agriculture. If there had been access to markets
all along, then how do we account for the low productivity?

New England rural society was radically reinterpreted with the appearance in 1970 of four books[15] that modeled the seventeenth-century

8. Grant, *Democracy in Kent,* 53.
9. Bushman, *From Puritan to Yankee.*
10. Battis, *Saints and Sectaries.*
11. "Free grace struck a responsive, if inarticulate chord among those who felt the attractions
of free trade" (Ziff, *Puritanism in America,* 76).
12. Hartz, *The Liberal Tradition in America,* 89.
13. "Ideas and attitudes as forces in history [had] returned and [were] now being explored as
explanatory categories in a novel way" (Hofstadter, *The Progressive Historians,* 443).
14. Hofstadter, *The American Political Tradition,* viii.
15. Lockridge, *A New England Town;* Demos, *A Little Commonwealth;* Greven, *Four Generations;* and Zuckerman, *Peaceable Kingdoms.* Strictly speaking, Demos's *Little Commonwealth*

Massachusetts town as an anthropologist might model a traditional peasant village:[16] a benign place, stable, disciplined, deeply religious, pa-
triarchal, homogeneous, self-sufficient and anxious to remain so, "a
christian, utopian, Closed, Corporate Community."[17] The coincidence
of simultaneous publication appeared to create a new paradigm, a new
consensus, and a metaphor—the "moral economy"—was transferred
from the anthropology of Southeast Asian peasant villages to early New
England historiography, where it has been dominant for two decades.[18]
That consensus was only reinforced by the nearly simultaneous publication eight years later of another cluster of works by moral economy
historians.[19] This time the other skein of Bidwell's braided argument
was allowed to drop. Access to markets was now beside the point; the
focus was on the low productivity, but this time it was a thing to be
celebrated.

II. THE MORAL ECONOMY MODEL

The moral economy model argues, by analogy from peasant, tribal, or
clan-based societies, that precapitalist rural communities, wherever they

---

is a study of conflict, not cooperation, but the conflicts are for the most part within families—a
product of the psychodynamics of the Puritan family—not among members of the community.

16. Among the more influential anthropological writings that might be cited are Scott, *The
Moral Economy of the Peasant;* Sahlins, *Stone Age Economics;* Wolf, *Peasants,* and "Closed,
Corporate Peasant Communities"; and the works of Karl Polanyi, among which are *The Great
Transformation, Trade and Markets in the Early Empires,* and *Primitive, Archaic and Modern
Economies.*

17. "But the origins of the Dedham commune ran deeper than the Puritan ideology, deeper
even than Christianity. . . . For the deepest secular origins of this Utopian Closed Corporate Community lay not merely in English villages but in a major strain of peasant culture also found in
medieval and modern villages of France and Spain, and in modern Indian and Javanese villages"
(Lockridge, *A New England Town,* 18).

18. A significant "break" in the consensus came with the publication of Stephen Innes's
Labor in a New Land. Innes appears, halfway through his book, to have been persuaded that the
Springfield he was describing could not be explained in terms of the communitarian model but fit
the older model—a model consistent with the works of Richard Bushman on Connecticut, David
Konig on Salem, Boyer and Nissenbaum on Danvers-Salem, Rutman on Boston, Battis on Boston,
and Powell on Sudbury, among others—of the colonial New England town as a dynamic, disputa-
tious, difficult place, a place designed to play a role in the British imperial ambitions that had
financed its settlement, a part of the modernization process almost from its very beginnings (see
Konig, *Law and Society in Puritan Massachusetts;* Boyer and Nissenbaum, *Salem Possessed;*
Rutman, *Winthrop's Boston;* and Powell, *Puritan Village*).

19. Henretta, "Families and Farms"; Merrill, "Cash Is Good to Eat"; Clark, "Household
Economy, Market Exchange, and the Rise of Capitalism"; and Mutch, "Yeoman and Merchant in
Pre-Industrial America."

are, are primarily collective arrangements for the economic and social security of all members of a group very much at risk, an arrangement "to guarantee subsistence as a 'moral claim' or as a 'social right' to which every member is entitled."[20] Such a social contract will have some or all of the following features.

1. The members, being risk averse, make collective decisions that favor minimizing expected losses over maximizing expected gains, subsistence crops over cash crops, and self-sufficiency (at the household or village level) over gains from trade.

2. Utility maximization, whether at the individual or the household level, is subordinated to community norms; this is to say that a premium is placed on conformity and that the transactions costs of individual initiatives are made very high.

3. There may be a two-tier system in which exchanges *within* the village (which are governed by "need" or "use value" rather than by profit or advantage) are insulated from exchanges with the *outside* world that alone inhabit "the privileged domain of market exchange transactions."[21] The "prices" at which goods exchange within the village are therefore mere "cultural constructs," their levels fixed by custom, not market outcomes.

4. "The two institutional pillars of the market system—the rule of contract and private property—are conspicuously absent."[22] As a consequence, what is exchanged are not "commodities" (things over which owners have rights of possession, transfer, or alienation) but "gifts" (a web of reciprocal claims on persons).[23] "The aim of a transactor in such

20. Platteau, "Traditional Systems of Social Security," 3.

21. Ibid. That there were conspicuously export-oriented, staple-producing sectors in the colonial economy is, I think, not in dispute. Built ships, naval stores, dried codfish, pine masts, shoe leather, fattened livestock, and beaver furs were quite evidently produced for the intercolonial, West Indian, and overseas trade—to which can be added wheat, horses, beef, pork, and flaxseed (see Schumacher, *The Northern Farmer and His Markets*). That trade, at least for the period 1768–73, is abundantly documented in Customs 16, vol. 1, at the Public Record Office in London. The moral economy model, at least in its more knowing formulation, is prepared to countenance such trade if it is confined to *external* relations, those between the rural village and the rest of the world. These outward-facing market transactions have, however, been characterized by moral economy anthropologists in pejorative terms: "self-interest-seeking with guile," "negative reciprocity," "agents seek[ing] personal advantage by using any kind of means at their disposal, including 'lying, stealing, and cheating' as well as more 'subtle forms of deceit' " (Platteau, "Traditional Systems of Social Security," 3).

22. Platteau, "Traditional Systems of Social Security," 7.

23. Note that to maintain that the gift creates a debt is *not* the same as maintaining that the debt creates a gift. That the "world of the account book" is a world of reciprocal debt has been used by some communitarian historians as presumptive evidence with which to argue, in effect

an economy is to acquire as many gift-debtors as he possibly can and not to maximize profit."[24]

This model—this "molly-coddled world of anthropological ideas"[25]—has proved to be far more resilient and polymorphic than one might have imagined. It has been applied to phenomena as varied as crowd actions in eighteenth-century England, Vietnamese and aboriginal peasant villages, the New York City working class in the 1830s, the towns and villages of New England, Hudson River Valley towns, the "task system" on southern slave plantations, communities of freed blacks in the lowland counties of South Carolina, agrarian populism in Texas, new settlements on the Illinois frontier, the conflict over fishing rights in eighteenth-century Rhode Island, the conflict over fencing laws in the postbellum Georgia up-country, and "stone age economies."

It is an idea born of the marriage of cultural anthropology and Marxism. From Marxism comes the vocabulary, the target, and the epistemology. The moral economy is a standing rebuke to capitalism, to its exploitation, alienation, "commodity fetishism," emiserating competition, and disempowerment of the producing classes. From anthropology comes the generic universality of "the village": the notion that all villages everywhere are, in some important sense, alike.[26] The villages of rural New England, like those anywhere in the peasant world,[27] are al-

---

backward, that what are being exchanged are not commodities but "gifts," i.e., claims on personal relationships. This, it seems to me, is not only a serious logical error but also a serious misreading of the nature of account book transactions in Massachusetts.

24. Gregory, *Gifts and Commodities,* 19.

25. Platteau, "Traditional Systems of Social Security," 6.

26. "Robert Redfield . . . in 1954 was the first to suggest that all villages share something of a common culture. In his 1956 book, *Peasant Society and Culture,* Redfield wrote, 'Peasant society and culture has something generic about it. It is some kind of arrangement of humanity with some similarities all over the world'" (Critchfield, *Villages,* 341). Critchfield defines the lineaments of this "universal village culture" and concludes, "It just could be the most harmonious way of life for human beings who choose to live in groups" (p. 346).

27. There have been some demurrals within the ranks of those I am calling "moral economy" or "communitarian" historians with respect to employing the aboriginal peasant village as the template for understanding Massachusetts towns. James Henretta, e.g., writes of Kenneth Lockridge's work, "Dedham was simply not analogous to the subjugated aboriginal settlements which Eric Wolf depicted as 'closed corporate peasant communities'. A more realistic comparison is with the peasant societies of *early modern* Western Europe; and the differences are sufficiently great as to render use of the term [*peasant*] unwise in the American context" ("Families and Farms," 19, n. 42). Later, in this same footnote, Henretta writes, "If a historical analogy is required, then the 'post-reform' peasant societies of *19th-century* Western Europe are the most appropriate, not those of the ancien regime" (p. 20, n. 42; emphases added).

Whether it is appropriate to call Massachusetts farmers *peasants* at all depends, of course, on how *peasant* is defined. If a veneration for ancestral lands and ancestral ways of doing things is

leged to have been communities in which the exchange transactions among "ancient and petty producers" created, not a market economy, but a thickly textured web of reciprocal obligations, binding one to the other and to something more than a place: to a "dense collective experience"[28] of reciprocity, mutuality, and kinship.

The moral economy model rejects on principle the notion that onto this material substratum could be grafted a market-oriented *mentalité* that is both inconsistent with and dysfunctional to it, for to attempt to do so violates the canons of Marxist epistemology according to which the structure of "ideology" (ideas, beliefs, values, consciousness, *mentalité*) is functionally rooted in the material substratum, that is, in the mode and social relations of production.[29] Ideas cut loose—like the ab-

---

central to, or even part of, the definition (as it is for Redfield and Critchfield), then applying the word to New England yeomen is, it seems to me, indefensible. But Massachusetts farmers—before 1750—may fit the definition of peasants as "family farmers only partially integrated into incomplete or imperfect markets" (Ellis, *Peasant Economics,* xii, and passim). The fit, however, will not be a good one, for Ellis means to include, among the imperfect markets that peasants face, "complex traditional rights of access to land which prevail over and constrain the operation of freehold land markets. In some countries these traditional land rights are inalienable, and in others transfers of land outside ties of family are rare even though freehold markets do exist" (p. 8). Hindrances of these kinds did not constrain land transfers in Massachusetts.

28. This useful phrase is from Arensberg, "American Communities," 1150.

29. "The only way to reconcile the contradiction [between evidence and theory] is by imputing to the market theorists a belief that there is a *disjunction between mentality and social structure,* that there can be profit-maximizing behavior in the absence of an economy in which profit was a meaningful concept" (Mutch, "Yeoman and Merchant in Pre-Industrial America," 285; emphasis added).

Although criticized by a Marxist reader of this chapter, my characterization of Marxist epistemology with respect to the rootedness of "ideology" in the material relations of production is, I think, defensible. I cite the following "celebrated passage" from Marx's *Critique of Political Economy:* "In the social production which men carry on, they enter into definite relations that are indispensable and independent of their will; these relations of production correspond to a definite stage of development of their material powers of production. The sum total of these productive relations constitutes the economic structure of society—the real foundation on which rise legal and political superstructures, and to which correspond definite forms of social consciousness. The mode of production in material life determines the general character of the social, political and spiritual processes of life. It is not the consciousness of men that determines their existence, but on the contrary their social existence determines their consciousness" (the passage is quoted, and characterized as "celebrated," in Berlin, *Karl Marx,* 132–33).

Marx's views on "the autonomy of thought" are further spelled out in *The German Ideology:* "Morality, religion, metaphysics and all the rest of ideology as well as the forms of consciousness corresponding to these, thus no longer retain the semblance of independence. They have no history, no development; but men, developing their material production and their material intercourse, alter along with this their actual world, also their thinking and the product of their thinking" (quoted in Elster, *Making Sense of Marx,* 468). The functional dependence of ideology on the material relations of production, and therefore the correspondence between them, was, however, not simple:

stract idea of a market economy or the seventeenth-century synthesis of religious, philosophical, and political ideas that placed the individual at the center of social action—are not forces in history, and ideas, being themselves determined, cannot be explanatory categories.

Notice that the moral economy argument is quite different from Bidwell's even though the world being described—an economy outside the market—appears superficially similar. Bidwell had in fact been speaking within a neoclassical framework: he *deplored* the lack of markets within a feasible range of most New England farms. Explicit in his work is the conviction that, had markets been accessible, the rationalization they impose would have liberated farmers trapped in woeful suboptimalities. The moral economy argument finds the same absence of a market, but *celebrates* it, as it celebrates the integrity of precapitalist, cooperative societies generally.

Can the moral economy model of the New England village be empirically tested? While deeply grounded in untestable assertions about values, attitudes, and *mentalités,* it is sufficiently multidimensional to exhibit facets that can themselves be tested.[30] The discussion in the remainder of this chapter "will hold, as 'twere, the model up to nature." It will ask, Can peasant producers be maximizers? How peaceable can Massachusetts "kingdoms" have been in the face of evidence of individuation, faction, "commercialization," and schism? Were farm-gate prices market outcomes or merely "cultural constructs"? Does market involvement require the capacity to produce surpluses? Did the structure of property rights in commonalty inhibit the "commodification" of pro-

---

"In the attempt to convince themselves that their acts are determined by reason or by moral or religious beliefs, men have tended to construct elaborate rationalizations of their behavior. Nor are these rationalizations wholly powerless to affect action for, growing into great institutions like moral codes or religious organizations, they often linger on long after the social pressures, to explain away which they arose, have disappeared. Thus these great organized illusions themselves become part of the objective social situation, part of the external world which modifies the behaviour of individuals, functioning in the same way as the invariant factors, climate, soil, physical organism, already function in their interplay with social institutions" (Berlin, *Karl Marx,* 135).

Ideas are not only *shaped by* interests, they *serve* interests (Elster, *Making Sense of Marx,* 465). In this guise, the ruling class "generate[s] ideas, values, laws, habits of life, institutions . . . the whole purpose of which is to prop up, explain away, defend, their own privileged, unnatural, and therefore unjustified, status and power" (Berlin, *Karl Marx,* 139). Thus, illusion, deception, self-deception, myth, and wishful thinking also come between ideology and fact.

30. For an excellent criticism of the moral economy model in the context of the debate between Samuel Popkin and James Scott on Southeast Asian peasant communities, see Feeny, "The Moral or the Rational Peasant?"

ductive resources? Finally, how well does the moral economy work as an explanatory model?

III. Peasant Motivation: "The Optimising Peasant"[31]

Recent studies of peasant and primitive economies have succeeded in blurring the sharp distinctions that anthropologists used to make between the attitudes that inform nonmarket and market, traditional and modern, peasant and capitalist modes of social organization. This is not to say that no such distinctions exist, only that they are no longer so clear cut and cannot be understood to have obvious behavioral consequences.

Ever since Max Weber, it has been taken for granted that certain attitudes—close calculation of profit and loss, systematization, rationality,[32] a belief in the effectiveness of individual action, future-time preference, maximization—were paradigmatic features of modern capitalism. But many of these same attitudes have been observed by anthropologists in premodern societies all over the world. Maximizing—in the narrowest sense of maximizing money income as well as in the broader sense of "seeking maximal advantage" or "acquisitive competition at some level"[33]—has been widely observed in the market-place behavior of countless peoples.[34]

31. This phrase is taken from Lipton, "The Theory of the Optimising Peasant."

32. By *rationality* is meant a consistent, ordinal ranking of preferences and the inclination to weigh the costs and benefits of pending actions.

33. The phrase is used by Raymond Firth in "A Viewpoint from Economic Anthropology," 31. "Seeking maximal advantage," whether on behalf of individual households or descent groups, has been found to characterize the market-place behavior of aboriginal Maoris, the Ifugao of the Philippines, the Afikpo, Esusu, Yoruba, Hausa, Tiv, and Dahomean peoples in West Africa, the northeastern Malays, the Haitians, Javanese, Trobriand Islanders, and the Highland Guatemalan Indians. There is even evidence, particularly widespread among the West Africans, of a delight in speculative profit taking on seasonal price differentials and, among Javanese peasants, of trading relations that are as "specifically impersonal, achievement-oriented, and socially neutral" as they are in highly developed economies (Geertz, *Peddlars and Princes*, 46–47).

"Maximization is a primary and valid psychological assumption. . . . The characterization of primitive and peasant societies as being uninterested in maximization is demonstrably false" (Belshaw, *Traditional Exchange and Modern Markets*, 77, 109).

That many of these cultures have institutionalized complicated leveling mechanisms to skim off differential wealth and redistribute it among households, far from repudiating, only confirms the existence of differential private gain and the troublesome persistence of the incentive to "seek maximal advantage" at the expense of, or in defiance of, community norms.

34. Perhaps the most scrupulously documented case is the Panajachelenos of Guatemala. "The Indians talk about markets, and prices, more than anything else, and merchandising activities

But we, who understand so little of our own attitudes and values, stand to gain little from arguing about the attitudes and values of societies utterly remote from ours. Much more fruitful is an approach that is prepared to countenance a typology of peasant villages, operating under a variety of constraints, with a variety of household-level strategies, each of which will have behavioral consequences that can be observed (and on the basis of which it may then be possible to infer values and attitudes). Such an approach is found in Frank Ellis's *Peasant Economics* (esp. pt. 2), which presents five models of peasant household economic behavior, all of which are amenable to neoclassical economic analysis because they all assume that peasants maximize (or minimize) something—even if not the same thing—that can be expressed as a function of something else (or several other things): output per acre as a function of manhour inputs, leisure hours as a function of wages forgone, output mix as a function of relative prices, and so on.

a) The profit-maximizing peasant. Behavior is said to be profit seeking, or profit maximizing, when the peasant can be seen to adjust outputs or inputs to give his household "a higher net income whether measured in money or physical terms, and this applies equally to a near subsistence household as to a fully monetised one." Sensitivity to the behavior of prices is required for the profit-maximizing peasant: the need for adjustment may in all likelihood have been triggered by relative price changes, and the inputs or outputs that are adjusted must be valued in terms of some kind of prices. If we use Ellis's definition of peasants as "family farmers only partially integrated into incomplete or imperfect markets," then it is clear that this kind of peasant lives closer than other peasants to a world of markets that function, perhaps not well, but less imperfectly than other peasant markets.[35]

The adjustment of the profit-maximizing peasant household toward the attainment of an *economically efficient* level of output can be completely described by marginal productivity theory, where marginal product is the slope (at a point given by the relative prices of labor and of output) of the total product curve, which, in turn, is estimated from survey data.

---

are well known." "The Indian is perhaps above all else an entrepreneur, a businessman always looking for new means to turn a penny . . . he is on the lookout for new and better seeds, fertilizer, ways of planting; and always new markets." "As will be seen, the Indians do not quite measure every economic activity by its money value. But they come close." (Tax, *Penny Capitalism,* 132, 12, 108.)

35. Ellis, *Peasant Economics,* 64, xii.

b) *The risk-averse peasant.* The potential for catastrophic loss is greater in the tropics, where most peasants live, than in temperate climates because in the tropics peasants are far poorer, weather patterns are far more volatile, and market information is far more inadequate than elsewhere. Under these circumstances, some peasants will seek to minimize the risk of disaster rather than maximize real incomes. Where allowed by landlords to make their own cropping decisions, they will put more acreage in subsistence crops and less in cash crops, and they will plant a mix of crops in each field—as many as eight or nine!—in a scattering strategy analogous to medieval strip farming. But risk-averse peasants facing these constraints are not beyond the reach of neoclassical analysis. Decision theory—specifically, the application of game theory to the maximization of expected utility under conditions of risk and uncertainty—is used, with the observed variances of rainfall, crop prices, and yields as variables. It predicts that most such peasants will produce subefficient levels of output. It should be emphasized that not all peasant households will be risk averse when the risks are desperately high. As will be discussed in section VII below, "some poor farmers are prepared to take an enormous gamble by which they either prosper or end up as penniless landless labourers."[36] Risk aversion may rise with wealth, decline with wealth, be a U-shaped or an inverted-U-shaped function of wealth, or be a state of mind independent of wealth.

c) *The drudgery-averse peasant with no labor market (the Chayanov model).* This model focuses on the decisions as to crop outputs and labor inputs made within a peasant household that cannot hire in or hire out wage labor. It uses indifference curves to analyze the trade-offs between the utility gains from increased output and the utility losses from decreased leisure. The point of tangency of the highest attainable indifference curve with the highest attainable total product curve will determine the level of output/income (and, by inference from yields, the acreage under cultivation) and hours of work/leisure. Since by assumption there is no hiring in or hiring out of labor, and since male and female workers are assumed to be interchangeable—it is, after all, a Russian model—the major determinant of performance will be the size (and age structure) of the peasant household.

This model appears to come closest to describing the so-called household (or peasant, or domestic, or family) mode of production that moral economists celebrate and posit as distinct from, and alternative

36. Ibid., 95.

to, the capitalist mode of production. But peasant agriculture on the Chayanov model "does not occur independently of the dominant capitalist mode except in the extreme (and entirely theoretical) case of pure subsistence agriculture. As soon as households buy or sell in the market place they confront prices and costs which are established in the larger capitalist economy." Chayanov-type decisions, if aggregated to the level of a *mode of production,* would be an economy "stagnated in every sense: no markets, no exchanges, no wider social forces causing movement and change in any direction."[37] As a model of Massachusetts agriculture at any time, it would appear to be, of all peasant models, not the best, but the *least* good fit.[38]

d) The farm household peasant with a labor market. There are four variants of this model, in which value of output (or household income) and hours of work (or leisure) are determined from the tangency of indifference curves and total product curves to the income or budget constraint, where both curves have been redrawn to embody the insights of Gary Becker's so-called new home economics.[39] When the resulting consumption and production decisions, which are jointly made, are analyzed, it turns out that the results for the peasant household are indistinguishable from the results under the neoclassical theory of the firm. This has implications for the Chayanov model:

> The purported uniqueness of peasants which is the cornerstone of the Chayanov model is seen to be entirely dependent on the assumed absence of a labour market. As soon as a labour market is permitted the production decisions of peasant households revert to the same economic calculus as other enterprises in the capitalist mode of production. *This result seems to confirm that what is distinctive about peasant forms of production is not a unique economic rationality common to all of them, but rather their partial integration into markets, and the degree of imperfection of those markets.* What the Chayanov model describes is nothing more nor less than a singular market imperfection; that of no labour market.[40]

e) The sharecropping peasant. Sharecropping introduces new analytic problems not shared by other models of peasant behavior. (1) Wage

---

37. Ibid., 116–17.

38. These issues are discussed further in sec. IX below.

39. That is, the household is seen not only as a consumer of purchased goods, valued at market prices, but also as a producer of final goods that take time to prepare, and time has an opportunity cost (see Becker, "A Theory of the Allocation of Time," and *A Treatise on the Family*).

40. Ellis, *Peasant Economics,* 137; emphasis added.

costs are ignored, and land rents, which are ignored in other models, enter as the major cost item. Unlike other land tenure arrangements, farming on shares means that, although the share is fixed (at least for the duration of the contract), the absolute level of rents varies with the level of output. (2) Much of the odor of exploitation that attaches to sharecropping comes from its association with "interlinked" transactions. When labor, land, credit, seed, and crop markets are defective, "interlinking"—access to these resources through, and only through, the intervention of the landlord—*may* act to equalize the distribution of scarce inputs but introduces an element of coercion, particularly with respect to crop mix, that pushes peasants into producing more of the cash crop than they would have preferred. (3) Sharecropping is a risk-sharing strategy, but the efficiency of its outcomes depends on who makes the decisions. If the major decisions are made by the tenant who gets to keep only a fraction of output, then "the equating of fractional marginal products to the market prices of inputs results in sub-optimal levels of resource use."[41] On the other hand, if the major decisions are made by the landlord, then, like a capitalist firm operating with wage labor, the outcome may be "efficient," but the social costs of domination, intimidation, and unequal access will have been ignored.

In this section, I have deliberately deflected the argument from one about maximizing *attitudes* to one about maximizing *strategies*, from one that drew on the observations of cultural anthropology to one that drew on the abstractions of neoclassical economics. But anthropology comes into its own in the next section, for the greatest lesson it has to teach economic historians is that the economic activities of all cultures, our own no less than those of others, must be "understood in the social setting and appraised by the values of the society in which they take place."[42]

The so-called New England debate is not about the universality (still less, the "innateness") of the profit motive but about the economic behavior of farmers in preindustrial New England. Anthropology, properly used, should teach us to ask, What is the culture, and what are the values within which *that* behavior took place? Was that culture and were those values inhospitable to individual- and household-level maximization? What role did communities play as purveyors of a coherent culture?

---

41. Ibid., 157. One of the underutilized resources may be labor-displacing technology, the introduction and diffusion of which may be retarded or halted where sharecropping tenants have a voice in decision making (see Whatley, "Southern Agrarian Labor Contracts").

42. Nash, *Primitive and Peasant Economic Systems*, 14.

IV. The Process of Individuation and
the Stability of Community

The historical emergence of market processes has frequently been identified with the rise of individualism. Evidence of increasing personal autonomy in the period under consideration would pose a challenge for the moral economy model.

Daniel Scott Smith has documented with great care and skill the individuation process unfolding in the demographic history of Hingham, Massachusetts,[43] and there is at least the presumption that this could have been happening throughout rural Massachusetts. In index after index there is clear evidence, beginning in the 1740s, of a movement in the direction of privatizing the decisions of adult life in repudiation of community values and parental control. There is a shift away from parent naming and Bible naming after 1750, a major increase in daughters marrying out of birth order after 1740, a decline in age at marriage, and a sudden increase in the out-migration of sons born to marriages in the 1740–60 cohort. Among those sons who remain, there is a slowing down of what Smith calls "intergenerational property mobility," a major increase in the inequality of the wealth distribution between 1711 and 1779, and, with population pressing on town lands, a great increase in propertylessness among males. Finally, a surge in premarital pregnancies between 1760 and 1800 suggests tellingly the loss of parental and community controls.

That these indexes of individuation are linked to the turbulent religious upheaval of 1740–45, the Great Awakening, suggests to Smith that the cause common to both is the *breakdown of community solidarity* and that this breakdown in turn can be traced to rapid population growth, the pull of new opportunities, and the dislocations and the anxieties of a developing economy. With the Awakening, the assault on religious orthodoxy, the "defiant individualism," and the unquiet shifts in traditional patterns of family governance that it legitimated[44] all combined

43. Smith, "Population, Family and Society in Hingham, Massachusetts."

44. The Great Awakening "liberated conscience from passive obedience to rulers and mounted a model resistance movement against vested authority. . . . Of greater lasting significance than its impact on churchgoing . . . was the Great Awakening's corrosive effect on . . . traditional injunctions of obedience to settled institutions. . . . Urging people to judge their spiritual estates themselves and to act appropriately, even if it meant traducing traditional arrangements, [the revivalists] fostered a 'defiant individualism' capable of operating outside the values of the old religious consensus and having . . . political repercussions too" (Cohen, "Onward Christian Politicos," 550, 552, 553).

with a subtle transformation of exchange relations within the economy to produce in mid-eighteenth-century Massachusetts a transitional period severe enough to be called a "crisis."

How did the village communities of Massachusetts withstand the crisis of individuation? If they were moral economies before the 1740s, did they remain so? In Yeats's terms, did the center hold? Kenneth Lockridge and Philip Greven have each formulated tests of community stability that consist of measuring persistence rates (or the inverse, out-migration rates) over time, in Dedham and Andover, respectively. Discovering the proportion of ratable polls who remained in the community—who appear on successive tax lists—to have been significantly higher in their towns than in the English parish town of Clayworth confirmed (they said) the greater stability, order, and traditionalism not only of Dedham and Andover but (they generalized) of colonial American society generally. Thus, geographic immobility was made a test, an observable correlate, of a moral economy—the closedness of the Christian, utopian, corporate communities.

Once persistence is identified as a test of the moral economy model it can be replicated by others. This W. R. Prest has done,[45] but with quite different results, which suggest that Lockridge had failed to distinguish, in his measures of persistence, between death and out-migration, so that Dedham's "radical underrecord[ing]" of deaths had contributed to Lockridge's radical overestimate of persistence, and that Greven's and Lockridge's estimates, taken at face value, "do not fit well" with other estimates of out-migration and persistence in seventeenth-century New England.[46] Furthermore, in comparing the social effect of out-migration from English and Massachusetts towns, Greven and Lockridge had failed to recognize that the out-migration of servants (who were the leavers in Clayworth) affected community stability far less than the out-migration of family heads (who were the leavers in Dedham and Andover). A still more pointed critique of their empirical work is its failure to control for size of town of origin. Dedham may have had a high persistence rate because its seventeenth-century land grant was an area of two hundred square miles—one could move very far indeed and still be a persister among the ratable polls of Dedham; Clayworth, however, was a small parish, and a short move made one an out-migrant.

But a critique of persistence as a test of community harmony can

45. Prest, "Stability and Change in Old and New England."
46. Thus, e.g., half the householders who settled Gloucester, Massachusetts before 1650 had moved out by 1660 (Heyrman, *Commerce and Culture*).

cut far deeper. In the first place, what in fact does persistence measure? Lockridge himself coined the invidious term *Europeanization* to describe the process of overcrowding, conflict, litigiousness, rising mortality rates, and fractionalization of landholdings that began to blight this community by the end of its first century. If successive generations refused to leave Dedham, it testifies to something, but to what?[47] By remaining, they exacerbated internal conflicts over rights in and division of the commons, the seating at the Meeting, the selection of town officers, the support of the minister, the growing number of uncovenanted (and therefore disfranchised) members of the community, and so on. In Sudbury, such a crisis had been averted by the large-scale out-migration of the grown children to found the town of Marlborough.[48] Which community—Dedham or Sudbury—had the more harmonious "collective experience"?

And what, finally, is "the community"? The land granted to the proprietors of the town of Dedham, like many of the early town grants, was later subdivided into four towns, each with its own church and school. Is the secession, or "hiving off," of new towns from old towns to be interpreted as increasing or decreasing persistence? as increasing or decreasing community stability? as increased heterogeneity or "enhanced homogeneity"?[49] The question can be asked in more general terms. What happens to the notion of "community" when, in fact, it is the exit option that is used to resolve community discord, rather than the affective bonds of voice and loyalty?[50]

V. The Market as the Agent of Community "Breakdown"

If ever there had been a time when one could have said of a Massachusetts town, "There is a we-ness" here such that "the sense of self and of

---

47. Perhaps persistence testifies less to harmonious relations and more to the burden that the costs of moving would impose on household wealth. In a recent study of nineteenth-century migration on the southern frontier, "More than 70% of the difference in wealth [between migrants to the frontier and nonmigrants] is explained by the unequal initial endowments of the migrants and the nonmigrants and the cost of migration" (Schaefer, "A Model of Migration and Wealth Accumulation," 148).

48. Powell, *Puritan Village.*

49. *Enhanced homogeneity* is the term Christine L. Heyrman uses to interpret the "hiving off" of Annisquam from Gloucester. The term *enhanced homogeneity* enables Heyrman to assimilate secessionist impulses into her "stable community" model. It also begs the question (see *Commerce and Culture,* 86).

50. Hirschman, *Exit, Voice, and Loyalty.*

community may be difficult to distinguish,"[51] then there was also a time when that ceased to be true. The communitarians see that as a time of irretrievable loss, of collapse, of fall, of a great divide between before and after. Borrowing heavily from Talcott Parsons and the typologies of German sociology, the historical experience of community breakdown in America has been dichotomized into polar ideal types: local versus cosmopolitan; primary versus secondary; rural-folk versus urban-industrial; status versus contract; community versus society; affective versus neutral; ascriptive versus achievement; traditional versus modern; *Gemeinschaft* versus *Gesellschaft*.[52] However the dichotomy is conceptualized, there are always two points in time—a before and an after—joined with a straight line representing a process, to use Perry Miller's term, of "declension."

It is a narrative strategy employed by virtually all American historians, in one way or another, but if one examines the array of proposed breakdown dates—the 1650s, 1690s, 1740s, 1780s, 1820s, 1850s, 1880s, 1920s—one cannot help but wonder which date is nearer the mark. After all, "How many times can community collapse in America?"[53]

There is a second narrative strategy: continuity without breakdown. It has been utilized by both sides, made to fit both the moral economy paradigm and its opposite. It views New England history, or the history of any New England town, as continuous: either as continuously commercial or as continuously noncommercial. It follows that, if the emergence of the market economy is a catalyst for breakdown, then a narrative that denies breakdown must locate the emergence of the market out of sight: either (like the consensus historians) at the very beginning, its

---

51. Bender, *Community and Social Change in America*, 7–8.

52. For an eloquent critique of the dualistic typologies in terms of which community breakdown has been structured, see ibid., chap. 2.

53. Ibid., 46. I would add to Bender's question another one. Why is the intrusion of market relations always held responsible for the breakdown of community? I find much of value in Bruce Mann's notion of "the newer community of the marketplace," which created a wider community extending beyond town lines to include strangers as well as neighbors: "The eclipse of the town as the primary focus of community did not necessarily mean that community declined" (*Neighbors and Strangers*, 166, 167).

In the following, substitute the word *market* wherever Mann has *legal*: "The gains in certainty, predictability, and uniformity that accompanied the formalization of legal practice and procedure allowed people from different communities to deal with one another within the common framework of an integrated legal system." The fact that certainty, predictability, and uniformity "also allowed people to treat their neighbors as they did strangers" (p. 168) places rural New England in what Benjamin Nelson called that transitional process "from tribal brotherhood to universal otherhood" fundamental to the economic development of early modern Europe.

effect felt continuously from the moment of earliest settlement, or after the curtain, figuratively speaking, has been rung down.[54]

A third, and bolder, narrative strategy has been to acknowledge the "commercialization" of the local economy as a turning point of some kind but to insist that it was one that *made no difference* to the structures of the community—primarily the church—that *really* matter; that, on the contrary, "the survival or resurgence of a communitarian culture limited the impact of commercial development." An example of this strategy is Christine L. Heyrman's study of the Massachusetts fishing towns of Gloucester and Marblehead. "Instead of confirming the conventional view that the Puritan communal order collapsed under the pressure of economic expansion," she writes, "the evolution of Gloucester and Marblehead illustrates the strength and resilience of traditional patterns of association and inherited beliefs and values." As she tells it, in spite of increasing commercialization throughout the 1730s, both towns "subside[d]" into "piety" in the 1740s, and "commercial expansion was contained within and molded by an older structure of relationships and beliefs."[55]

That Heyrman ends her narrative with the decade of the 1740s reminds us that it is no less true of narrative history than it is of statistical time series that the story one reads in the evidence depends on one's selection of its terminal dates. Propositions are robustly confirmed only when parameters in the research design—in this case its time frame—are biased *against* the hypothesis. Had she pushed her study beyond 1750, beyond "the intolerable zealotry and enthusiasm"[56] of the Great Awakening, would she still have found that spiritual concerns remained central? Had she taken a longer view, would piety still be seen to have triumphed? Would she still have characterized the entire colonial period "as not secularization but something like its opposite"?[57] Even more to

---

54. Thomas Bender puts a subtle spin on the continuity narrative: "Americans did not lack rationality, a concern for efficiency, or a willingness to work hard in behalf of their self-interest. What they lacked, from a modern perspective, was an autonomous economic institution legitimizing and facilitating the pursuit of economic goals outside of the web of social networks and cultural traditions. This was the market. . . . The market was primary in the transformation that separated the late eighteenth century from the late nineteenth century" (*Community and Social Change in America,* 113). In Bender's rendering, the institutionalized market lies (in some sense) outside eighteenth-century culture, yet there is the suggestion of an easily negotiated transition in the notion of a preexisting "readiness" with which market institutions, when they emerge, will not be uncongenial.

55. Heyrman, *Commerce and Culture,* 19, 18, 414.

56. Wilson, *The Benevolent Deity,* 120.

57. Heyrman, *Commerce and Culture,* 411.

the point, is her assumption that an increase in piety strengthened the bonds of community to go unchallenged? Since the Awakening shattered virtually every congregational polity in Massachusetts, in what sense can "triumphant piety" be said to have *preserved* the communal order?

VI. THE BEHAVIOR OF PRICES: "CULTURAL CONSTRUCT" OR MARKET OUTCOME?

Evidence of statutes, resolutions, and community pressure to fix, regulate, or control prices on both the province and the town levels in Puritan Massachusetts—like evidence of customary prices in traditional societies and of just prices in medieval Christian societies—has reinforced the view of moral economists that exchanges under such conditions were nonmarket events, their prices merely "cultural constructs."

But a market economy can coexist with a price-fixing regime as long as buyers and sellers are free to adjust *quantities* produced, bought, and sold to the fixed prices. This is demonstrably so in the most sophisticated economies at the present day, when planning and regulatory agencies find that controlling output indirectly (with no loss of efficiency) by fixing prices can be "a powerful and flexible instrument for rationally allocating resources."[58] Even under the medieval doctrine of the just price, considerable real-price flexibility entered in three ways: (1) while bread *prices* were fixed, the *weight* of the "farthing-loaf" was not; (2) while *bread* prices were fixed, *grain* prices were not; and (3) municipal authorities were permitted to adjust the level of bread prices with reference to a notion of "permanent costs of production," which of course included the price of grain.[59]

Philip Curtin has identified the same flexible response to market forces in the traditional "fixed-price" regimes of the fifteenth-and sixteenth-century Senegambian slave trade. In precolonial West Africa the buyer paid "the traditional number of measures, but var[ied] the quantity actually paid per measure. After a good harvest, the container

---

58. Weitzman, "Prices vs. Quantities," 477.

59. Pierre Goubert, in *Beauvais et les Beauvaisis de 1600 à 1730*, estimated that a French peasant in the seventeenth century purchased and consumed two to two and a half pounds of bread a day and his household ten pounds of bread a day! Since most French peasants (and English too) did not have ovens in their huts and cottages, it is small wonder (even if the diet of the English laboring classes was a bit more varied) that the regulation of bread prices was of the utmost importance throughout most of Europe. On the other hand, the appalling consequences of fixing bread prices in famine-stricken Milan in the 1620s is the subject of the remarkable chap. 12 of Alessandro Manzoni's *I promessi sposi* (The betrothed), first published in Italy in 1827.

used for measuring grain, for example, would be full to overflowing
. . . while in the hungry season before the harvest is in, the container
might not be even one-third full. . . . This type of *quantity bargaining
to allow for market price adjustments* on a seasonal or daily basis was
so common in precolonial West Africa that it can be taken as the dominant system in local markets."[60]

The output and allocation of goods and services under a regime of
fixed prices tests the efficiency of such a market not through the price
response to the quantities demanded and supplied but through the demand and supply responses to the administered, and therefore expected,
price. There is no question but that price flexibility *can* be used to identify the emergent hegemony of market forces—indeed, that is the principal diagnostic tool of my own work—but price flexibility is only a
sufficient condition, not a necessary one. The necessary condition is the
responsiveness of demand and supply to price.

Let us now proceed to examine the specific case of price regulation
in the Puritan commonwealth. In 1635, after a brief experiment in leg-
islating prices and wages at the provincial level, that responsibility de-
volved by statute on the towns.[61] It is likely that these less remote, more
informal—and, in a "shame culture," more effective—pressures from
the community acted to fix customary prices for some time.[62] The question is, For how long a time?

60. Curtin, *Economic Change in Precolonial Africa*, 239–40; emphasis added. Curtin criti-
cizes Polanyi for having sought to distinguish between "price" as a competitive market phenomenon and "equivalency" as a nonmarket phenomenon (what I have called a "cultural construct").
The actual terms of any bargain in precolonial Senegambia "were formed under market influences
in most recognizably commercial circumstances." Those terms include not only price but "the
number and size and quality of units to be exchanged, as well as the terms of payment" (p. 240,
n. 8).

61. See Hughes, *Social Control in the Colonial Economy*, 99 and throughout, and "Transference and Development of Institutional Constraints upon Economic Activity," esp. 53–60. A brief
discussion of colonial statutory wage fixing appears in Bureau of Labor Statistics, *The History of
Wages in the United States from Colonial Times to 1928;* and in Wright, *History of Wages and
Prices in Massachusetts*.

The social control of prices and wages was attempted not only in the seventeenth and early
eighteenth centuries but in a burst of price-setting "conventions" called during the revolutionary
war and early postwar years, especially throughout Worcester County. On these conventions, see
Brooke, *The Heart of the Commonwealth*, chap. 7.

62. In at least one community, local control of prices through the force of custom appears to
have continued at least as late as 1755. The following passage was found in the account book of
Henry Eames of Framingham, Massachusetts: "Mr. Bridg came into the town meeting and there
declard that he Bought rie of me and was obliged to give 44 shiling a bushel and I tolld him that
was not so for I never Sold aney above 40 shillings a bushel. He Replied and said he had but 2
bushels of me because he found that they sold chepr at mill and for 42 shiling a bushel. Deacon

According to the argument to be presented in chapters 4 and 6, the *increased scattering* of farm prices and of farm wages after 1750 constitutes evidence that the regime of socially controlled prices was beginning to break down by the mid-eighteenth century. By 1800, the dispersion, the scattering, the variance of prices (measured as the coefficient of variation), had peaked, and farm prices and wages had begun to converge, but this time under the hegemony of a market process.

When, and to what, shall we attribute the shift in regimes, circa 1750? Many historians have found in the Great Awakening an upheaval profound enough to have shattered the consensus that had upheld "constraints of commonwealth and moral economy," exposing a host of fault lines along which fractured communities polarized into new coalitions.[63]

But at least as great a threat to the regime of social controls came from the acute inflationary pressures acting on New England prices in the 1740s. The volume of paper currency (bills of credit) outstanding, which had approximately doubled each decade from 1710 to 1739, exploded fourfold between 1740 and 1749.[64] The several New England paper currencies (which can be treated as a whole because they traded at par)[65] depreciated in value from 5.00:1 to 10.33:1 against the British pound sterling in the 1740s alone.

To cope with "the Excessive high price of Provisions for Two Years past [that] has exceedingly Impoverish'd the Town," the record commissioners can be seen in the Boston town records of 1742–57 gradually relaxing controls over the Faneuil Hall market. In 1742, there was still a tax on country people bringing produce to the Boston market, and the

---

and Left. Sloan mad anser that they never had more than 40 shilings a bushel. Mr. Bridge said that he might be mistaken. June 23, 1755. Henry Emmes atest." (These prices are stated in old tenor currency; 40s. old tenor = 5s4d. lawful money = $0.89.)

In a revealing addendum, Eames wrote elsewhere on the page, "If we cannot stand before ouer Enemies in this world because of ouer Sins howe much Less shall we be abele to stand before the just Judge in the Greate day if theay are not pardon'd thro' the Blood of Christ." Eames's account book is in the Manuscript Collection of Baker Library, Harvard Business School.

63. Brooke, *The Heart of the Commonwealth*, 83–84.

64. McCallum, "Money and Prices in Colonial America," table 2, p. 11. McCallum's thesis here is that the "genuinely excessive" note issue in New England would have had an even more inflationary effect had "bad money" (paper) not driven out "good money" (silver). The increase in M1 equaled the emission of bills of credit minus the drain of specie (where M1 measures the supply of money as coins + paper currency + checking accounts in banks).

65. Rhode Island's note issue was considered a rogue currency as it flooded into Massachusetts. It is hard to see how it could trade at par when, at least by one estimate, it exchanged against the British pound sterling at 26:1 in 1760, ten years after Massachusetts had resumed a specie standard (ibid., 36, n. 20).

market was allowed to open only three days a week, and on those days only until noon (a proposal to extend the hours to one o'clock having been defeated). But the next year the tax was abated "as it disserves the town," and in 1757 it was ordered that Faneuil Hall market was to be kept open every day (except the Lord's day) from sunrise until one o'clock and on Saturdays until sunset.

Inflation not only overwhelmed efforts at price and wage fixing but also undermined the position of the elites.[66] The institutions that had forged the consensus in which the market was "embedded" were coming apart at the seams, and the transformation can be read in the evidence, beginning in 1750, of increasing variance of prices as they left a regime of social controls to enter the radically different world of a market process.

VII. THE ASSUMPTION OF SELF-SUFFICIENCY

The capacity to produce surpluses, whether at the household or the village level, is often treated as so necessary a condition of trade that the moral economists infer the absence of marketing solely from calculations that the local resource base would have been insufficient to produce surpluses. This, in my view, is the principal misconception in the historical literature on markets, yet it continues to dominate the debate.[67]

---

66. In the absence of a price index for Massachusetts before 1750, the severity of the inflation of the 1740s has to be inferred. Evidence from rates of exchange on the British pound are relevant only to the prices of internationally traded goods. One clue to the inflationary pressures is the increasingly importunate petitions of the clergy to their congregants and to town meetings for raises in salary. For instances in which the minister of Westborough found himself in the undignified position of begging, demanding, cajoling, and nagging his parishioners for an increase in salary and in firewood, see Walett, ed., *The Diary of Ebenezer Parkman,* entries for 9 January, 5 March, and 9 September 1744, 11 January, 8 February, and 7 August 1745, and 3 February, 1 April, and 24 October 1746, among others.

The difficulties that ministers confronted in the 1740s were exacerbated after the Revolution. To the extent that the breakdown of the "moral economy" can be read in the demeaning of elites, the evidence appears incontrovertible. The clergy lost their veto over congregational matters, their security was reduced from lifetime tenure to one held only at the will of church members, religion was disestablished in Massachusetts, they lost to other professionals—particularly lawyers—their monopoly of learning and the status that went with it, the education of children was handed over to teachers and academies, and with the proliferation of post offices and newspapers they lost their pivotal position in the dissemination of information (Brown, *Knowledge Is Power,* 78–81).

67. "The notion of economic surplus is extremely tricky, and it is doubtful whether it has much significance except in its meaning of unexpected windfall excess. . . . A man may not have enough grain to maintain his family and meet his kinship obligations to the extent that his values dictate; he has no surplus grain. But he may be in considerable need of an iron tool to enable him to continue to produce or to expand production. He may thus market grain, which was by no means

Implicit, and often explicit, in this argument is the unexamined premise that households and villages evolve from self-sufficiency to market involvement, that self-sufficiency always precedes market involvement, that markets are for the disposal of surpluses and are therefore accessible only to those who are sufficiently endowed to be able to produce a cash crop above and beyond the requirements of household (or village) subsistence.

On the contrary, exchange in simple economies arises from deliberate social decisions to forgo household (or village) self-sufficiency in favor of the gains from specialization and trade. Exchanges may in fact be sought first and most urgently by those who are inadequately endowed.[68]

The assumption that the poor take refuge in self-sufficiency ignores the market dependence of those at the very lowest levels of income and wealth, a phenomenon that has been documented for southern sharecroppers,[69] northern tenant farmers,[70] "cobblers whose children have no shoes," medieval English peasants,[71] sixteenth- and seventeenth-century

---

surplus, in order to obtain the wherewithal to purchase an iron hoe from a blacksmith" (Belshaw, *Traditional Exchange and Modern Markets*, 77–78).

68. That, e.g., is the conclusion of Bettye Hobbs Pruitt from her examination of the 1771 tax valuations of Massachusetts towns (see her "Self-Sufficiency and the Agricultural Economy of Eighteenth-Century Massachusetts").

69. Wright and Kunreuther, "Cotton, Corn and Risk in the Nineteenth Century."

70. Jeremy Atack, in his studies of farm tenancy in the North in 1860, compared tenant farmers with yeoman farmers with respect to two measures of self-sufficiency: home manufactures and diversification away from cash crops (hay, corn, wheat, and dairy products). He found that "the yeomanry produced far more home manufactures, indicative of a higher level of self-sufficiency, than tenants . . . [while] the data clearly show the greater degree of specialization of tenant farms compared with those of yeomen. . . . In both regions [Northeast and Midwest], tenant farmers concentrated more on cash grains than other crops. This is consistent with their greater need for cash to meet their periodic obligations" ("The Agricultural Ladder Revisited," 21–22 [I refer here to the unpublished version of this paper; the published version omits the discussion of the robust association found in the regression analysis to obtain between tenancy and specialization in cash crops]). See also Atack, "Tenants and Yeomen in the Nineteenth Century," table 4, p. 27, where logit regressions explaining farm tenancy in the North, 1859–60, produced coefficients that were large, positive, and highly significant on variables measuring specialization in cash crops.

Specialization in cash crops is linked to the production of surpluses: "Tenants in both regions [Midwest and Northeast] generally produced larger surpluses than owner-occupiers. In the Midwest, for example, tenant farms of every size produced more than comparable ones operated by the yeomanry. Indeed, those of 31–40 acres produced almost three times the surpluses of owner-occupied farms of the same size. . . . The product mix of tenant and yeoman farms in both regions accounts for this differential between them" (Atack and Bateman, *To Their Own Soil*, 219).

71. "The places and times in which inequalities were worst and the manorial and fiscal obligations heaviest were also periods and places in which men had the greatest need to produce for the market and to trade" (Postan, *The Medieval Economy and Society*, 201).

English wage earners,[72] settlers on the Maine frontier,[73] and Massachusetts farmers.[74] Dependence on the market can be a safety-first strategy for those who cannot afford *not* to take risks and hence, as Gavin Wright found for the postbellum South, may well be a U-shaped function of wealth or of size of farm.

What I am arguing is this: that "time's arrow" may very well have gone *from* marketing *to* self-sufficiency (whether defined on the household or village level) rather than the other way. If that is the case, the timing of market involvement cannot be made to wait upon the technological capacity or resource abundance to produce surpluses. Once market forces govern the trade between buyers and sellers, self-sufficiency itself becomes a market decision, not an ideological one.

VIII. THE PRIVATENESS OF PROPERTY RIGHTS

Still another test of the empirical content of the moral economy as a model of eighteenth-century New England towns might concern itself with examining the "absence of genuine rights of private property in productive assets"[75] that is assumed to be characteristic of the generic village. This assumption, even when not made explicit,[76] is the key to the moral economists' assault on the "commodification" of the means of production under a market economy.[77]

The issue of property rights and their role in economic development has been attracting a good deal of attention both in the law-and-economics literature and in the so-called new institutional economic history.[78] It deserves extended treatment that I am not expert enough to

72. Recall the discussion in chap. 1 of Shammas's *Pre-Industrial Consumer in England and America,* in particular her statement that "being poor and being a consumer, it turns out, were not mutually exclusive conditions" (p. 1).

73. Farmers settling the Maine frontier in 1790 with an initial allotment of 150 acres of land were found, as much as twelve years later, to have cleared and farmed only three acres, having devoted most of their land and labor not to subsistence farming but to producing a cash crop (lumber) for merchants shipping corded wood and ship masts to Boston (Taylor, " 'A Struggle of Finesse' ").

74. Pruitt, "Self-Sufficiency and the Agricultural Economy of Eighteenth-Century Massachusetts."

75. Platteau, "Traditional Systems of Social Security," 10.

76. It is, however, made explicit in Mutch, "Yeoman and Merchant."

77. In chap. 1, I cited Polanyi's *The Great Transformation* as one statement of the view that "labor, land, and money are obviously *not* commodities. . . . To allow the market mechanism to be sole director of the fate of human beings and their natural enviornment, indeed, even of the amount and use of purchasing power, would result in the demolition of society" (p. 72–73).

78. See, e.g., the following three books in the Cambridge University Press series on the political economy of institutions and decisions: North, *Institutions, Institutional Change and Eco-*

give, but I will relate some of this work to the evolution of property rights in early Massachusetts.

The most compelling evidence in support of the moral economy claim that ownership of the means of production was not privatized but was held in common by members of the community in early Massachusetts is the number of towns that at first settlement located their house lots in nucleated villages, farmed in strips or on unfenced lots in common fields, and grazed their cattle on common lands. Although not all towns were laid out in this way, the open-field system was widespread, particularly for towns settled in the seventeenth century.[79]

Private property, the rights that attach to it, and the institutions that secure those rights emerged as part of an evolutionary process—"the traverse along [a] continuum"[80]—in historical time. In open-field towns, rights to the usufruct of the land became rights to the land, to its use, transfer, donation, sale, disposal, alienation, "commodification."[81] As the common arable was progressively divided into smaller and smaller lots to be fenced and farmed in severalty, what had begun as "cow rights" in the common pasture and a share in governing the common

---

nomic Performance; Libecap, *Contracting for Property Rights;* and Barzel, *Economic Analysis of Property Rights.*

79. The variety of settlement patterns adopted by the proprietors of Massachusetts towns has been explained by the extent to which open- or closed-field systems predominated in the regions of England from which they came (see Allen, *In English Ways*). The classic study of open-field settlement and its transformation is Sumner Chilton Powell's history of Sudbury, *Puritan Village.* J. Ritchie Garrison, in his dissertation "Surviving Strategies," contrasts the seventeenth-century settlement of the Connecticut Valley town of Deerfield on the open-field system with the eighteenth-century settlement of the hill town of Conway on the closed-field system.

80. Field, "The Evolution of Property-Rights Institutions," 6. The discussion of common lands that follows owes much to, and draws heavily on, the work of Barry Field. See also Field and Kimball, "Agricultural Land Institutions in Colonial New England."

81. As far as Massachusetts inheritance law is concerned, the restrictions that the moral economists would place on the alienation of land in the early New England village do not apply. The English common law of primogeniture and entail was abandoned on first settlement in Plymouth and in 1641 in Massachusetts Bay with the publication of Nathaniel Ward's *Body of Liberties.* With respect to both intestacy and wills, the partible inheritance of land by all children (with, until 1789, a double portion for the eldest son) permitted no restrictions on its subsequent sale (except by the widow of her dower, which she held in trust for her husband's children). (See Haskins, "The Beginnings of Partible Inheritance in the American Colonies.")

But on reflection it is not even clear which—primogeniture or partibility, entail or alienability—is more "pro-capitalist." Moral economists, who see in the "commodification" of productive assets a sinister capitalist ploy, might ponder the role that dynastic concentrations of entailed land played in capitalist accumulation: "The distribution of land . . . is really only one part of a larger issue: the degree to which family capitalism required the unequal distribution of all property, both realty and personalty, to heirs" (Shammas, Salmon, and Dahlin, *Inheritance in America,* 42).

arable emerged as farms held in private.[82] This simple sketch of a linear transition is complicated by the fact that the word *commons* was applied to two types of collective tenures: common lands (mostly for grazing) and common fields (mostly for tillage). Both referred to acreage fenced in common, but a right in the common lands carried the legal status of a "tenant," whereas a right in the common fields carried the legal status of an "owner." The continuum then is a complicated one: a linear movement in time from commonalty to severalty, intersected by a cross-sectional shift between the uses of common lands—from pasture to arable and back to pasture, with rights shifting from tenant to owner and back to tenant—each with different mixes of public and private.

The institution of the commons may have come to these shores as the cultural baggage of East Anglian settlers who had known only open-field farming since the Middle Ages, but it persisted here because it was as well adapted to the danger of Indian attack, the acute scarcity of labor, the prohibitive labor costs of fencing, the low yields, and the poor nutritional quality of native fodder grasses as it had been in the Middle Ages to the management of risk. But holding land in common disappeared in one New England town after another when the conditions to which it was adapted disappeared:[83] when the free-rider problem, particularly with regard to fencing, became an acute source of strife;[84] when

82. Even the "purest" property rights are constrained by the "pure" property rights of others. Blackstone's famous definition of private property as "the sole and despotic dominion which one man claims and exercises over the external things of this world, in total exclusion of the right of any other individual in the universe," establishes, by the very absolutism of its language, the contingent nature of property rights. Within fifty years of Blackstone's utterance, state courts in New York and New England began the process of compromising farmers' property rights in favor of industrial property rights.

83. There was an alternative to closing the commons, and that was for each new generation (and its herds) to "hive off," to clear, found, and settle new towns, and to devise new strategies to accommodate growing populations. This was Sudbury's solution (see Powell, *Puritan Village*).

84. Fencing is a particularly vivid opportunity for free-rider problems because fences have the character of a public good. An abutter may refuse to pay his share of a fence, but, once erected, there is no way he can be excluded from the benefits of being on the other side of one. "It is noteworthy that [a] 1643 act specified that [if] an individual wanted to fence his property and the abutter(s) wished to keep their land in common use, the individual doing the fencing had to bear all of the fence costs." By the end of the eighteenth century, methods for apportioning and assigning fencing costs among commoners, establishing a grievance procedure, and monitoring compliance were fully in place (Field, "The Evolution of Property-Rights Institutions," 20–23).

The incidence of fencing costs also figured in conflicts between farmers and cattle raisers in the postbellum Georgia up-country. For Steven Hahn, the decision to shift the burden of fencing costs from farmers to cattle raisers (i.e., to vote the so-called stock laws) represents the triumph of capitalist values over the "moral economy" values of the "commonwealth of producers." Hahn

the natural increase of population and of livestock pressed upon grazing rights; when crops became sufficiently varied and husbandry sufficiently heterogeneous that uniform times of opening and closing the commons could not be maintained; when cultivated English grasses that were both nourishing and nitrogen fixing in rotation took over; when fencing costs fell; when labor productivity rose; when transactions costs—in particular, the costs of exclusion, of decision making, and of enforcement—rose.[85]

The dissolution of the commons can be seen as a special case of the role of transactions costs in the evolution of private property rights. It is not clear how a moral economy model, which would deny to these costs a market valuation, making of them a mere "construct," can help us understand this process better. The closing of the common may have had something to do with "the breakdown of community," but what? Was it cause? effect? symptom? synonym? If we want to *explain* it, we certainly have to do better than that.

IX. THE MORAL ECONOMY AND ECONOMIC DEVELOPMENT: THE PROBLEM OF HISTORICAL EXPLANATION

Suppose the preindustrial rural villages of New England really were moral economies. What is the force that would have pushed them off

---

deplores the shift from fencing out to fencing in as yet another instance of the privatization and "commodification" of a public good—the open range (see *The Roots of Southern Populism*).

For a reinterpretation of the Georgia fence-law conflict outside the moral economy paradigm, see Kantor and Kousser, "Common Sense or Commonwealth?" Kantor and Kousser find that the Georgia vote on the stock law cannot be explained by class (tenants and laborers against yeomen), or by culture (the conflict between the moral economy and the market); it is explained by the distribution of benefits: "The bitter conflict over the fence law had its roots not in a struggle to preserve a cooperative 'moral economy', but in the straightforwardly materialistic goals shared in common by those who expected to win and those who expected to lose by this institutional change. It was a conflict not of cultures or classes, but of interests" (p. 24).

85. "As a first approximation we can say that property rights will be developed over resources and assets as a simple cost-benefit calculus of the costs of devising and enforcing such rights, as compared to the alternatives under the status quo. Changes in relative prices or relative scarcities of any kind lead to the creation of property rights when it becomes worthwhile to incur the costs of devising such rights" (North, *Institutions, Institutional Change and Economic Performance*, 51). North is at pains to point out, however, that property rights are not necessarily progressive. A more realistic approximation will take account of the persistence of inefficient property rights. "The high transaction costs of political markets and subjective perceptions of the actors more often have resulted in property rights that do not induce economic growth, and the consequent organizations may have no incentive to create more productive economic rules." "The efficiency of the political market is the key" (p. 52).

center, that would have raced the engine and kicked it off its complacent, static suboptimality? If the market had been co-opted to serve communitarian ends and its capacity to initiate transformational change blunted in the interests of "older structures of relationships and belief," then where is the mechanism for change when we know that there was change? What can be built into the communitarian model of the Massachusetts rural economy to account for what we know to have been its dynamism? How did the transition to capitalism take place?

To ask the question still more generally, What should be the place in social science history of a model that fails to explain a phenomenon in such a way as to predict its observed transformation? Should not all models of the historical past be such that we can use them to ask, "Under what conditions, with the evidence in hand, might we have predicted the observed outcome?"[86] Somewhere Sir Peter Medawar, Nobel Laureate in biology, has written, "Most of the day-to-day business of science consists in trying to find out if our imagined world is anything like the real one." (A historian would add, ". . . is anything like one out of which the real one could predictably have emerged.") "If it is not," Sir Peter continued, "we have to think again."

The moral economy model imagines a world divorced from the market. If the real world presents evidence of the synchronous and convergent movement of prices, then the imagined world is (with respect to the market at least) nothing like the real one, and "we have to think again" about the premise that the market was absent or malfunctioning. If prices both converged and moved synchronously—that is, if they behaved *as if* they were determined in a market—then the burden of proof rests on those who insist that they were not. The behavior of prices— that is, the onset of synchronous and convergent behavior in the prices of farm commodities, farm labor, and rural savings—can be used to date the emergence of a market economy in the countryside.

Using the behavior of farmers' own prices to diagnose the emergence of a market economy does not mean that I have to impute modern economic motivations to the individual farmers whose account books I used. Prices are not a phenomenon of individual decision making but are themselves a collective "fact," the resultant of a social process. Although the market process has great implications for individuals, the individual is not the unit of analysis.[87] Prices are. The clues to the mar-

---

86. Conrad and Meyer, "Statistical Inference and Historical Explanation," 38–39.
87. The ideas in this paragraph owe a great deal to Smith, "A Mean and Random Past."

ket process lie hidden in the *pattern* of prices. Individuals do not experience "the past as pattern," but prices do. "People can have inadvertent, weak, or heterogeneous intentionality, yet certain results emerge in the aggregate. Out there—beyond the individual—there are mechanisms that ensure stable and predictable results on the average."[88] This relation between individual randomness and aggregate stability is called Quetelet's paradox. "The process, as Quetelet implied, may be stochastic, but the mean has meaning."[89] In just such a way were Massachusetts farmers involved in, oriented toward, under the hegemony of, a market economy.

It is likely that, even in the face of challenges to it as a model, the "moral economy" will continue as a metaphor to exert a powerful hold on the imagination, for it is only partly about early New England villages. It is mostly about what we, as Americans, have become, about a world, it is said, we would be better for having lost than for never having had at all.[90] Much as we may need such a "usable past," that is not, it seems to me, a burden the past need bear; nor do historians fulfill their responsibilities to the present by inventing it.

X. Conclusion

But is the application of a moral economy model to Massachusetts rural villages really only an "invention"? The studies in this book will attempt to present rigorously empirical evidence to date the emergence of a market economy. One of the principal diagnostics will be the convergence of farm account book prices and wages. But before prices and wages

---

88. Ibid., 146.

89. Ibid. "Mathematical patterns are pure, timeless concepts, uncontaminated by reality. Yet the outside world is so structured that these patterns in the mind apply to it with eerie accuracy. Nothing has more radically altered human history than this uncanny, to some inexplicable, interplay of pure math and the structure of whatever is 'out there'. The interplay is responsible for all science" (Gardner, "Count-Up," 34).

90. "If—as some of us are now arguing—there was not only a strong anti-capitalist sentiment in the US but also non-commercial and therefore non-capitalist ways of organizing economic activity which provided a lived and viable alternative to capitalist relations, institutions and practices, the entire story takes on a new aspect. Alongside the world of capital and its ways we would point to an alternative world of labor and its ways; alongside the world of cities built on money and contract we would point to an alternative world of the countryside built on personal credit and mutual obligation; alongside a government designed to secure to the few the opportunity to rule the many . . . we would point to an alternative government designed to secure to the many the chance to rule themselves" (Merrill, "The Ghost of Karl Polanyi," 66–67).

could have been so acted upon, before they could have been arbitraged into convergence, they had to be shaken loose from constraints of custom, law, and regulation, and the evidence shows that that process of price *divergence*—should we call it a *proto-market* process?—was happening in 1750.[91] Much supporting material has been presented in this chapter to suggest that the 1740s were indeed a turning point: the several indexes of individuation, the schisms exposed during the Great Awakening, the paper currency inflation of the 1740s, the relaxation of administrative and statutory controls over the Boston market.

But when did that proto-market process *begin*? Were social controls effective enough to hold off emergent market forces until 1750? Was there *ever* a moral economy in Massachusetts? Or was the proto-market carried, so to speak, to New England aboard the *Arbella*?

A study—like this one—that uses the behavior of relevant prices as the principal diagnostic is constrained by the fact that there are very few price observations for years before 1750 because there are very few farm account books (or very few surviving account books) before 1750.[92] It appears that the keeping of farm accounts was itself a cultural artifact with a time-path of its own: they appeared in about 1750, became more plentiful after 1760, peaked between 1790 and 1840, and then gradually disappeared as farmers turned to keeping cash books instead. The lack before 1750 of sufficient farm prices from which to discern a pattern of convergence threatens to leave the years before 1750 a "black box," and that opens the possibility that there may have been a time, before the emergence of the proto-market by 1750, when the moral economy model—or at least fragments of the model—may in fact have fit the New England village economy. Given the data we now have, that surmise cannot be dismissed out of hand. What can be said with confidence is that the kinds of empirical evidence marshaled here certainly will not support the application of a moral economy model to Massachusetts rural towns after 1750.[93]

91. Some "moral economists" themselves concede a turning point ca. 1750. Among them are Lockridge (*The First Hundred Years,* 177–80) and Henretta, who writes of the northern colonies generally that "a commercially oriented agriculture began to develop after 1750" ("Families and Farms," 16).

92. A notable exception is the six volumes of John Pynchon's account books, 1652–1702, in the Connecticut Valley Historical Museum, Springfield, Massachusetts. These were the archive used by Stephen Innes for his *Labor in a New Land.*

93. In a private communication to the author, John J. McCusker writes, "I find almost everything you are saying was the case in the last half of the eighteenth century to have been true as well

Great importance, therefore, attaches to the sources of evidence used in these studies, to the archives from which they come, and to the constraints they impose. These are discussed in chapter 3.

---

of the first half of the seventeenth century." By way of summary, McCusker adds, "I take as my text the statement (lament!) by John Winthrop: 'it being the common rule that most men walked by in all their commerce, to buy as cheap as they could, and to sell as dear'" (the quotation can be found in Hosmer, ed., *Winthrop's Journal,* 2:20).

3

Sources for the Study of Rural Economic History

I

My Research Design—to Confirm the Emergence of a Market economy from the market-like behavior of the relevant prices—depends for its data on the exploitation of farm account books, probate inventories, administration accounts at probate, and town tax valuations.[1] While many new studies in economic history continue freshly and fruitfully to mine published sources of macro-level data,[2] there has been much interest in recent years in finding and exploiting archival materials of, by, and about individuals, to build data bases that can generate new insights into "the past as pattern."[3]

For the identification of an emergent capital market in the rural economy—the concern of chapter 5—administrators' and executors' accounts at probate offer a way, without equal, into the preindustrial world of dyadic credit relationships. Administration accounts, filed in county probate courts as debts were paid by and to the estates of the deceased, are final reckonings. A decedent whose inventoried possessions may have included a "mansion," a piano, wallpaper, portraits on the wall, carpets on the floor, curtains at the windows, morocco-bound volumes in the library, silver shoe buckles, velvet waistcoats, a sword and sheath, a matched pair of carriage horses, a dozen head of cattle, claims to a thousand acres in the wilderness, and a share in a merchant ship can emerge from these accounts insolvent, his heirs forced to make

1. Only briefly discussed in this chapter, administration accounts are discussed in greater detail in the appendix to chap. 5. In addition to farm account books, probate inventories, and administration accounts at probate, town tax valuations for 1771, 1786, 1792, and 1801 are used in chap. 8 to provide independent confirmation of the timing of transformation in the rural economy. I do not discuss tax valuations in this chapter because (with the exception of that for 1771) they are a macro-level data source, and a very familiar one to historians of the Massachusetts economy.

2. I have in mind such macro-level sources as town tax valuations, state and federal censuses of population, manufacturing, and products of agriculture, prices current, freight loadings, ton-mile hauling rates, the McLane Report on Manufacturing, Patent Office records, balance of payments accounts, customhouse receipts, foreign exchange rates, receipts from public land sales, bank reserves, bank deposits, currency in circulation, national income accounts, military personnel records, reports of persons and articles hired at U.S. Army forts, retail and wholesale prices, and coastwise shipping manifests. All these data sources, and more, are used in such new studies as Thomas Weiss's revised estimates of the nineteenth-century labor force, Robert Gallman's revised estimates of the nineteenth-century capital stock, Kenneth Sokoloff's new work on patenting activity and manufacturing productivity growth, Lee Soltow's new studies of nineteenth-century income and wealth distributions, Robert Margo's new series of civilian real wages, and the new work of Richard Steckel on height, nutrition, mortality and morbidity (all these studies appear in Gallman and Wallis, eds., *American Economic Growth and Standards of Living before the Civil War*).

3. Elton, "Two Kinds of History," 77.

their own way in the world and his creditors unable to recover more than a few shillings on the pound. It is in these documents that one finds interest rates, a traffic in promissory notes, endorsements, and evidence of the expanding network of increasingly remote credit partners that defines a capital market.

For studies of farming practices and farm price and wage behavior—the concerns of chapters 4, 6, and 7—farm account books are without equal.[4] For a glimpse into the kind of information they provide, consider the account book of John Baker, a farmer in Ipswich, Massachusetts, from 1769 to 1834.[5] Open the box in which his large hidebound book is kept. The faint smell of manure, over 150 years old, still rises from thick yellowing pages, and you begin to live his life. In his book can be found every debt transaction to which he was a party for sixty-five years, the farm-gate price and quantity of everything he bought and sold, the price of every pair of shoes he made, the name of every person with whom he traded and in many cases the town in which that person lived, the labor he did for others, the goods and services he

4. Strictly speaking, few, if any, of the books we call "account books" are in fact that. Accountants distinguish between memorandum books, journals, and ledgers. In the terminology of accountancy, only ledgers are properly called account books. Most farm record books were memorandum books arranged in a bilateral form of single-entry bookkeeping. Entries were made in the order in which transactions occurred for each person with whom the farmer dealt; the left-hand page recording the transactions *to* which that person was a debtor ("Dr.") with respect to the farmer, the right-hand page recording the transactions *by* which that person was a creditor ("Cr.") with respect to the farmer. Debts and credits accumulated, sometimes for several years, until at some point in the history of the relationship the entries on the Dr. side and those on the Cr. side were summed, a balance taken, and a reckoning made either with a cash payment or with a promissory note. The account was then marked "settled," with both parties signing that it was so, on the date and at the place of reckoning.

Considerably more sophisticated than any others in my sample, vol. 2 of the books of Charles P. Phelps of Hadley (courtesy of Manuscripts Division, Baker Library, Harvard Business School) is, strictly speaking, a journal, a more advanced double-entry bookkeeping tool, to which each transaction posted from the memorandum book was both debited and credited to functional accounting categories: to "Sundries," to "Household Expenditures," to "Produce," to "Stock," even to "Profit and Loss." By Max Weber's definition of a *rational capitalistic enterprise* as "one which determines its income yielding power by calculation according to the methods of modern bookkeeping and the striking of a balance," Charles Phelps was well on the way to running such an enterprise as early as 1829 (the quote from Max Weber is given, without citation, in Corbin, *Accounting and Economic Decisions,* 212).

Advanced industrial and commercial enterprises would have posted their debits and credits from the journal to a T-styled ledger with assets on the left and liabilities plus equity on the right.

I ask the reader's indulgence as I follow conventional usage and apply the term *account book* to all manuscript books, of whatever form, in which farmers recorded bilateral debt transactions against the names of their credit partners.

5. John Baker's account book is in the Manuscript Collection of the Baker Library, Harvard Business School.

provided his widowed mother and what he charged her for them, the weights of the hogs and cattle he bought and sold and butchered, the ton-mile rates he charged for hauling loads, the destinations to which he hauled them, the man-days (or, in the case of contract labor, the man-months) of labor he hired, the tasks he hired it to do, the wages he paid, whether the hired hand was a man or a boy, whether the fellow came with his own team, wagon, and plow or used Baker's, and whether Baker provided dinner or the hired man "found" for himself. And because he sold milk, eggs, butter, and fresh meat, we know that his farm produced them, although they are too perishable to have been appraised in his inventory.

Farm account books are a treasure of rural history—the material in them "has the decisive advantage of being hard and exactly dateable FACT relating to the business activities of the central entrepreneurial figure in agriculture, the farmer"[6]—but used alone they leave many questions unanswered. In this respect they are like all sources of data in that they offer both opportunities and limitations; they both widen and constrain any inquiry based on them. The most significant limitation of account books is that they record only transactions: there are no aggregates. There is no record of total inputs, only hired inputs; no record of total outputs, only sold outputs. Total costs cannot be calculated because account books do not record the farmer's own labor, the unpaid labor of his family, the use of his own implements, or the working time of his own oxen. We learn a great deal about the farmer whose books we study, but not the most fundamental things. Is he well off, or is he poor? How much land does he farm? What yields does he get? How many head of cattle does he have? What implements does he have? How many sons and of what ages does he have helping him? What labor do his womenfolk do?

Probate inventories can fill some of these lacunae. Farm account books are best understood when compared with probate inventories, for the two archives complement one another. Account books are to inventories as income statements are to balance sheets, as flows are to stocks. Probate inventories are perhaps the most bountiful source for economic and social history to be mined in recent years. With the careful techniques developed by Gloria Main and Alice Hanson Jones to correct for the wealth bias imparted by their age skewedness, we have learned to reconstruct a whole world of the living from the real and personal prop-

---

6. Jones and Collins, "The Collection and Analysis of Farm Record Books," 87.

erty owned by the dead.[7] Inventories have been used to estimate the
level, distribution, and rate of growth of wealth; to note changes in diet
and to relate these to other data on heights and mortality; to identify
features of preindustrial consumption, savings, investment, and credit;
to trace patterns of geographical and social mobility; to relate rural savings to nonagricultural investment; to study levels and changes in living
standards; to examine links between the emergence of capital markets
and the fertility transition. From probate inventories we can track the
diffusion of a new technology, discover the books people read, mark
some of the changes in law and custom regarding the testamentary position of women, reconstitute families, and, because slaves were inventoried by name and age in the personal estates of their masters, sharpen
our understanding of slave demography.

It is just because probate inventories are so powerful that we need
to remind ourselves that they too have limitations. Even at its very best,
an inventory is but the still life of an enterprise, a farm, a household
stopped in time, its ongoingness frozen at the moment of death. Flows
are stilled, observable only after the fact as stocks. Allocation, production, exchange, and distribution have ceased to be activities unfolding
in time and can be observed only as the (perhaps inadvertent) consequences of interrupted processes.

Although probate inventories, unlike account books, do record aggregates, they have a built-in tendency to err with respect to both outputs
and inputs, making it hazardous to use them to calculate agricultural
production functions. They understate current *farm output* by frequently
omitting to inventory crops standing in the fields[8] and provisions consumed by the family or sold off the farm before appraisal. At the same
time they overstate current output by inventorying provisions held over
from previous years, harvested from leased acreage, or, of course, purchased.

Probate inventories tend to understate the *land input* by omitting

---

7. Jones, "Estimating Wealth of the Living from a Probate Sample," and *American Colonial
Wealth;* Main, "The Correction of Biases in Colonial American Probate Records."

8. A rare opportunity to appreciate the magnitude of this understatement is afforded by the
probate records of one William Stone of Watertown, Massachusetts. The provisions remaining at
his death in 1808 were valued in his inventory at $38.00, but, subsequently, in administering the
estate, the accountant estimated "the value of produce of the real estate from April 11, 1809 to
April 1, 1810, amounting . . . to the sum of $789.55" (from Middlesex County Court of Probate,
First Series, no. 21742).

British appraisers were instructed not to overlook standing grain. "Corn growing upon the
ground ought to be put into the inventory," according to Richard Burn's *Ecclesiastical Law* (1763,
cited in Allen, "Inferring Yields from Probate Inventories," 118).

leased land while at the same time overstating the land input by including all acreage whether used in current production or not.[9] And while the acreage in meadow, pasture, woods, and marsh is usually reported, the curious failure to report the number of acres in tillage precludes the estimate of crop yields from probate inventories.[10]

The investment of *capital* in agriculture takes several forms: structures, husbandry tools, working livestock, and (if not already accounted for in the value of land) the accrual of improvements to the land. The omission from inventories of any and all hired implements and of the hired services of working animals means that capital inputs are seriously understated. Many Massachusetts farmers—perhaps nearly half in 1771—owned neither plows nor oxen. They tilled the soil with hired capital that will appear only as transactions in their account books.

With respect to the (free) *labor input,* probate inventories are, of course, silent. These data are not merely biased downward; they are lacking altogether.[11] The need for hired help varied widely from farm to farm, but it is likely that no farm was run entirely without it even in the eighteenth century, and hired hands became a more and more important element in the operation of a farm after 1800. Farm account books are the only source for hired labor, as genealogies, vital records, and censuses are for family labor. Here the complementarity between archival sources is most keenly felt.

II

I began by saying that farm account books and probate inventories are complementary resources, that the lacunae in each could be filled by

9. I am speaking of northern inventories here; southern inventories did not include number of acres and valuation of real estate.

The question of how to value land in a production function is complicated. Its market price in a probate inventory is a mix of an economic rent to location—proximity to markets, e.g.—and the marginal value product of its soil quality. The need to distinguish between these two components of farmland value is discussed in David and Temin, "Slavery, the Progressive Institution?," 771–74.

10. Two recent studies have developed techniques for estimating grain yields from English probate inventories (see Overton, "Estimating Crop Yields from Probate Inventories"; and Allen, "Inferring Yields from Probate Inventories"). "For many farms it is possible to compute the value per acre of wheat, barley, or other grain in the fields. If these valuations are divided by prices, should this not produce implicit estimates of expected yields?" (Allen, "Inferring Yields from Probate Inventories," 118). This suggests that English inventories not only included standing "corn" but also gave acreage in each crop.

11. Slaves were inventoried, of course, because they were part of the personal portable wealth of their masters.

reference to the other. But that is not entirely true. There are critical magnitudes that neither one can supply. Farm account books lack aggregate outputs and inputs, but probate inventories that have them systematically err. Farm account books will not permit the calculation of per acre yields, but neither will inventories.[12] We are left to wonder why Massachusetts farmers did not find it useful—nay, imperative—to calculate and record outputs, crop yields, revenues, and costs in their account books when such information could have been used as a tool to inform and direct the activities of their farm.[13] Why, instead, were their account books merely records of debt?

There are those who would argue that this preoccupation with debt is yet further evidence that Massachusetts farmers lived in a moral economy isolated from the rationalizing imperatives of the market, that debt bound them to one another in a web of reciprocity quite unlike a market relationship.

On the other hand, the case can be made that the ubiquity of debt accounting, far from arguing aloofness from the market, can argue its very dominion, that costs were not "accounted for" because those farmers—like any producer in perfect competition—took their costs, like their prices, from markets over which they had no control. In ordinary parlance, *to account for* means to explain; to explain is to control; and what can be controlled will determine what is to be accounted for. Modern accounting makes it possible for the knowledge of unit costs to be used in the determination of factor proportions, levels of output, and product prices, but this assumes a degree of control over product and factor markets that would have been quite alien to early New England

12. In the Massachusetts inventories I have examined, tillage acreage, even as a whole, much less by crop, is consistently omitted.

13. Robert Loder, an English "improving" farmer of the early seventeenth century, included in his accounts at year's end the seed sown in each crop, the total harvested in each crop, the ratio of seed to yield, the value of crops sold, the value of the seed, the labor and livestock costs of each field, and the calculation of rents and interest forgone on each field under his own cultivation. He weighed the costs of wintering his stock against the imputed return he realized from retaining their dung, milk, and labor services. He compared piece rates with per diem wages. And he kept a close record of household expenditures (Fussell, ed., *Robert Loder's Farm Accounts*).

It would appear, however, that Loder's account book was not typical even in its own time and place. Despite a long history of bailiffs' manorial accounts, the English custom of keeping full farm records was apparently abandoned sometime between the late Middle Ages and the late eighteenth-century (Allen, "Inferring Yields from Probate Inventories," 117).

The manuscript collection at the Old Sturbridge Village Library contains an anonymous account book and daybook from Hampstead, New Hampshire (1817), that is as detailed as Robert Loder's. But "Anonymous," calculating perhaps that the cost of calculating outweighed its benefits, abandoned the effort after only one year!

farmers. The point deserves emphasis: what was alien was the control over the market, not the market itself.

We can ask the same question about double-entry bookkeeping: why was it so rare among farmers?[14] Of my sample farmers, only Charles P. Phelps of Hadley (in 1829) set up his book with separate accounts for produce, sundries, farm, family, notes receivable, (live)stock, cash, notes payable, and profit and loss. Every transaction, written in an exquisite hand on pale blue lined paper, was debited to the appropriate account as an increase in assets or a decrease in liabilities and simultaneously credited to another account as a decrease in assets or an increase in liabilities. Phelps separated the household accounts from the farm accounts; he struck a balance; and at the end of the year he posted his net position to profit and loss.

Double-entry bookkeeping was certainly not new: according to Raymond de Roover, it had arisen among Genoese or Florentine merchant venturers in the late thirteenth or early fourteenth centuries.[15] Had it been as useful to New England farmers as the bilateral, single-entry record keeping—learned, somehow, by all my sample farmers—they would have learned double entry the same way. Was it not useful because they were outside the market? Or was it not useful because they were not modern? The two questions are not the same.

The failure of my sample farmers to adopt double-entry bookkeeping is matched by the failure of entrepreneurs generally to adopt it before the Industrial Revolution. This is to say that double-entry bookkeeping is a tool of modern capitalism, not of market capitalism.

According to Donald Corbin, double entry is necessitated by the following conditions of the modern enterprise: the need to distribute profits among many absentee shareholders; the production of joint outputs among which costs must be allocated and separable decisions about profitability made; the need to put a value on unsold inventory (which is not the same as having unsold inventory); the need to allocate to each time period the slow depreciation of long-lived assets; the separation of ownership and control and hence the need to publish financial reports to absentee owners; the taxation of corporate profits (after 1913); the government regulation of financial markets; the growth of scientific management and the efficient monitoring of through-put at each stage of production; and the growth of the business machine industry, which, by

14. See n. 4 above.
15. de Roover, *Business, Banking and Economic Thought in Late Medieval and Early Modern Europe*, chap. 3.

selling the tools for record keeping, created its own demand.[16] As Sidney Pollard wrote about capitalist manufacturers in the Industrial Revolution, who also did not use double-entry bookkeeping, "It may be legitimate to judge that if reliable overall cost accounts are not further developed the chances are that the need for them could not have been felt very strongly."[17]

In order, then, to understand the preoccupation with debt, we must look again at account books, this time not so much as repositories of hard and datable fact but as artifacts of a culture at a specific time and place. Debt is a fact of life in all agricultural economies where very long production periods combine with periodic natural catastrophes to introduce dire uncertainty. But for Massachusetts farmers, debt was also a tactical response to the currency inflation before 1750,[18] to the chronic dearth of specie after 1750, to the currency hyperinflation during the Revolution, to the hard times, hard money, and hard taxes after the Revolution, and to the absence of banks doing business with farmers until the 1840s. Recourse to private indebtedness served at least to stabilize, if not to increase, the real money balances of farmers.

As rural indebtedness grew more ubiquitous, so did the incidence of rural record keeping, which is to say, the keeping of account books by Massachusetts farmers has a history, a time shape, of its own. As was mentioned at the end of chapter 2, there were very few before 1750, more in the mid-1760s, many between 1790 and 1840, and then few

16. See Corbin, *Accounting and Economic Decisions.*

17. Pollard, *The Genesis of Modern Management,* 248.

18. It will be recalled from the discussion of socially controlled prices in chap. 2 that the face value of paper currency in circulation in Massachusetts doubled in the 1710s, the 1720s, and the 1730s but quadrupled in the 1740s. As a consequence, it was suggested, specie was withdrawn from circulation as bad money drove out good. This "Gresham" effect, drawing down the quantity of money in circulation, may have muted the inflationary pressure but did not counteract it. The rapid devaluation of the Massachusetts pound against the pound sterling—from 5:1 to 10:1 in ten years—is proof of that.

Another view is offered by Charles Calomiris. Calomiris examined paper currencies issued both before 1750 and during the Revolution and found in both cases that the emissions were not excessive. Had the province provided for the redemption of both new tenor and the continental and accorded to both the status of legal tender in payment of taxes, the inflationary consequences of both episodes would have been neutralized (Calomiris, "Institutional Failure, Monetary Scarcity, and the Depreciation of the Continental," 47–68).

Here, again, the time boundedness of farm account books is to be regretted. Because there are few farm account books from the 1740s in my sample, I have few price observations for the 1740s in my price index and cannot track the inflation in farm prices of the 1740s. On the other hand, the hyperinflation of the revolutionary war does not appear at all in farm account book prices. This is because, being a repository of debt, accounts were kept, not in continentals, but in old tenor, a stable unit of account.

again after 1840, by which time they were being replaced by cash books that recorded transactions merely as inflows and outflows of cash "rather than [as] components of dyadic relationships between households."[19] With the innovations of cash books and of double-entry bookkeeping, accounting could evolve beyond mere record keeping to become for modern farmers—as it became for modern firms—a tool.

III

A discussion of sources in historical research must confront the possibility of selection bias. This section examines the argument that a sample of account books overrepresents literate, numerate, and therefore, presumably, wealthier farmers, much as a sample of probates overrepresents older and therefore, presumably, wealthier decedents. Does the keeping of accounts itself suggest a level of calculatingness that is "entrepreneurial"? Does the very fact of keeping records constrain the open-hearted sharing that is supposed to make a community and presclect for the kind of shrewd, calculating Yankee who is at odds with the community and therefore hardly representative of it?[20] (The reader will recognize, of course, that this is just the opposite of the argument at the beginning of section II that the very fact of debt accounting proves this same sample of farmers to have been *un*-entrepreneurial!) If so, then the selection bias in our source would have favored our hypothesis, and our results would have been compromised.

There are three kinds of evidence that might shed light on this question. One is the enormous range of writing, spelling, and number skills shown in the books, which, one supposes, must reflect an equally broad spectrum of education (and, by association, of wealth, enterprise, or "achievement orientation"), bounded on the lower end only by the fact

19. Larkin, "The World of the Account Book."

20. Thus, e.g., in "It Wasn't Me," one of Wendell Berry's short stories, Wheeler Catlett explains to Elton Penn, a young farmer he has helped, why Penn is not obliged to him: "I know that if you bought a calf from Nathan Coulter you'd pay him for it, and that's right. But aside from that, you're friends and neighbors, you work together, so there's lots of giving and taking without a price—some that you don't remember, some that you never knew about. You don't send a bill. *You don't, if you can help it, keep an account. Once the account is kept and the bill presented, the friendship ends, the neighborhood is finished*" (quoted in McKibben, "What Are People For?" 34; emphasis added).

If that is the way indebtedness is handled in Wendell Berry's community (Port William, Kentucky) today, it is certainly not the way indebtedness was handled in Gotham Brigham's Marlborough, Massachusetts, in 1804 when he charged his father's estate $0.50 for time he spent sitting with his mother at his father's funeral!

that all are to some degree literate and numerate. Copies of some pages from a few account books reflecting that range are presented in the second appendix to this chapter. At one extreme are the books whose spelling, numeracy, and flourishing penmanship speak of the courtly elegance of gentlemen farmers. But there are books in which the handwriting is barely legible, the spelling idiosyncratic (even by eighteenth-century standards), and a 1688 entry in which tallies were used instead of numbers. Given this broad range of record-keeping skills, the fact that the books are strikingly similar in format—two facing pages for each account; name of debtor, "Dr.," and *to* each debt transaction on the left-hand page; name of creditor, "Cr.," and *by* each credit transaction on the right-hand page; dates in the left margin of each page; a common vocabulary used for periodic reckonings—suggests that farmers were somehow taught the conventions of keeping accounts and that these conventions figured in the intergenerational transmission of a literate and numerate culture.

The second kind of evidence that could speak to the question of a possible wealth bias would be to locate each account book–keeping farmer in either the 1771 tax valuations, the 1850 Manuscript Census, probate inventories, or periodic town tax lists so that they may be positioned along a wealth continuum.[21]

21. While this exercise should in principle be doable for the whole sample, it was found in fact to be unsatisfying for a number of reasons. There can be several men with the same name in a town, some, presumably, father and son, but others not. Not all sample towns were towns in 1771. Not all town valuations in 1771 remain extant. Of the towns with extant valuations a goodly number have torn or missing pages. "The extant lists thus encompass 62 percent of the towns and 54 percent of the rateable polls" (Pruitt, "Agriculture and Society in the Towns of Massachusetts," 2, n. 2).

But the principal hurdle is the existence of an archival "black hole" for the eighty years between 1771 and the Manuscript Census of 1850, during which time a farmer could have been born, lived, and died without appearing in a comparable record.

By *comparable,* I mean to draw attention to the two qualities of completeness and *disaggregation* in the 1771 valuations. Each household head is separately listed by name and characterized with respect to the number of adult males in his household; annual worth of his real estate; number of outbuildings, vessels, wharf footage, stock in trade, money at interest, and acreage in tillage, pasture, meadow, grain yields, and head of livestock.

The manuscript returns for the Seventh Census (1850) list each household member by name, age, occupation, and birthplace. Of particular use is the schedule Products of Agriculture, which lists by owner each farm "the produce of which amounts to $100 in value" and provides acreage by land use and the value of tools, of real estate, of livestock, of home manufactures, and of orchard and dairy produce.

There were disaggregated valuations at this level of detail done in 1784, but they survive in the Massachusetts State Library for fewer than twenty eastern towns. There were also valuations at this level of detail done in 1786, 1792, 1801, and 1831, but they were not disaggregated; i.e., they record only town totals. The occasional disaggregated town tax lists that survive for other years rate each household only as to "total personalty" and "total realty."

A third line of defense against the charge that a sample that is manifestly literate and numerate and unforgiving of debt is unrepresentative of the population from which it was drawn consists in recognizing the generally widespread access to public education in early Massachusetts. Unique among the regions of colonial America, in New England, from the early seventeenth century on, the household, church, school, college, and printing press together articulated a common vision according to which "the diurnal life of the community became educative, in that [education] was explicitly seen as the proper means of forming human beings to live according to God's law." [22] This assessment of early Massachusetts's commitment to education is confirmed by recent quantitative studies that find a high and positive level of association between literacy and the following variables: population density, Puritan domination (or, alternatively, the presence of influential Quakers), access to and investment in schools, wealth, economic development, individualism, urbanization, and a complex interaction between center and periphery that one sociologist calls the "urbanization of the countryside" (in contradistinction to the southern "ruralization of the town"). [23] It is obvious that these so-called independent variables are collinearly related to one another. It is also obvious that colonial Massachusetts would score high on all counts.

Of course, literacy is not the same as numeracy. [24] If the early education (in Dedham) of Hingham's minister, the Reverend Ebenezer Gay, is any guide, the grammar school curriculum, between 1700 and 1710, consisted in mastering the *Sententiae pueriles* and translating the *Colloquies* of Erasmus, the *Metamorphoses* of Ovid, and the New Testament in Greek. It is entirely possible that arithmetic got short shrift. But by 1713, a telescope had been installed at Harvard, Newton's *Principia*

---

22. Cremin, *Traditions of American Education,* 19.

23. See Gallman, "Changes in the Level of Literacy in a New Community of Early America"; and Richardson, "Town versus Countryside and Systems of Common Schooling," esp. 416, 426.

24. In *A Calculating People,* Patricia Cline Cohen dates the emergence of widespread numeracy in America generally to the 1820s and 1830s, by which time " 'their minds', Tocqueville said, were 'accustomed to definite calculations' " (p. 3). Cohen attributes the "sudden" emergence (p. 4) of numeracy to the shift in schools from Roman to Arabic numerals, to increased access to schools, to the introduction of arithmetic into school curricula, but most of all to what she calls the "expanding domain of number": of quantification, of censuses, of private and social accounting, surveying, engineering.

But Cohen also would have us reflect on what we mean by numeracy. What is it? The ability to count, surely, but how far? To write symbols, but Roman or Arabic? To perform some arithmetic manipulations, but which? To use an abacus? To keep a tally? Is there, she asks, a threshold between numeracy and its opposite? And what is its opposite?

had been assimilated into the so-called New Learning, and "Harvard students began the serious study of algebra, trigonometry, and fluxions (calculus)" for the first time.[25] Since it was customary for Harvard graduates to "keep school" for a time before being called to a church, one can presume that, as early as the second decade of the eighteenth century, schoolchildren in Massachusetts were being exposed to the "domain of number." Taught, as they were, by Puritan divines, they were certainly not learning that "man is the measure of all things." But they could still have been learning that he is the measurer.

IV

I conclude this discussion of sources by recalling the distinction made at the outset between the stock magnitudes in probate inventories and the flow magnitudes in farm account books. The distinction is of great significance. My decision to rely principally on account books rather than probate inventories is not a decision to answer the same questions with new data: it is a decision to ask different questions.[26]

Examining the rural economy through the prism of probate inventories explains the growth of per capita output as a production function, that is, as a consequence of the quantitative and qualitative growth of inputs, technological change, total factor productivity growth, and scale economies. Examining the rural economy through the prism of exchange transactions, on the other hand, explains the growth of per capita output as a consequence of wider, better integrated, more highly articulated markets.

Obviously, the choice between these two scenarios of the growth process must not be determined by the choice of archive, but the other way round. How in fact did this economy grow?

The remaining chapters of this study will find that the agricultural economy of Massachusetts became integrated into a system of produce, capital, and labor markets within a few years of the Revolution. At the same "moment," this economy began to experience a steady growth of measured labor productivity, that is, of output per worker. In the observed absence of any technological change over the period,[27] we can

25. Wilson, *The Benevolent Deity*, 20.

26. Account books provide the principal data in chaps. 4, 6, and 7. Administration accounts at probate provide the data on debt and credit in chap. 5. Probate inventories provide the wealth variables for the regression and quartile analyses in chap. 5. Town tax valuations are used in chap. 8 to confirm the timing and identify the productivity consequences of the transformation to a market economy.

presume a "Smithian" process in which the wider market increased the degree of specialization and division of labor, increased both the number of manhours and the intensity with which they were worked, and increased the efficiency of farm management.[28]

APPENDIX A: MANUSCRIPT SOURCES

Farmer	Town	County	Dates of Book	Archive
A Market Gardener	W. Cambridge	Middlesex	1836–50	OSV
A Farmer	Vernon	Vermont	1840–49	OSV
Adams, John Gray	Amherst	Hampshire	1845–81	HD
Allen, Timothy	Sturbridge	Worcester	1811–45	OSV
Arms, Daniel & Aaron	Deerfield	Franklin	1783–1806	HD
Arms, Ebenezer	Deerfield	Franklin	1750–68	HD
Bacheller, Elijah	Charlton	Worcester	1800–21	OSV
Baker, John	Ipswich	Essex	1769–1834	HBS
Barnard, Joseph	Deerfield	Franklin	1738–69	HD
Barnard, Joseph, Jr.	Deerfield	Franklin	1768–1805	HD
Bartlett, Luther	Conway	Franklin	1801–35	HD
Bartlet, Preserved	Northampton	Hampshire	1794–1828	OSV
Bartlett, Wm. & Solomon	Westhampton	Hampshire	1753–1832	HBS
Bassett, William	Bridgewater	Plymouth	1810–41	HBS
Beals, Jeremiah	Bridgewater	Plymouth	1790–1822	SPNEA
Boardman, Elijah	Rutland	Vermont	1831–58	HBS
Boynton, Isaac	Pepperell	Middlesex	1809–56	OSV
Bull, Nehemiah	Westfield	Hampden	1727–39	HD
Burke, Jonathan	Bernardston	Franklin	1762–87	HD
Burnham, Jonathan	Ipswich	Essex	1723–87	EI
Chamberlain, Samuel	Westborough	Worcester	1788–1856	OSV
Chapin, Herman & William	Springfield	Hampden	1782–1866	HBS
Chase Family	Haverhill	Essex	1771–1904	HBS

(*continued*)

27. In a careful study of close to one thousand farmers' probate inventories in eastern Massachusetts between 1730 and 1855, I have found no horse rakes, only a few grain cradles, and only three cast-iron plows, none before 1844. On the other hand, in the account book of Samuel Boardman of Rutland, Vermont, I found the following entries: "By a cultivator without the potatoe scratch 4.75" and "By a wire tooth horse rake 9.00." But both entries are for July 1848.

Andrew Baker, of the research staff at Old Sturbridge Village, has informed me that he has found some cast-iron plows in Worcester County probate inventories, but none before 1830. With the exception of the replacement of two-wheeled carts by four-wheeled wagons, there was, it appears, no technological change in farm implements ca. 1785–1800, the period that will be identified as the productivity transition.

28. For a similar process in the early iron industry, see Paskoff, "Labor Productivity and Managerial Efficiency against a Static Technology," and *Industrial Evolution*; in early American industry generally, see Sokoloff, "Productivity Growth."

Farmer	Town	County	Dates of Book	Archive
Childs, Erastus	Deerfield	Franklin	1824–50	HD
Childs, Henry	Deerfield	Franklin	1833–67	HD
Clapp, John	Deerfield	Franklin	1796–1826	HD
Clark, Horace	E. Granby	Connecticut	1821–34	OSV
Cobb, Joseph	Cape Elizabeth	Maine	1755–56	HBS
Cook, Aaron	Harvard	Worcester	1797–1833	HBS
Craig, Robert	Leicester	Worcester	1757–81	OSV
Dickinson, Consider	Deerfield	Franklin	1806–23	HD
Dole, Stephen	Newbury	Essex	1738–90	EI
Eames, Henry	Framingham	Middlesex	1752–59	HBS
Eaton, Joseph & Samuel	Haverhill	Essex	1771–1807	HBS
Ely, Nathaniel	Longmeadow	Hampden	1800–1808	HD
Everett, Aaron	Wrentham	Norfolk	1797–1826	HBS
Fairbank, Josiah	Milton	Norfolk	1840–58	OSV
Farnum, John	Douglas	Worcester	1790–1820	OSV
Fay, Nahum	Northborough	Worcester	1788–1832	HBS
Field, Moses	Northfield	Franklin	1750–95	HD
Fish, Thaddeus	Kingston	Plymouth	1767–80	OSV
Foster, Abraham	Rowley	Essex	1754–72	EI
Foster, Amos & Aaron	Danvers	Essex	1798–1816	EI
Freeman, Comfort	Sturbridge	Worcester	1773–1807	OSV
Fuller, Aaron	Deerfield	Franklin	1822–61	HD
Goodale, David	Marlborough	Middlesex	1819–58	OSV
Goodrich, Phineas	Acton	Middlesex	1818–30	HBS
Gould, Rufus	Oakham	Worcester	1832–55	HD
Griffin, Jonathan	(Unknown)	N.H.	1757–69	OSV
Griswold, Joseph	Buckland	Franklin	1798–1804	HD
Hawks, Zur	Deerfield	Franklin	1810–26	HD
Hayward, David	Braintree	Norfolk	1787–1813	OSV
Hayward, John	Braintree	Norfolk	1770–1813	OSV
Heald, Joseph	Pepperell	Middlesex	1808–13	HBS
Hebard, Eleazer	Sturbridge	Worcester	1789–1805	OSV
Hinsdale, Ebenezer	Hinsdale	N.H.	1746–55	HD
Hitchcock, Henry	Deerfield	Franklin	1840–46	HD
Hosmer, William	Westfield	Hampden	1842–53	HBS
Hovey, Luke	Boxford	Essex	1698–1792	EI
Howard, Harrison	N. Bridgewater	Plymouth	1801–61	HBS
Hoyt, David	Deerfield	Franklin	1751–1803	HD
Hoyt, Jonathan	Deerfield	Franklin	1800–1810	HD
Hyde, Alvan	Lee	Berkshire	1793–1833	HD
Hyde, Joseph	Hopkinton	Middlesex	1784–91	HBS
Jacobs, Michael	Plymouth	Plymouth	1835–59	OSV
Lee, Joseph	Newton	Middlesex	1823–29	EI

Farmer	Town	County	Dates of Book	Archive
Lincoln, Caleb	Hingham	Plymouth	1795–1812	HBS
Little, Moses	Newbury	Essex	1724–78	EI
Low, Jabez	Leominster	Worcester	1813–47	OSV
Martin, Nathaniel	Bridgton	Maine	1817–76	HD
Marvel, Pascal	Shutesbury	Franklin	1834–56	OSV
Nash, Eber	Greenfield	Franklin	1835–48	HD
Newton, John	Greenfield	Franklin	1786–98	HD
Nims, Hull	Deerfield	Franklin	1784–1834	HD
Nye, Jonathan	New Bedford	Bristol	1796–1816	HBS
Odiorne, William	Billerica	Middlesex	1848–56	HBS
Parker, James	Shirley	Middlesex	1770–1829	AAS
Phelps, Charles Jr.	Hadley	Hampshire	1805–54	HBS
Plumer, William & Samuel	Epping	N.H.	1793–1847	HBS
Plummer, Enoch	Newbury	Essex	1748–95	EI
Poor, Jonathan	Newbury	Essex	1762–1808	EI
Porter, John	Wenham	Essex	1770–74	EI
Robbins, Julius	Deerfield	Franklin	1840–82	HD
Sanger, Abner	Keene	N.H.	1774–94	Keene
Sheldon, John	Deerfield	Franklin	1741–92	HD
Sheldon, Seth	Deerfield	Franklin	1808–32	HD
Sherman, Otis	Grafton	Worcester	1823–43	HBS
Sloper, Samuel	Blandford	Hampden	1772–1802	HBS
Smead, Ebenezer	Deerfield	Franklin	1723–99	HD
Smead, Joseph	Deerfield	Franklin	1783–96	HD
Smith, Alexander	W. Springfield	Hampden	1797–1836	HBS
Smith, Asahel	Dedham	Norfolk	1811–45	DHS
Starkweather, Charles	Northampton	Hampshire	1814–49	HD
Starkweather, Haynes	Northampton	Hampshire	1849–86	HD
Stebbins, Dennis	Deerfield	Franklin	1838–41	HD
Stone, Nehemiah	Charlton	Worcester	1773–1830	AAS
Thayer, Isaac	Braintree	Norfolk	1769–99	HBS
Whiting, Harrison	Holliston	Middlesex	1828–49	HBS
Williams, Solomon	Deerfield	Franklin	1786–1836	HD
Wolcott, William	Windsor	Connecticut	1744–98	HD

Note: Manuscript sources consist chiefly of farm account books but also of journals, diaries, day books, and memorandum books.

Key to abbreviations of archives: EI = Essex Institute, Salem; OSV = Old Sturbridge Village Library, Sturbridge, Mass.; HBS = Manuscript Division of Baker Library, Harvard Business School, Cambridge, Mass.; SPNEA = Society for the Preservation of New England Antiquities, Boston; HD = Historic Deerfield's Pocumtuck Valley Memorial Library, Deerfield, Mass.; DHS = Dedham Historical Society, Dedham, Mass. The towns given are in Massachusetts unless otherwise indicated in the "County" column. In this table, towns are assigned to counties according to the modern map of Massachusetts.

APPENDIX B

The facsimile pages reproduced below are from the following account books and appear here photographed by and with permission of the archives in which they are held. Bracketed page numbers indicate placement in this volume.

1. Henry Eames of Framingham. Courtesy of the Manuscripts Division, Baker Library, Harvard Business School, Cambridge, Massachusetts. His little account book is catalogued as 1752–54, but it contains entries, as here shown, from 1688. Note the tallies. [p. 73]

2. William Bartlett of Westhampton. Courtesy of the Manuscripts Division, Baker Library, Harvard Business School, Cambridge, Massachusetts. Bartlett was a farmer who did a good deal of tailoring. These entries are from 1765–69. Note the spelling. [p. 74]

3. Nahum Fay of Northborough. Courtesy of the Manuscripts Division, Baker Library, Harvard Business School, Cambridge, Massachusetts. These entries are for 1788. Fay's is the most elegant single-entry book in the sample. [p. 75]

4(*a*) and (*b*). Thaddeus Fish of Kingston. Courtesy of Old Sturbridge Village Research Library. Photos by Thomas Neill (*left,* B27811; *right,* B27812). In these entries, probably from 1770, we appear to be catching Fish in the act of becoming a calculating profit maximizer! [p. 76]

5. Charles Phelps, Jr., of Hadley. Courtesy of the Manuscripts Division, Baker Library, Harvard Business School, Cambridge, Massachusetts. Phelps was the wealthiest and most sophisticated of the farmers in the account book sample. One of his entries is for tickets to hear Jenny Lind sing in Boston. His books exhibit double-entry bookkeeping in farm accounts as early as 1829 [p. 77]

6(*a*) and (*b*). Dennis Stebbins of Deerfield. Courtesy of the Pocumtuck Valley Memorial Association Library, Deerfield, Massachusetts (photos courtesy of Historic Deerfield, Inc.). Stebbins's book is for the years 1838–41. This is not an account book but a farm journal or day book for the years 1833–41. Stebbins uses an "Alphabet of Characters" (6*b*) to encode the labor done by paid hands and family members each day. Note the large amount of broom work done. [p. 78]

In the year 1764 one
Sim: Strong deter to me
for Coting 2 Cafes and 3 Loams   0 5 0
Yo Coting 3 pigs   0 02 0
1765 Yo 3 barrels of sider   4 00 0
Yo Coting 2 pigs and 2 Rams   0 03 9
1766 Yo Coting Kev and pigs   0 03 0
1767 Yo Coting 2 pigs   0 01 6
Yo dent dresing flex one day 0 015 0
Yo Coting Jouf and Lam   0 0 9 0
Yo Liling 2 Hogs   0 010 0
Yo Coft Coting   0 0 9 0
the balance is on
the fide a count is   0 019 4

December the 6 then   7 14 11
Rakned with
Simon Strong and
Due to him on a Stene   0 02 9

1769 Simon Strong deter to me
for whele lash timber   1 00 0
Yo bent Keggsford in the
woods   0 015 0
Yo Coting   0 02 6

In year 1725
Qurtas Pomroy deter to me   0 0 00 0
for 2 goflons of methegln
1730 Yo 3 then
Qurtas Pomroy Dr
for 1 buffhel of turnips   0 1 6
for 1 buffhel of turnips   0 6 0
for parstring Mare & Colt   1 10 0
Yo one basket a ton y
Qurtas pomroy deter me
three galons of me   0 015 0

1764 then settled all accounts with
Qurtas Pomroy
13 By a Note

The Golden Rule Three

A woman Brought 150 Eggs of a Contry man
for 7. 8. 5 Shillings worth the quad 2d for 3
qd for ye Rest a pany for 2 egg then the sold
thereof again 5 egg 3d of teman is know
whether She Lost or gained by hur eggs

1770 november the 24
matter holms Dor for holding
Plow one half Day   12 - 6

Cr   matter holms
Dor timber Sixteen and Eight
Pence

A man Spens in his family 485-11-11-3 2
in a year Demand how much that one
Days with another 485-11-11-3 2

9711
112
19433
29711
116543
4

So 4661 75
365) 4661 75 = 1
1

365) 4661 75 (4) 1277 (12) 319 (2) 26l
362   24   078   2 0
1011   1277   76   078   01
0730   1255   36   01
0801 7   0 2625
0 655 5   25 55
0   0 7 10 0 0 7 0

1 - 1277 - 365
365
3 85
7662
3831
20 97 10 (485   1 4661 05 (4661 05
180
010
010

4 4661 05 (10) 116 526 (9) 710 (8)
4   3 85   8 2
76   24   0 1 2
24   0 20   0 00
0 21   0 00
0 24

1829
Dec. 31.   Expense   Dr to Produce X

For sundry produce expended
in the family this year off the
Farm . estimated at .. .   300.—

X Mrs P.s Portion Dr to Profit & Loss X
    This sum to balance ..   368.91

X Farm   Dr to Sundries
X House Expense .. for one year   1315.94
X Farm Expenses ..   do. ..   270.13
X Labor .. ..   .. do. ..   306.18
                                 1892.25

Sundries   Drs to Farm   X
X Produce .. for one year ..   1054.26
X Stock ..   do. 65.95
X Profit & Loss .. do. 711.26
                                  1831.47

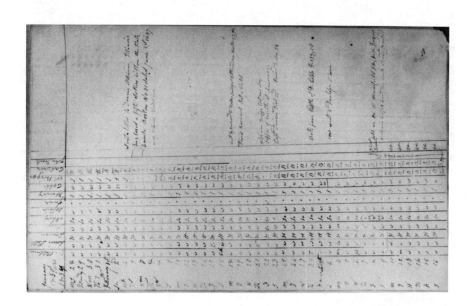

4

The Development of
Commodity Markets

THE PEOPLE WHO SETTLED MASSACHUSETTS BAY CAME, NOT FROM
risk-averse or Chayanov-type peasant villages, but from a tradition of
market crosses, market days, servant markets, corn markets, hay markets, cattle, wool, cheese, linen, silk, and produce markets, itinerant
peddlers, stalls, shops, and fairs. "Eight hundred fairs and markets were
held regularly in every part of the English realm."[1] The British investors
who financed the "planting" of colonies in New England, the royal pat-
ents under which they raised the capital, and the merchant-entrepreneurs
who organized, financed, and directed the settlements—the Pynchons
in the Connecticut River Valley, the Willards in the Merrimack River
Valley, the Winthrops in Ipswich, Boston, and New London, the Otises
in Barnstable, and "some two dozen" others—had in mind from the
very beginning the full integration of Massachusetts Bay into British
imperial trade,[2] that "Boston may be esteemed the mart town of the West
Indies!"[3]

Some places, like Boston, Salem, and Springfield, were born commercial, entrepôts of worldwide empire trade from their very beginnings. Others were folded into the domestic market as nodes in a dendritic pattern linking local market-places. Still others held on longer to
the social controls that regulated the market-place. How much longer?
When can the rural economy of Massachusetts be said to have become
part of a market economy?

We now embark on a variety of empirical exercises to document and
date the emergence of a market economy from the observable, behavioral correlates of market orientation that can be found in farm account
books and daybooks. Subsequent chapters will investigate rural capital
and labor markets; we shall be concerned in this chapter to determine,
from the spatial pattern in which farmers moved their produce and from
the intricate behavior of farm-gate prices, the extent to which Massachusetts farmers were involved in and oriented toward markets for their
output. The argument will proceed by testing the following indicators.

1. Russell, *A Long, Deep Furrow,* 58. Virtually everyone of the seven hundred market towns
in England, however small, had at least one retail shop by 1700, and 75 percent of the smaller
market towns in East Anglia (the origin of most of Massachusetts's early settlers) had at least one
retail shop as early as the sixteenth century (Shammas, *The Pre-Industrial Consumer in England
and America,* 248, 227).

2. See Innes, *Labor in a New Land,* 171–84; McCusker and Menard, *The Economy of British
America,* chap. 5; and Morison, *The Maritime History of Massachusetts,* chap. 2.

3. Edward Randolph writing in 1676, quoted in Morison, *The Maritime History of Massachusetts,* 17.

Farmer's records of marketing trips. Farm account books and day-books record the trips farmers actually took to sell and to buy farm produce. Nearly two thousand wagon trips "with loads" recorded by the farmers in this sample were analyzed by frequency of origins, destinations, and miles traveled. The expansion of markets can be observed in both the increasing proliferation of destinations and the increasing concentration of trips to those destinations that emerge as "central places."

Farmers' records of transport costs. The high cost of overland transport to coastal markets was identified by Bidwell and has long since been considered the primary constraint on the development of Massachusetts agriculture.[4] By providing the costs of the separate components of the hauling package—wagon, team, driver—account books allow us more accurately to estimate the burden of hauling costs to farmers and the savings that could be realized from the use of owned rather than hired components.

The convergence of farmers' prices. Economic theory defines a market as a place in space and time where prices of the same good tend toward uniformity. Thus, it should be possible to test for market influences on farm-gate prices by testing for the convergence of those prices in time and space.

The slaughter weight of hogs and feed and meat prices. It has proved possible to determine that the ratio of feed (corn) to meat (pork) prices played, over time, an increasingly significant role in farmers' decisions respecting the weight at which to slaughter hogs. If the method stands scrutiny, it will be one of the few instances where a test of supply elasticity can be made for individual farmers in this period.

The cyclical synchronicity of farm account book prices and big city prices. A price index constructed on Massachusetts farmers' account book prices is seen to exhibit a pattern of cyclical fluctuations and of responses to the major macroeconomic shocks of the period that is markedly and visibly synchronous with indexes of wholesale prices for agricultural and manufactured goods in the major urban markets of Philadelphia and New York City.[5]

4. See the discussion of Bidwell's influence on the historiography of the debate in chap. 2, sec. I.

5. For the construction of my Massachusetts farm price index and a detailed comparison of it with the Warren-Pearson (New York City) and Bezanson (Philadelphia) wholesale price indexes, see my "A Price Index for Rural Massachusetts."

I. Traveling to Markets

In farm account books and daybooks are found the records of the trips farmers made off the farm to buy the things they did not produce (molasses, sugar, coffee, tea, rum, dry goods and notions, indigo, salt, fish, flour and meal, lime, shingles, iron, bricks) and to sell the things they did produce (corn, small grains, hay, meat, livestock, butter, cheese, potatoes, apples, cider, wool, hops, flax, timber and wood products, potash, and dung). Of course, as repositories of debt transactions, account books recorded only those trips that required the hiring of a wagon, team, or driver from someone else. As a consequence, transport services that the farm family performed for itself, with a wagon and team it owned or paid for in cash or barter, went unrecorded. Furthermore, if the farmer sold "at the barn" to a buyer who hauled the goods back himself, the cost of that trip will not appear in either the seller's or the buyer's accounts. Thus, to an unknown but probably large extent, account books understate the movement and the volume of market hauling, serving to set only a lower bound to our estimates of the movement of farm commodities in trade. Daybooks, diaries, and personal journals are more generous, and I have relied heavily on those I could find.

In the quantitative analysis that follows, only those trips are called *marketing trips* that specify hauling off the farm, "with a load," to a stated destination or a stated number of miles, by wagon, sled, or sleigh "with team." Journeys by chaise, by carriage, or on horseback were not included. I hoped thereby to exclude visiting, going to church or to meetings, arbitrating disputes, attending to paupers, appraising inventories, administering estates, surveying, assessing—all the myriad responsibilities a farmer bore in his community that would have taken him away from home, but not to markets. In doing so, however, I am sure that I both excluded too much[6] and included too much.[7]

The procedure with respect to each hauling trip was first to measure on a map the mileages between towns of origin and towns of destination, in each case as straight-line distances, and then to multiply by 1.6, the

---

6. Thus, Joseph Lee of Newton wrote, "Nov. 4, 1823: R.S. went to Boston *in the carriage* and . . . bot 113 lb beef @ 3, 28 lb Pot ashes @ 10. Bot at City Mills 23 bu rye meal 68, 2 bushels Indian meal 65" (emphasis added).

7. I assumed, e.g., that all trips in which livestock were being hauled were to markets. Some of these, the daybooks make clear, were rather to winter the animals or to have them mated.

ratio Robert Fogel found, from a random sample, to obtain between modern highway distances and bee-line distances.[8] Since old roads were far more winding than modern highways, the calculations that follow understate true mileages. Towns of origin and destination of each trip were then coded as to region: East or West.[9] The load being hauled, where given, was also coded and each trip entered in one of six time-period subfiles: 1750–75, 1776–90, 1791–1805, 1806–20, 1821–35, and 1836–55.[10]

The results from analyzing the trip data bear on three questions. How far did farmers travel to market their goods? To which towns did they travel? Which towns emerged as the principal market towns?

Figure 2 is a frequency distribution of the distances farmers hauled their loads in different time periods. In light of the argument that prohibitive hauling costs placed much of Massachusetts agriculture beyond the feasible reach of markets, figure 2 is of great interest. Although varying widely in length, the number of very long journeys is astonishing.[11] Panel A of table 1 presents mean and median distances for each period for all observations; panel B presents the same data for a sample of trips truncated to eliminate long-distance outliers. This last was done on the assumption that many of the longest journeys (particularly in the fourth period, when many were unusually long) were undertaken once—to visit relatives, say, rather than as part of a marketing pattern. But these misgivings may have been overcautious. Bricks, shingles, livestock,

---

8. Fogel, *Railroads and American Economic Growth,* 67. Unfortunately, the 1789 *Survey of the Roads of the United States of America,* by Christopher Colles, contains no Massachusetts roads!

9. Towns in Essex, Middlesex, Suffolk, Norfolk, Plymouth, and Bristol counties in Massachusetts and towns in Rhode Island, New Hampshire, Maine, and Vermont were called *East;* towns in Worcester, Franklin, Hampshire, Hampden, and Berkshire counties in Massachusetts and towns in Connecticut and New York were called *West.*

10. The periodization is not arbitrary. The first is the colonial period; the second is the years of Revolution, postwar depression, and constitutional crisis; the third will be identified in this study as a time of pivotal transformation in the rural economy. The fourth—1806–20—was dominated by the domestic consequences of war in Europe—of isolation from it, involvement in it, panic and depression after it. The fifth period is identified by most other writers as the beginning of market agriculture in New England. The sixth period is dominated by the railroad: the beginning of full-time freight and passenger railroad service from Boston to Worcester, on the way to Albany (an event of great significance to Massachusetts agriculture), and when the railroad came to most of the sample towns in this study.

11. In his *Change in Agriculture,* Clarence Danhof suggests a maximum distance of twelve to fifteen miles. In "The Farm Enterprise," Danhof put it a bit differently: "Land lying within a few miles—a half-day return trip by road or water—of an urban market offered an acceptable cost of transportation" (p. 162).

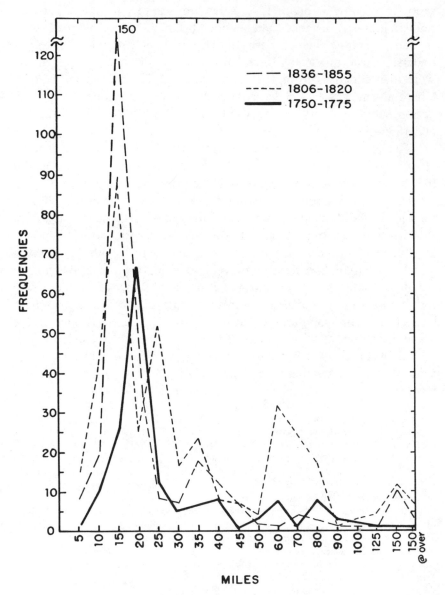

Fig. 2 Frequency distribution of distances farmers traveled with wagon loads, 1750–1855.

Source: Farmers' accounts and daybooks.

Note: For method of measuring distances, see text.

Table 1   Length of Hauling Trips

Item	Time Period					
	1750–75	1776–90	1791–1805	1806–20	1821–35	1836–55
A. All trips:						
Number of trips	156	233	271	355	526	286
Average mileage[a]	26.7	22.4	31.0	50.5	21.0	24.8
Median mileage[b]	18.7	18.0	19.6	24.0	14.4	14.0
Range of miles[c]	5–175	5–150	5–150	5–200+	5–200+	5–200+
SD	22.2	18.0	27.0	65.4	26.9	33.0
B. Truncated distribution:						
Number of trips	151	227	259	329	508	271
Average mileage[a]	23.7	18.7	27.0	24.5	18.7	17.2
Median mileage[b]	17.8	17.3	17.7	18.9	12.7	13.6
Range of miles[c]	5–80	5–80	5–80	5–80	5–80	5–85

Sources: Account books and daybooks. The measurement of origin-to-destination distances is described in the text.

[a] The mean and median were calculated from mileage weighted by frequencies.

[b] The median is given because the distribution is skewed to the right.

[c] Farm-to-town trips, the shortest, are assumed to be five miles.

hay, barrels, "freight," ashes, corn, fish, molasses, and potatoes were all hauled one hundred miles or more at one time or another, in which case panel B may not be any more typical for having been truncated.

From the pattern of mean distances over time it appears that marketing perimeters shortened during the Revolution and immediate postwar years, widened markedly to 1820, when over 20 percent of the 355 trips were between fifty and three hundred miles in length, and shortened just as markedly thereafter. According to figure 2, the modal hauling distance decreased from twenty miles in the second period to ten miles in the fifth—which I attribute to increasing *proliferation,* that is, more market towns. And it increased again in the last period to fifteen miles—which I attribute to the increasing *concentration* (i.e., drawing power) of the bigger market towns.[12]

12. It is worth emphasizing that it was not short hauls to a railroad depot that pulled the average mileage down from 50.5 to 21 between the fourth and fifth periods. The fifth period predates the arrival of railroads to sample towns: Framingham, 1835; Ipswich, 1839; Braintree, 1845; Westborough, 1835; Biddeford (now in Maine), 1842; Oxford, 1840; Middleborough, 1846; Marlborough, 1855; Grafton, 1835; Springfield, 1841; Acton, 1844. I am grateful to Charles J. Kennedy of the University of Nebraska for supplying me with these dates when the railroad appeared in several of our sample towns.

The initial proliferation and eventual concentration of destinations are demonstrated with three measures of increasing precision. A first approximation counts the number of trips to destinations that were common to two or more origins in each time period (table 2).[13] A second approximation selects those destinations that were common to ten or more trips in each time period (table 3).[14] A third approximation measures the proliferation and concentration of market destinations most accurately by calculating an index of inequality (a Gini coefficient) for each time period.[15] The coefficients, and the Lorenz curves derived from them, are of great interest, particularly with respect to regional differences. As measured by the destinations of hauling trips, markets in the western part of Massachusetts became more concentrated only gradually—moving from a G of .460 in the first period to a G of .755 in the last. But the market destinations of eastern farmers were highly concentrated ($G = .633$) from the first, Boston dominating all other destinations until the last period, when, with the relative decline of Boston and the spread of market-places, very nearly the same level of dispersion ($G = .487$) appears as in western Massachusetts a century earlier (see fig. 3).

That the concentration of marketing trips proceeded at such different rates in East and West has implications that will be strongly confirmed in the different patterns of regional price convergence to be discussed later.

13. *Origins* refers to the home towns of the sample farmers.

14. The enduring importance of Boston, the emergence of Concord, and the retreat of Salem will come as no great surprise to historians of Massachusetts, but the importance of some of the smaller towns may. In Shrewsbury, Artemas Ward had a general store in the 1750s to which farm produce came from all over Worcester County and beyond. In Rainbow, Connecticut, there were, in the 1820s and 1830s, at least four grist mills, and it was to one of these mills that Horace Clark of East Granby sold about five hundred bushels of corn and the same amount of rye each year. For a single mill regularly to buy such a large quantity from a single farmer suggests that that tiny town (near the Connecticut River, midway between Springfield and Hartford) had access to or was itself a regional entrepôt of importance for flour, meal, and grain.

15. Gini coefficients measure the relation between the cumulative percentage of total trips (P) and the cumulative percentage of total destinations (Y). G lies between zero and one: i.e., if there were an equal number (and, therefore, an equal percentage) of trips going to each destination, the Gini coefficient would be zero. If all the trips were to one destination and none to any other, the Gini coefficient would be one. The higher the Gini coefficient, the greater the inequality (or concentration) of trip destinations.

Gini coefficients are typically used to measure inequality (or concentration) in the distribution of income or wealth. I am using Ginis here because a finding of increased concentration of destinations suggests the emergence of what economic geographers call *central places*. Central places are themselves an important part of the development process because they generate final-demand linkages of their own through the marketing institutions that tend to cluster there.

Table 2 Destinations from Two or More Origins

1750–75		1776–90		1791–1805		1806–20		1821–35		1836–55	
Boston	4	Dedham	3	Northampton	5	Springfield	2	Springfield	2	Westfield	6
Shrewsbury	18	Ipswich	3	Providence	3	Northampton	5	Northampton	7	Northampton	2
Springfield	2	Braintree	3	Woodstock, Conn.	2	Dedham	2	Roxbury	2	Roxbury	2
Leicester	5	Roxbury	2	Dedham	3	Acton	5	Acton	5	Boston	5
Hadley	2	Worcester	2	Boston	9	Boston	9	Boston	10	Mansfield	4
N	114	Leicester	4	Ipswich	3	E. Cambridge	3	Harvard	3	Hadley	2
		Boston	2	Northborough	4	Charlestown	2	Concord	2	North Andover	4
		N	116	Boltor	2	Concord	2	Littleton	2	Arlington	5
				Salem	2	Groton	2	Sudbury	2	Worcester	3
				Grafton	2	Harvard	3	Roxbury	2	Westborough	8
				Princeton	2	Littleton	2	Mansfield	6	*N*	186
				Westborough	2	Lunenburg	2	Newton	2		
				Taunton	3	Ipswich	3	Hadley	2		
				N	180	Hadley	2	Marlborough	2		
						Salem	2	Brighton	2		
						Leicester	2	Worcester	2		
						Sutton	2	Grafton	2		
						Worcester	3	Lancaster	2		
						Easthampton	2	South Hadley	2		
						South Hadley	2	Ware	2		
						Southampton	2	Duxbury	2		
						Wendell	2	*N*	239		
						Williamsburg	2				
						Templeton	2				
						Pepperell	2				
						N	218				

Sources: Account books and daybooks.

Table 3   Principal Destinations, by Frequency of Trips

Time Period and Destinations	Number of Trips	Percentage of Total Trips Made
1750–75 (N = 156):		
Boston	12	7.7
Salem	37	23.7
Shrewsbury	18	11.5
Percentage of total		42.9
1776–90 (N = 233):		
Boston	24	10.3
Salem	99	42.5
Percentage of total		52.8
1791–1805 (N = 271):		
Boston	56	20.7
Salem	17	6.3
Kingston	17	6.3
Providence	13	4.8
Northampton	15	5.5
Northborough	15	5.5
Southampton	10	3.7
Roxbury	12	4.4
Ipswich	10	3.7
Percentage of total		60.9
1806–20 (N = 355):		
Boston	100	28.2
Concord	16	4.5
Kingston	17	4.8
Northampton	21	5.9
Harvard	12	3.4
Sutton	10	2.8
Waltham	12	3.4
Percentage of total		53.0
1821–35 (N = 526):		
Boston	74	14.1
Concord	27	5.1
Newton	37	7.0
Rainbow, Ct.	96	18.3
Grafton	33	6.3
Northampton	15	2.9
Petersham	13	2.5
Acton	10	1.9
Littleton	11	2.1
Percentage of total		60.1
1836–55 (N = 286):		
Springfield	112	39.2
Boston	20	7.0
Westfield	17	5.9

Table 3   (*Continued*)

Time Period and Destinations	Number of Trips	Percentage of Total Trips Made
1836–55 (*N* = 286):		
Suffield, Ct.	12	4.2
Westborough	10	3.5
Percentage of total		59.8

Sources: Farm account books and daybooks. See text.
Note: N = total number of trips in each time period. Principal destinations are those common to ten or more trips in each time period.

II. TRANSPORT COSTS

It is difficult to understand how farmers could have afforded to haul bulky farm produce as far as is shown in table 1 if transport costs were as high as those found in some of the published records.[16] In fact, so constraining have they been thought to be that most estimates of a feasible market range are calculated from given ton-mile wagon rates. At hauling costs of twenty cents per ton-mile, the marketing perimeter for, say, a wagon load (forty bushels) of corn, selling for fifty cents a bushel, could not have exceeded twenty miles.[17] This is indeed a tight constraint, yet throughout the second half of the eighteenth century, when corn did sell for fifty cents (three shillings) a bushel, farmers' trips were on the average longer than twenty miles. How can we explain this?

To minimize high teamster rates farmers had at least three options.

16. Twenty cents per ton-mile in McClelland, "Railroads, American Growth and the New Economic History"; thirty to seventy cents between 1800 and 1819 and fifteen cents in 1853 in Taylor, *The Transportation Revolution,* 133, 442; thirty to seventy cents typically, with some exceptions—twelve cents in 1822, twenty to fifty cents by turnpike, ten to fifteen cents by macadam road in 1839, and 23.5 cents Boston to Providence in late 1820s—in Pred, *Urban Growth and the Circulation of Information,* 112; twenty-five cents for 1906, reduced 17.6 percent in a backward extrapolation to 1890, in Fogel, *Railroads and American Economic Growth,* 71; and eighteen cents Boston to Worcester in 1832 in Salsbury, *The State, the Investor and the Railroad,* 122. These may be the rates of specialized teamsters. Some of the farmers in my account book sample acted as teamsters, providing wagon, team, and themselves as driver. Isaac Bullard of Dedham charged twenty to twenty-five cents between 1789 and 1803; John Baker of Ipswich charged nineteen to twenty-two cents during the 1790s; Robert Craig of Leicester charged twenty-one cents in 1778; and John Heald of Pepperell charged twenty cents in 1808–13.

17. Danhof suggests that an "acceptable" cost of transportation must be less than 20 percent of the value of the produce ("The Farm Enterprise," 162).

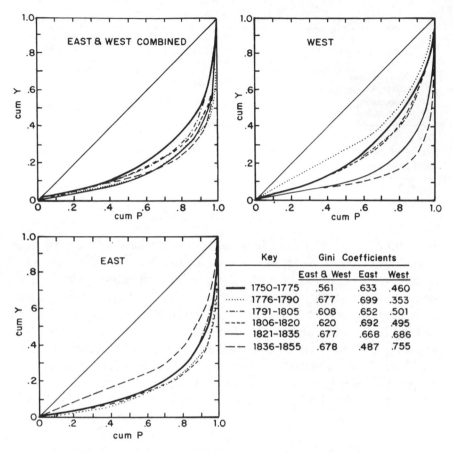

Fig. 3   Measuring market concentration, 1750–1855.
Source: Farmers' accounts and daybooks.
Note: "Cum P" measures the cumulative percentage of total trips. "Cum Y" measures the cumulative percentage of total destinations. The towns were divided between East and West as described in the text.

The first was to sell "at the barn"—f.o.b. pricing—where the buyer assumes the hauling costs. One finds this mentioned fairly often in the sources, particularly with respect to meadow hay, a bulky thing and expensive to haul relative to its value. The second option was to "shop around," selling in markets where product price was highest, transport costs lowest, or both. Markets exist in space, which is to say that transport costs, whether borne by buyer or seller, will be a consideration in any market transaction.[18] What we may be observing in the multitude of destination vectors along which each farmer traveled to market (see fig. 4) is the process of making distance into an economic variable.

The third option was for the farmer to provide at least some of the transport inputs himself. This is not a new insight.[19] But what farm account books can tell us are the costs of the inputs when they are hired separately and their opportunity costs when they are owned.

The prices farmers charged each other for supplying wagons and teams appear in the account books, along with clues—destination, mileage, or time—that allow us to calculate ton-mile rates.[20] These rates can equally well be used to impute the value of the wagon and team when the farmer provided them for himself. The imputed value of the farmer's services when he does his own driving must also be calculated and should in some sense be set equal to the value of his farm labor forgone.

Cognizant of opportunity costs, most writers have assumed that market journeys were made in winter when farmers were less occupied and the sledding was easy. At random, I made a note of the months of 636 trips. Twenty-seven percent (172) were undertaken in the winter months of November, December, January, and February, but 73 percent (464) were made between March and October. In fact, fewer trips were made in December and January than at any other time, and more trips— twice as many—were made during a harvest month than during any other month. Yet almost none of these journeys, undertaken at the farmers' busiest season, involved the hiring of a driver. Therefore, any calculation of the true cost of hauling must include a wage imputed to the driver that is at least equal to the farmer's highest alternative wage.

One way to do this is to award to the farmer-qua-driver in each period the highest wage paid to hired farm labor in that period. The wages of hired farm labor, as will be seen, were differentiated by task, the highest wages going to haying and reaping labor.[21] Averaging these wage observations for each of the six periods and assuming one ton per load and ten-miles per day (an assumption that remains to be discussed

18. See Greenhut, *A Theory of the Firm in Economic Space,* chap. 4.
19. See Fogel, *Railroads and American Economic Growth,* 71.
20. Ton-mile rates are calculated on the assumption that a full wagon load weighed one ton.
21. See fig. 10 below.

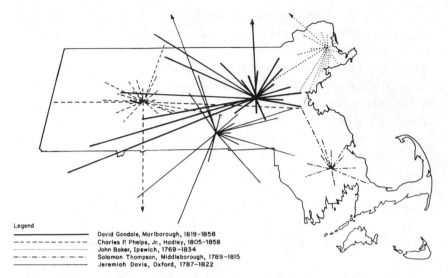

Legend

———————————— David Goodale, Marlborough, 1819–1858
– – – – – – – – – – – Charles P. Phelps, Jr., Hadley, 1805–1858
·· John Baker, Ipswich, 1769–1834
–·–·–·–·–·–·–·– Solomon Thompson, Middleborough, 1789–1815
———————————— Jeremiah Davis, Oxford, 1787–1822

Fig. 4   *a,* The pattern of marketing trips of five Massachusetts farmers. *b,* The pattern of marketing trips of four Massachusetts farmers.
Source: The account books of the farmers.

below) gives to farmers the ton-mile wage imputed to drivers that is shown in table 4.[22]

It is now possible to compare ton-mile rates calculated here with the teamster rates from other published sources that appeared in note 16 above. When the out-of-pocket costs and opportunity costs are summed across the three components of the hauling package, ton-mile rates in current dollars approached twenty cents and climbed above it in the sixth period (see table 4). But in *constant* dollars they stayed well below twenty cents throughout. Because the deflator—my price index—is built on the product prices of the same farmers whose hauling costs we are now calculating, the costs in constant dollars are the appropriate measure of the real burden of transport costs to Massachusetts farmers.

22. The issue of opportunity costs applies to owned oxen as well. Suppose, e.g., that the farmer has his own team and that the team recorded in his account book were hired to augment his own team for long, heavy, uphill trudges. Then we should double the cost of animal power in our calculations of his true hauling costs. (I have come across a haul using *eighteen oxen* in the 1770s.) No adjustment could be made in table 4 for such eventualities, i.e., for doubling, or more than doubling, oxen "wages." On the other hand, many farmers did not in fact have their own teams. A survey of the 1771 valuations reveals that, in most rural communities, between 20 and 35 percent of farmers (i.e., those reporting both acreage in tillage and bushels of grain) had no oxen, and that proportion went as high as 40 percent in Ipswich and 48 percent in Hadley.

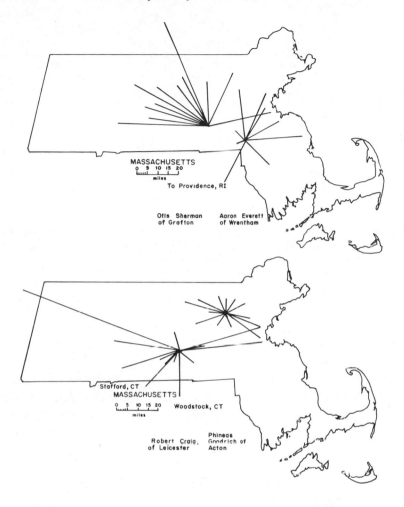

The evidence in the previous section that marketing trips on average exceeded twenty miles suggests that our sample farmers made, in some sense, the same calculation.

While we have focused our attention on minimizing the upward pressures on transport costs, have we ignored the downward pressures? With improvements in road-building techniques over this century of rapid change, might we not have expected hauling costs actually to fall? Putting it another way, have I overstated transport costs by assuming no increase in miles traveled per day throughout the period?

There were two bursts of road building in Massachusetts in our period: the private turnpike era of 1790–1808 and the public-road-building

Table 4   Average Per Ton-Mile Costs of Hauling,
by Component (dollars)

Time Period	Yoke of Oxen[a,b]	Vehicle[a,b]	Driver[b,c]	Total Cost	
				Current	Constant[d]
1750–75[e]	.031	.015	.049	.095	.151
1776–90[e]	.049	.029	.073	.151	.177
1791–1805	.044	.032	.067	.143	.146
1806–20	.083	.027	.072	.182	.156
1821–35	.074	.033	.074	.181	.171
1836–55	.085	.027	.108	.220	.180

Sources: Farm account books and daybooks.
[a] Costs of hiring wagons and oxen come from farm account books.
[b] Inputs hired by the trip adjusted to per mile rate by dividing by straight-line mileage between towns, multiplied by 1.6. Ton-mile rates calculated from the assumption that a full load is one ton. Inputs hired by the day adjusted to per mile rate by assuming ten miles traveled per day. To the extent that this assumption understates distance, the estimates overstate cost.
[c] Very few drivers were hired for hauling. This is the driving wage imputed to the farmer and calculated from the per day wage for the highest paid labor hired on the farm: in the early years carting, in later years haying.
[d] The total in current dollars is deflated by my price index.
[e] Currency is old tenor adjusted to lawful money at 7.5:1, then adjusted to dollars at 1s. = \$0.1667.

era of the 1820s and 1830s. The first of these brought major improvements in the straightening of roads, the second in the surfacing. Turnpikes strove for a Roman straightness that considerably shortened distance, but at the expense of steep grades that slowed the movement of heavy loads considerably, a grade of 5 percent adding 5 percent to the weight of the load. "Straight roads over high hills involved the expenditure of more horsepower in travelling than did winding roads over level ground between the same two points."[23]

The major innovation in road surfacing was macadam. Macadam roads were introduced in this country in 1820, but by 1851 "there were not a dozen miles of macadam road in all the New England states."[24] The diffusion of macadamizing had to await the invention of the mechanical stone crusher, and that was not until 1858. All Massachusetts country roads and most turnpikes were, throughout our period, dirt roads requiring constant and expensive maintenance; they were therefore allowed to deteriorate—despite the knowledge of crowning and ditching, sluiceways and macadamizing. Winter travel by sled or sleigh

23. Taylor, "The Turnpike Era in New England," 173.
24. Parks, "The Roads of New England," 193.

was, as a rule, faster than wagon and allowed the transport of much heavier loads.[25] But winter travel on the improved turnpikes could be worse than on the old country roads because their very straightness produced a wind-tunnel effect, blowing bare the high crowns and making them impassable for sleds.

Perhaps what speaks most unambiguously to the issue of road improvement is that, of the 1,827 trips analyzed in this chapter, there is only one entry for a turnpike toll.

III. PRICE CONVERGENCE

The role of price convergence as a diagnostic of market integration has already been introduced. In chapter 1, the narrowing of wheat price differentials suggested the emergence of a market economy in much of Europe by the end of the seventeenth century. In chapter 2, price convergence as an experimental design was compared with the moral economy model, which, by contrast, was found to be either untestable or, in the context of Massachusetts after 1750, inapplicable. Evaluating, in chapter 3, the several archives on which this study depends, farm account books alone yield up a sufficient number of price and wage observations to date the onset of the convergence process.

To use the narrowing of price differentials over time as a measure of the extent and timing of market function is yet another way of arguing inferentially from observable correlates of market integration to phenomena—*mentalités*—that otherwise cannot be observed. But price convergence is more than a proxy; it is an experimental design, an operational formulation of the market hypothesis that can be confirmed or refuted by the experiment.

"Economists understand by the term *market*," wrote Alfred Marshall in 1890, quoting Cournot, "not any particular market place in which things are bought and sold, but the whole of any region in which buyers and sellers are in such free intercourse with one another that the prices of the same goods tend to equality easily and quickly."[26] It is not

25. "On sleds drawn by two horses, farmers could carry 30 bushels of wheat (three-quarters of a ton) 20 miles and return the same day" (Schumacher, *The Northern Farmer and His Markets,* 68).

26. Marshall, *Principles of Economics,* bk. 5, chap. 1, p. 324. The price of a good to which all others converge—the tendency within a single market toward a single price that equilibrates supply and demand—is net of transport costs: "The more nearly perfect a market is, the stronger is the tendency for the same price to be paid for the same thing at the same time in all parts of the market: but of course if the market is large, allowance must be made for the expense of delivering

hard to think of modern complexities that distort market outcomes and render Marshall's definition inadequate, but that is not, I think, true of the application we will make of it here. In the farm commodity markets of New England in the century before the Civil War, there were few, if any, oligopolistic elements. And a "good" was for these farmers—as it is for most farmers—a standardized, recognizable "thing," a commodity bounded on all sides by a gap in the chain of substitutes. That is, there was, for farm commodities, little deliberate effort at product differentiation in order to introduce elements of monopolistic competition.

But here one must pause to note the product differentiation that did in fact exist. There were two grades (or qualities or kinds) of beef and of pork, salted and fresh, and there were two grades of cider, new and old (or water and clear). By 1762, two qualities of hay were being grown and sold, English upland and fresh meadow, the price of the first usually double the price of the second. In all the calculations that follow, each of these differentiated products has been treated as a separate good.

In addition, there was product differentiation that cannot be so easily handled. In the 1840s, account books begin suddenly to distinguish several varieties of potatoes, differing in size, in color ("blue potatoes"), in name ("English," "Rohan," "Chenango," "merino," "Carter"), and in price, a differentiation that may have become feasible when, after the blight of 1843, potatoes suddenly became very expensive.[27] Similarly, after 1840, increased urban demand drove up the price of the English hay supplied to livery stables, thereby increasing the variance of English hay prices as a function of proximity to urban places. English hay and

---

the goods to different purchasers; each of whom must be supposed to pay in addition to the market price a special charge on account of delivery" (p. 325).

In addition to allowing for differential transport costs, convergence to an equilibrium price takes place in *time:* "Again, markets vary with regard to the period of time which is allowed to the forces of demand and supply to bring themselves into equilibrium with one another, as well as with regard to the area over which they extend. And this element of Time requires more careful attention just now than does that of Space. For the nature of the equilibrium itself, and that of the causes by which it is determined, depend on the length of the period over which the market is taken to extend. We shall find that if the period is short, the supply is limited to the stores which happen to be at hand: if the period is longer, the supply will be influenced, more or less, by the cost of producing the commodity in question; and if the period is very long, this cost will in its turn be influenced, more or less, by the cost of producing the labour and the material things required for producing the commodity" (p. 330).

27. The potato blight, which was to have such momentous consequences when it struck Ireland two or three years later, appeared quietly in Massachusetts. Not dependent for their very lives on the potato, only one of the farmers in my sample, David Goodale of Marlborough, remarked in 1843 that "half the crop is black in the ground." Within a year the price of potatoes rose from one shilling (seventeen cents) to over $1.00 a pound.

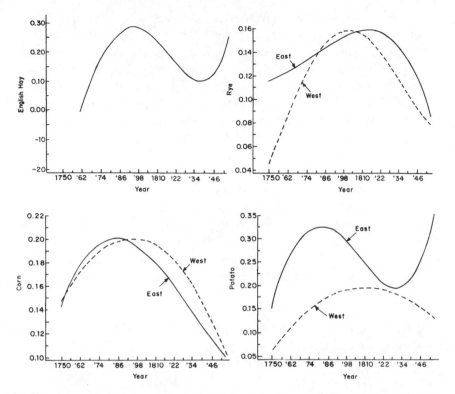

Fig. 5   Regressing the coefficient of variation of prices on time: corn, rye, potatoes, English hay.
Source: Price data come from farm account books
Note: Preparation of data described in the text. Coefficient of variation is the standard deviation of annual prices divided by the annual means of prices.

potatoes, each formerly a single "good," had each become a cluster of goods. Suffice it to say, the price consequences of product differentiation can play havoc with the convergence process (as can be seen in fig. 5 in the case of potatoes and English hay after 1840), forcing us to acknowledge that Marshall's description of a market process depends critically on defining a *good*.[28]

To test the pattern of price convergence over time, annual price data were collected from fifty-four account books and daybooks and from

28. The demand for higher quality both from abroad and from an increasingly urbanized population at home led to grading, and to the standardization of quality within grades, of American butter, flour, cheese, wheat, pork, wool, and tobacco (Danhof, *Change in Agriculture,* 43, n. 61).

over nine hundred probate inventories[29] for each of the following farm commodities: corn, potatoes, rye, oats, both hays, both kinds of beef, both kinds of pork, and both kinds of cider. Annual means and standard deviations of prices were calculated for each "good" in each region, and annual observations of the coefficient of variation (the standard deviation divided by the mean) were regressed on a nonlinear time trend for Region East, Region West, and the pooled sample. The regression results for corn, potatoes, rye, and English hay are presented in table 5 and, graphically, in figure 5.[30]

Inspection of figure 5 reveals that the onset of convergence—that is, of the downward-sloping portion of the regression plots, which, in turn, is our diagnostic for the effect of market integration on the behavior of prices—happened, in most cases, before 1790, shortly after the Revolution and several decades before the dates widely accepted as pivotal in the transformation of the rural economy of New England. This process is confirmed in the East, in the West, and in both regions pooled for each of the four principal crops.

I shall have more to say about convergence, but first our attention is directed to the *rising* portion of these regressions. How shall we explain *increasing* coefficients of variation between 1750 and the onset of the convergence process? (The same pattern will be found to obtain when, in chap. 6, farm wage rates are tested for convergence.) Coefficients of variation of farm commodity prices are an inverted-U-shaped function of time. If market orientation can be diagnosed by the convergence of prices, how shall we interpret the widening divergence that preceded it? As evidence of *withdrawal* from markets?

In a manner of speaking, yes. And the explanation that I shall propose hangs on the two senses in which I have used the word *market:* market-places and market economy. It will be recalled from the discussion of socially controlled prices in chapter 2 that early in the colonial period "markets-ouvert"—market-places or town fairs—were regulated

---

29. Six hundred of the inventories from Middlesex County had been gathered at random for each of three time periods—1764–76, 1789–96, and 1832–35—by Sarah McMahon, who very generously made the commodity price data available to me. As additional observations for the year 1855 I also used the commodity prices for each town in my sample that appear in the agricultural schedules in "The State of Industry in Massachusetts," which is, in effect, the 1855 state census.

30. The F-values on the regression equations in the cases of oats, meadow hay, beef, pork, and cider were not statistically significant at the 5 percent level. F-values on the regression equations given below for corn, rye, potatoes, and English hay were statistically significant at the less than 1 percent level; t-statistics on the coefficients were significant at the less than 2 percent level.

Table 5   Regressing the Coefficient of Variation on Time:
Prices for Selected Crops

	Potatoes	Rye	Corn	English Hay
Constant	−12.48	8.83	16.54	−79.66
	(1.39)	(4.04)	(6.24)	(3.36)
Time	2.71	.31	.25	5.18
	(4.49)	(3.22)	(2.17)	(4.04)
Time^2	−.052	−.003	−.003	−.08
	(4.45)	(3.18)	(2.76)	(3.84)
Time^3 × 10^{-2}	.029			.039
	(4.28)			(3.58)

Note: Absolute values of t-statistics are given in parentheses. "Time" is entered as (year − 1749).

by Massachusetts town governments, whose responsibility it was to open and close the market-place and to establish the terms of private exchanges. Along with statutory price fixing went laws against forestalling, engrossing, and regrating and a tight corpus of licensing, regulated weights and measures, and surveillance to ration supply and to restrict demand, regulations without which the fixed prices would not hold.[31] But, as we have already noted, by the mid-1740s the pressures building against such controls—pressures from currency inflation, from scarcities, from the Awakening's frontal assault on congregational orthodoxy—proved irresistible.[32]

What I think we are seeing in the increasing variance (the rising coefficient of variation) of farmers' prices after 1750 is a glimpse into the disarray between regimes, between the end of social control and the beginning of an equilibrium process, between the demise of one kind of market and the emergence of another. But, as was discussed in chapters

31. See Hughes, "Transference and Development of Institutional Constraints upon Economic Activity," and *Social Control in the Colonial Economy;* Brown, *Faneuil Hall and the Faneuil Hall Market.* Every May for a number of years after its founding in 1732, the town of Dudley met to choose selectmen and the following town officials "whose job it was to regulate a wide range of economic activities: the clerk of market, the brander of horses, the sealer of leather, the surveyors of shingles, the fence-viewers, the tything-men, the wardens, and the constables" (Brooke, *The Heart of the Commonwealth,* 20). In addition, the proprietors of the common lands and the proprietors of the common fields selected officers to regulate planting times, fencing, grazing, and opening and closing times, sue trespassers, levy taxes on themselves, and admit new proprietors (see Field, "The Evolution of Property-Rights Institutions").

32. "By the late eighteenth century it had become accepted American legal doctrine that the English law of markets overt did not apply in this country. The practices of medieval commerce died out under the more dynamic requirements of an utterly commercial society" (Hughes, *Social Control in the Colonial Economy,* 131). (Pace Michael Merrill, even I will not argue that rural society in eighteenth-century Massachusetts was "utterly commercial.")

2 and 3, without price observations (i.e., without farm account books) for the early eighteenth century, this must remain a surmise.

Price convergence is a necessary condition of a market process, but it may not be a sufficient condition. Two studies of the effect of late nineteenth-century railroad building on commodity prices, one in India and the other in Tsarist Russia, both found price convergence, but *without* market integration.[33] Regional price differentials narrowed, not because the regions were becoming integrated into a single market, but because in each case the building of a national railroad lowered transport costs between spatially separated markets. The prices that tend toward uniformity in Marshall's definition of a market are f.o.b. prices, *net* of transport costs (or transactions costs generally). We are fortunate in our choice of archive that the farm-gate prices in account books come to us uncontaminated with transport costs.

But even if these had been delivered prices, the onset of price convergence took place some three or four decades before the appearance of the railroad in Massachusetts. There are no railroad trips in this data base; the trips that have been analyzed in this chapter were all wagon trips. And although the period 1750–1855 saw some improvements in road construction, it is not clear, as was noted earlier, how or whether those improvements translated into lower transport costs. Finally, according to table 4, overland transport costs were not falling but were in fact rising, both in current and in constant dollars. Price convergence happened in the face of the rising costs of wagon transport. For many reasons, then, we can reject the argument that savings in rail transport costs were causing the price convergence observed in the data.

Confidence in price convergence as a diagnostic of market integration is enhanced if it can be demonstrated that farmers' production decisions led to increasing regional specialization. Following the experiment in Metzer's thesis, I compared 1855 production figures for corn, rye, oats, and English hay with 1801 production figures, for the forty-eight sample towns represented by the fifty-four farmers' account books and journals. The towns were grouped into counties, and the counties were used as surrogates for regions. Outputs in the sample towns in 1801 and in 1855 were averaged for each county and coefficients of variation calculated. If, under the influence of a market economy, regional specializations had been developing between 1801 and 1855, we should expect to see a *larger* coefficient of variation—an increased var-

---

33. McAlpin, "Railroads, Prices and Peasant Rationality"; and Metzer, "Some Aspects of Railroad Development in Tsarist Russia."

iance between counties with respect to crop-specific outputs—in 1855 than in 1801.

The results are given in table 6. Corn and, to a lesser extent, English hay exhibit moderate increases. In the case of oats there is no change whatever. But in the case of rye there is a marked change in the geographical distribution of rye production, confirmation of growing regional specialization. In the Russian case, "The observed increased in these dispersion measures between the two periods indicates that agricultural production . . . became indeed much more specialized in terms of its spatial distribution."[34] In the Massachusetts case, "much more" may be an exaggeration—perhaps only "more."

It is now possible to bring together the trip analysis and the price analysis and allow them to comment on each other. It will be recalled that there were regional differences in the pattern of marketing trips. Concentration—which in the terms of our earlier discussion meant a skewed distribution of trips to some destinations—characterized eastern marketing from the beginning but emerged only slowly and late in the West. The implications of this are now visible in the respective patterns of price convergence in East and West. The narrowing of price differentials is later and not as statistically significant in the West as it is in the East, reflecting the tardier emergence of important central places in the West. The mechanism that effected the link between observed travel patterns and observed price behavior was not the appearance of cheap transportation but rather the arbitraging activity of the farmers themselves, each of whom, in moving out from his farm along a multitude of "destination vectors," served to transmit the information that brought about price convergence.

IV. Supply Elasticity: The Case of Hog Weights

It if could be done, the most efficient test of market orientation would be to calculate supply elasticities, that is, farmers' decisions about what and how much to produce in response to changing prices. But the data for these calculations are so often just out of reach. The daybooks from which aggregate outputs can sometimes be derived seldom give prices; the account books from which prices can be derived seldom give outputs; and rarely do both sources exist for the same farmer.

It is presumably at planting time that one best captures the farmer

34. Metzer, "Some Aspects of Railroad Development in Tsarist Russia," 133.

Table 6　Regional Specialization, 1801–55, Average Production

Region[a]	Corn (bushels)	Rye (bushels)	Oats (bushels)	English Hay (tons)
Berkshire:				
1801 (2)	6,452.5	1,524.5	2,183.5	1,082.00
1855 (2)	8,196.0	787.0	6,534.0	2,484.85
Essex:				
1801 (5)	13,416.2	1,288.0	440.6	1,057.80
1855 (6)	9,768.0	1,079.0	1,616.5	1,598.18
Hampshire-Hampden-Franklin:				
1801 (7)	8,861.7	4,316.0	1,392.1	904.40
1855 (8)	21,850.0	6,979.0	4,037.5	2,545.70
Middlesex:				
1801 (10)	8,074.7	2,335.4	722.8	614.60
1855 (11)	11,241.0	1,180.0	3,266.6	1,947.30
Norfolk:				
1801 (4)	6,917.0	528.0	169.2	593.40
1855 (4)	8,090.0	481.7	484.5	1,457.20
Plymouth-Bristol:				
1801 (5)	12,739.2	2,066.6	2,158.0	1,088.70
1855 (5)	6,924.2	526.6	1,581.0	1,019.50
Worcester:				
1801 (12)	7,447.7	1,841.4	2,531.4	698.25
1855 (12)	11,108.0	963.0	6,131.2	2,030.65
Mean of all regions:				
1801	9,129.9	1,985.7	1,371.1	862.70
1855	11,025.3	1,713.8	3,378.8	1,869.05
Standard deviation:				
1801	2,813.0	1,183.5	944.8	223.60
1855	5,037.3	2336.7	2,334.2	552.90
Coefficient of variation:				
1801	.31	.60	.69	.26
1855	.46	1.36	.69	.30

Source: 1801 valuations, "State of Industry in Massachusetts, 1855."

[a] Numbers in parentheses are number of towns represented in the account book sample.

in the act of responding to changes in relative prices, but even if it were possible to recover the record of a farmer's planting decisions, to which prices would he have been responding? Current prices? Lagged price? Expected price? And in each case there is seldom a single price but rather a range, sometimes very wide, of seasonally fluctuating prices, the annual averaging of which might only obscure the very responses we are attempting to capture.[35]

Marc Nerlove has argued that farmers in fact do not respond, as is

35. Nerlove, *The Dynamics of Supply.*

neoclassically assumed, to *all* price changes, but only to those they expect to be permanent, that is, to changes in what he calls *expected normal price,* defined as "the average level about which future prices are expected to fluctuate."[36] Expected normal price is arrived at by a progressive and cumulative learning process in which past expectations are regularly scrutinized and corrected against past realities.[37] But given the inadequacies in our data, one despairs of being able to use Nerlove's elegant model in this study.

There is, however, one farm output that may lend itself to measuring price elasticities of supply without the complications that separable expectations introduce, an output that, in a manner of speaking, *embodies* the farmer's expectations. This is a commodity that does not ripen at an urgent moment in time: its growing season can be prolonged for years or cut short to a matter of days. Farmers are therefore in the position of being able to space the "harvest" in order to capture seasonal price advantages. True, it may have been customary to harvest this "crop" between Thanksgiving and New Year's, but that was never an imperative, at least in New England, and became less so over time.[38] I refer, of course, to the hog.

Although the conventional view is that hogs were butchered at eighteen to twenty months of age, there is evidence in the literature that as early as 1800 "some farmers kept their hogs over two winters, [while] others slaughtered at 8, 10, or 12 months."[39] Of the 556 slaughter weights of swine that I have collected from account books and daybooks, 190, or 34 percent, were of young pigs, while a great many others were so heavy (450 to 600 pounds) that they must have been considerably older than twenty months. If season and age did not set the time of butchering, what did? It should prove possible to locate the

36. Ibid., 25.

37. If P^*_t is the expected normal price in period t, then

(1) $P^*_t - P^*_{t-1} = B(P_{t-1} - P^*_{t-1})$,

where B, the coefficient of expectation, lies between zero and one, and

(2) $X_t = a_0 + a_1 P^*_t + u_t$,

where u_t is a random residual and X_t is output in period t. By substituting the term $[BP_{t-1} + (1 - B)P^*_{t-1}]$ from eq. (1) for P^*_t and introducing longer lags, Nerlove can, as it were, push back into insignificance the unobservable P^* term:

(3) $X_t = a_0 + a_1[BP_{t-1} + B(1 - B)P_{t-2} + (1 - B)^2 P_{t-3} + B(1 - B)^3 P^*_{t-4} \ldots] + u_t$.

38. For the months in which butchering actually occurred, see Rothenberg, "A Price Index for Rural Massachusetts," 999.

39. Bidwell and Falconer, *History of Agriculture,* 111.

determinants of age at slaughter (i.e., weight) in economic variables: perhaps in the price of corn (cost), the price of pork (revenue), and the ratio between them.

In the previous section we used regression analysis to distill, as it were, the time shape of price dispersion. We will now use regression analysis to test a causal hypothesis: that market-oriented farmers slaughtered their livestock in response to corn and pork prices. Then, by adding time dummy variables to the regression, we can determine in what time period our sample farmers began to "harvest" their pork "crop" in response to relative prices.

From the sample account books and daybooks the weights at slaughter of 366 adult hogs were collected, with year, town, and region.[40] But first a determination had to be made as to whether the weight given in the source was a live weight or a dressed weight, and there are virtually no clues in the sources themselves. My solution was to compare the per pound price of the hog (given or easily calculated) with the per pound price of fresh pork for that region in that year. If the per pound price of the hog was *less than* the price of fresh pork, the weight was called a *live weight* and entered as such into the data base. If the per pound price of the hog equaled or exceeded the price of fresh pork, the weight was called *dressed weight* and divided by 0.70 to standardize all weights as live weights.[41]

Regressions were then specified of hog weights on a variety of in-

40. The fact that many small pigs were butchered at a very tender age is certainly relevant to this inquiry, but because some of them were so very small (six pounds, e.g.), their presence would distort the results. Pigs therefore had to be removed from the sample. There is no firm line that separates pigs from hogs, and the decision had to be arbitrary. One dictionary defined *hog* as swine in excess of 120 pounds. Had I used that boundary, there would have been 384 hogs in my sample. I chose instead to set the boundary at 200 pounds live weight, with an N of 366.

41. The dressed weight/live weight ratio of 0.70 that I have used throughout is midway between the 0.75 or 0.76 used by Gallman ("Self-Sufficiency in the Cotton Economy of the Antebellum South"), Battalio and Kagel ("The Structure of Antebellum Slave Agriculture"), and Bateman and Atack ("The Profitability of Northern Agriculture in 1860"), and the 0.65 used by several of my account books and by Jay Adams, formerly principal farmer at Old Sturbridge Village, whose job it was to replicate to the minutest detail the farming practices of central Massachusetts in the period 1790–1840.

The procedure outlined in the text for distinguishing between dressed and live weights was generally followed, but exceptions were made. The manuscript records of a large-scale slaughterer in 1838–39 indicate that larger animals could command a higher per pound price than smaller animals simply because they were fatter, not because they were dressed. That is, the higher price reflected a difference in quality. Therefore, to avoid biasing the sample upward, swine weights were treated as live weights whenever to treat them as dressed weights would, when divided by 0.70, produce hogs that would have weighed in excess of seven hundred pounds when alive.

dependent variables, both deflated (by my price index) and not, in logs and not. The independent variables are corn price; the prices of fresh pork and of salt pork; the ratios of corn price to each pork price; and year. The regressions were run by region and for the pooled sample, with *year* entered both as a continuous variable and as period dummies to test a variety of time-period break points.

When *year* was entered as a continuous and linear variable, the results indicated that, while corn and pork prices may have played a role in the slaughter decisions of farmers, the most powerful explanatory variable was *year;* hog weights were manifestly an increasing function of time. Of course, time is hardly neutral with respect to market development: time can be regarded as a surrogate for market-validated changes in animal husbandry such as the emphasis on manures, which brought about stabling and penning, and the introduction of legumes and root crops into swine feed which enabled farmers to keep and fatten their stock through the winter. Time is a surrogate for the changes in relative prices that determined the allocation of corn between humans and animals. Time is a surrogate for the manifold effects of the proliferation, expansion, and accessibility of urban markets.

Pregnant with economic content as it is, however, the variable *year* had robbed the price variables of their power to explain hog weights and given us little in return. Considerably stronger R^2's and more significant coefficients are obtained when the price data are divided into time-period subfiles.[42] The best-fit regression results are shown in table 7. Again, the dependent variable is *hog weights.* Because the independent variables are not presented in this table in the order in which they were entered in the regression equations, a new column, "R^2 Change," indicates the increase in explained variation accounted for by the addition of that variable.

The results suggest emphatically that the time variables in the later

42. There are *regional* differences in the explanatory power of the price variables as well as temporal differences, and, in fact, the regional differences are more consistent. The time variables account for a smaller proportion of the change in hog weights, and price variables for a larger proportion, in the West than in the East. In view of our earlier findings of a slower pace of market development in the West than in the East, this curious finding deserves comment. We may be picking up the early specialization of Connecticut River Valley farms in livestock raising. According to Bidwell and Falconer, farms in and around Hadley were stall feeding oxen for the Brighton cattle market as early as 1700 (*History of Agriculture,* 109). Even if swine were not shipped to Brighton, one imagines that the habit of responding to market signals would spill over from cattle raising to swine raising.

Table 7   Multiple Regression of Hog Weights on Selected Prices,
Time Period Breakdowns, 1750–1855

	Coefficient	R^2	R^2 Change	Absolute Value of t-Statistic
Corn prices, East:				
1750–1820	− .690	.079	.006	1.36
1821–35	.736	.132	.132	1.39
Salt pork prices, West:				
1750–1810	− .077	.457	.055	.20
1811–30	− .295	.164	.164	1.14
Corn prices/salt pork prices, West:				
1750–1810	.496	.324	.012	1.65
1811–20	− 1.222	.339	.339	2.13
Time, East:				
1750–1820	.010	.602	.523	.94
1821–35	− .287	.167	.017	4.32

Sources: Prices and hog weights are from farm account books and day books.
Note: All hog weights and prices are entered in logs. Hog weights are entered as live weights, adjusted, where necessary, from slaughter weight or dressed weight to live weight as described in the text. R^2 change indicates the percentage increase in explained variation accounted for by the addition of each variable, one at a time.

periods are losing to price variables the dominance they had had in the early years. This shift of explanatory power from time factors to price (or market) factors can be seen in the increased size of the coefficients on all price variables, in the higher t-statistics on all price coefficients (i.e., the greatly diminished probability that there was in fact no relation between hog weights and price variables), in the sharply diminished R^2 change of all time variables, and in the sharply increased R^2 change of all price variables.[43]

While the growing strength of corn and pork price variables supports the hypothesis of growing market orientation, that support remains modest, and the turning point—roughly 1820—is considerably later than our other evidence. That could be due to the specification of the regressions. Corn is not in fact the basic feed of hogs. A diet rich in corn may have been given to swine only for the brief fattening period.[44] If hog

43. It is relevant to state here that only about one-sixth of the sample hog weights were drawn before 1820; five-sixths of the observations postdate 1820.

44. Although cattle weights may be more nearly a function of the hay cattle consume than are hog weights of the corn hogs consume, it does not follow that a regression of the slaughter weights of cattle on hay prices would have given better results than the hog weight regressions used here. Cattle, even if stall fed in winter, grazed free for much of the year, free in the sense that

weights depended more on feeds other than corn—for example, slops or skim milk—we have not captured that in these regressions.

In addition, the signs on the coefficients appear to run counter to intuition, at least for a static model. The implicit model being tested here assumes that the higher the price of corn (holding pork price constant), the earlier the farmer would butcher his corn-consuming animals; that the higher the price of pork (holding corn price constant), the heavier (older) he would allow his hogs to become; and that the higher the price of corn relative to the price of pork, the lower the weight of the butchered hog. Instead, the signs on the regression coefficients suggest that the very opposite holds true. If expectations played a decisive role here, as well they might, that too has not been captured in these regressions. A rise in the price of corn may have led to the anticipation of a rise in the price of pork fed on corn and therefore (contrary to the static model) to a delay in butchering; a rise in the price of pork may have led to immediate "cashing in" if that rise were expected to be short lived; and changes in the ratio of corn to pork prices may have generated uncertainties that induced the farmer to slaughter his hogs early, salt them down and barrel them, and await further price changes. Given the very long production periods in agriculture generally and in animal husbandry in particular, price-elastic behavior can give wildly different results depending on how anticipated revenues and the anticipated costs of withholding are calculated. But we still do not know on which prices farmers framed these calculations: current? lagged? expected? or what Nerlove calls "expected normal"?

"The time of killing beasts is to be regulated by the market," wrote Isaiah Thomas in 1803,

> and the advantage and convenience of the farmer. And the same things must fix the time, if he sells them to the butchers. Beef that is only grass-fed must be killed as early as the beginning of November, because after this time, grass will not increase the fatness of cattle. This may be afforded at the lowest price, perhaps 2½ pence per pound, without loss. Cattle that are fatted till December must have, besides grass or hay, corn or juicy vegetables, or both, to increase their fat-

pasture land was of such poor quality that it had virtually no alternative uses and therefore zero opportunity cost. In addition, cattle perform a wide variety of services throughout a long lifetime. It is unlikely that they were slaughtered for "light and transient causes" like a change in the relative prices of hay and beef.

ness. The price of beef therefore ought to be higher, by about two farthings. If not killed till January, the price should continue rising at least in the same proportion; and so on, till the time of fatting by grazing returns.[45]

V. FARMERS' PRICES AND THE TRADE CYCLE

The final exhibit—the behavior of my commodity-price index (see table 8)—is, in a sense, the first, for it was the discovery of synchronous cycles in the behavior of Philadelphia wholesale prices, New York City wholesale prices, and Massachusetts farmers' account book prices that plunged me into the present investigation.

Examine figure 6. Visible in the behavior of all the indexes are some inflation during the French and Indian War, the depression that followed the war and against the backdrop of which the imperial crisis was played out, the revolutionary war inflation and its deep postwar depression so aggravated by farm foreclosures, prosecutions for debt, hard money, and high taxes. Massachusetts farm prices led New York and Philadelphia prices by a year or two in response to the carrying trade prosperity of the mid-1790s, a prosperity interrupted by the Embargo, the effect of which was felt more keenly in urban markets than in rural, although it did register in Massachusetts farm prices in 1808. The high prices of the War of 1812 were followed in all three series by the depression of 1819, considered by some to mark the beginning of the modern trade cycle. The whole postwar decade of the 1820s was one of depression, not only in the urban centers, but on the farms of Massachusetts as well. The dramatic boom of 1836 appears, more or less dramatically, in all three series, followed by steadily falling prices through the lean and hungry 1840s, relieved only momentarily in 1847—again in all three indexes— by the prosperity of the Mexican War. By 1853, California gold was responsible for the assertive recovery visible in New York, in Philadelphia, and on the inland farms of Massachusetts. "From 1849 to 1859," writes Albert Fishlow, "the total money supply increased from approximately $354 million to about $767 million on the impulse of the California gold discoveries. It requires no rigid adherence to the quantity theory of money to anticipate the direction of the effect upon the price

45. Thomas, "Agriculture," in his *Massachusetts, Connecticut, Rhode Island, New Hampshire and Vermont Almanack,* n.p. I am grateful to Sarah McMahon for bringing this passage to my attention.

Table 8 Weighted Index of on-the-Farm Prices Received by Massachusetts Farmers, 1750–1855 (1795–1805 = 100)

Year	1800 Weights	1855 Weights	Year	1800 Weights	1855 Weights
1750	42.7	41.4	1795	103.9	98.0
1751	37.8	33.5	1796	98.6	91.4
1752	66.5	68.0	1797	99.0	85.3
1753	63.7	62.6	1798	94.8	99.8
1754	53.6	53.7	1799	98.7	111.7
1755	63.6	67.3	1800	109.1	109.2
1756	56.6	76.8	1801	88.4	91.9
1757	62.6	73.2	1802	97.1	86.8
1758	62.7	73.8	1803	91.1	96.0
1759	62.4	65.2	1804	107.3	115.2
1760	54.4	79.1	1805	111.2	117.6
1761	65.6	85.3	1806	116.4	130.3
1762	74.1	84.8	1807	110.6	108.1
1763	68.4	89.6	1808	98.6	98.5
1764	63.8	82.1	1809	110.1	114.1
1765	72.2	77.7	1810	111.8	112.7
1766	65.5	88.2	1811	112.5	99.7
1767	60.8	61.7	1812	111.5	112.9
1768	74.0	73.2	1813	120.0	114.8
1769	62.0	68.1	1814	121.9	120.5
1770	63.8	55.4	1815	123.6	122.5
1771	66.9	61.3	1816	124.8	130.5
1772	63.6	61.7	1817	134.3	131.1
1773	66.6	68.7	1818	126.2	112.5
1774	68.7	76.1	1819	121.4	119.9
1775	74.8	74.7	1820	105.3	104.8
1776	80.6	73.8	1821	101.4	111.2
1777	108.2	108.0	1822	104.1	112.6
1778	86.3	82.3	1823	104.0	110.1
1779	112.7	108.9	1824	100.3	112.8
1780	100.6	101.6	1825	103.2	109.1
1781	77.4	77.7	1826	106.3	117.4
1782	81.3	91.9	1827	105.6	118.9
1783	104.6	105.6	1828	106.4	113.9
1784	74.5	67.7	1829	95.8	108.2
1785	82.3	84.0	1830	103.1	98.8
1786	72.7	69.0	1831	100.3	99.9
1787	79.9	78.9	1832	112.8	110.4
1788	79.1	82.9	1833	115.2	122.5
1789	73.9	76.2	1834	113.0	114.9
1790	78.4	74.1	1835	118.1	128.6
1791	75.7	79.1	1836	136.6	151.7
1792	75.0	72.6	1837	140.1	146.7
1793	92.3	105.7	1838	130.4	130.0
1794	106.8	118.8	1839	128.6	139.0

Table 8   (*Continued*)

Year	1800 Weights	1855 Weights	Year	1800 Weights	1855 Weights
1840	108.6	110.5	1848	115.7	135.6
1841	120.1	121.9	1849	114.0	143.5
1842	102.4	110.5	1850	117.0	112.6
1843	96.8	95.0	1851	132.1	141.8
1844	97.4	97.7	1852	119.3	108.0
1845	104.3	110.3	1853	134.9	125.0
1846	123.4	121.3	1854	145.2	166.2
1847	130.5	129.4	1855	141.7	158.8

Source: For the construction of this index, see Rothenberg, "A Price Index for Rural Massachusetts."

Note: The reference base of the index is 1795–1805. The index was constructed with two weight bases to reflect the shift in the composition of Massachusetts farm output from 1800 (actually 1801) to 1855. For currency conversions, see notes to table 4.

level."[46] This, and the further stimulation of a European war in the Crimea, would appear to have been registered as sensitively in the account books of "isolated" New England farmers as in the ledgers of New York and Philadelphia mercantile houses and published prices current.

The synchrony of these price movements does more than merely "reaffirm the good news from Zion that economists have been hawking about the world for centuries."[47] It poses this challenge to the still skeptical: if the farmers whose account books were used to build this commodity-price index—middling farmers, widely scattered across the state, most from very small rural communities—were in fact "ancient and petty producers," isolated from distant markets by high transport costs and by a *mentalité* of self-sufficiency within a "moral economy," then by what conduit were these trade cycles and macroeconomic shocks to the general price level communicated to them?

46. Fishlow, *American Railroads and the Transformation of the Antebellum Economy,* 42.
47. Lebergott, "Comments on Measuring Agricultural Change," 227.

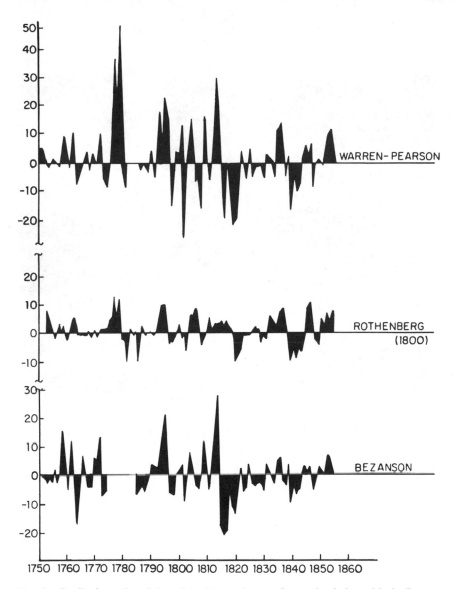

Fig. 6   Cyclical synchronicity of the Massachusetts farm price index with the Bezan-son index of Philadelphia prices and the Warren-Pearson index of New York City prices. *Source:* Rothenberg, "A Price Index for Rural Massachusetts." The Bezanson and Warren-Pearson indexes are presented and discussed in Cole, *Wholesale Commodity Prices in the United States.*
Note: Trend eliminated by calculation of first-differences. The Massachusetts index was first smoothed by a three-year moving average.

5

The Development of a
Capital Market

THE PROBLEM OF THIS CHAPTER IS TO CONFIRM AND TO DATE THE emergence in the farm economy of a capital market sufficiently evolved both to motivate rural savings and, by enhancing their liquidity, to channel them out of farming in pursuit of higher returns in the nonagricultural sectors. For it is the intersectoral shift of resources out of agriculture that transforms economic growth into the more dynamic process of economic development.

On the eve of the Revolution, New England had the lowest per capita wealth and "the most dismal outlook" of any colonial region.[1] Throughout the eighteenth century, the colonial South, embedded as it was in world commodity markets, had grown far more rapidly and was, on a per capita basis, far wealthier. Yet so rapid was the rate of growth in the North in the decades following independence that by 1840 per capita northern income was over 30 percent higher than southern. This remarkable reversal did not happen because southern growth had slowed—apparently it had not—but was due "entirely" to what had become, in barely two generations, "the extraordinarily high income of the Northeast."[2]

That impressive growth story was centered in Massachusetts with the industrialization of cotton-textile and machine-tool manufacture but had had its beginnings in the farm economy decades before, with the unheralded emergence, proliferation, and integration of local markets into a market economy—a thickening network in place, I argue, between 1785 and 1800. Less spectacular than the export-led growth of the South, Massachusetts's development pattern was ultimately a more fruitful one, nourishing "ramifying nests of symbiotic enterprises"[3] to cushion against the devastating consequences of western competition.

The challenges came from Vermont grain and dairy farms, from Pennsylvania and Genesee valley wheat farms, from Cincinnati hog markets. It came by coastal schooner, overland wagon, canal barge, railroad, and live on the hoof. Local markets relayed the shocks as changing relative prices, and resilient farmers responded by shifting from grains to hay, from hay to dairying, and finally from agriculture to commerce and industry.[4]

1. Jones, *Wealth of a Nation to Be,* 141.
2. Fogel and Engerman, *Time on the Cross,* I: 249.
3. This irresistibly apt phrase, taken out of its original context, appeared in Jacobs, "Why the TVA Failed," 45.
4. The shifting composition of Massachusetts agriculture during the first half of the nineteenth century can be demonstrated by comparing the two weight bases I constructed for my farm price

Central to such a transformation must have been the development of an effective mechanism for increasing the liquidity of the regional economy, for motivating the accumulation of capital in the farm sector, and for channeling savings through credit networks that became increasingly multilateral and impersonal, out of declining sectors on the fringes of the development process and toward higher returns generated in the commercial, infrastructure, and manufacturing sectors. The mechanism to effect that transformation is a regional capital market.[5]

I. FORMULATING TESTS OF CAPITAL MARKET FUNCTION

Because the test of capital market function most often used—the convergence of risk-standardized rates of return—cannot be documented for the rural economy in this period, this study tests for the appearance of three other attributes of market penetration that can be documented.

1. A developing capital market alters what I am calling the structural (or institutional) elements of the capital-transfer process. Interest rates are freed to behave like market-clearing prices, credit instruments become more fully negotiable, and new investment opportunities appear, accompanied by new financial intermediaries to service them.

2. A developing capital market is accompanied by decreasing transactions costs, evidence of which can be inferred from the increasing size and widening geographical spread of individual credit networks.

3. A developing capital market enhances the liquidity of financial instruments and therefore the propensity of rural wealthholders to substitute them for physical assets. This may be the most important role the capital market played in the transformation of the agricultural economy, and it is tested here in two ways. The first is a wealth-quartile analysis of shifts in portfolio composition over time. The second is a regression analysis identifying the determinants of that shift.

---

index. They are calculated as the proportion each commodity was of total value of net output in Massachusetts, first in 1801, then in 1855 (see table 8).

5. That the southern economy was unable in the antebellum period to generate a comparable growth spurt may have been due to its failure to evolve a comparable capital market, a failure due, perhaps, to the anomaly of increasing risk aversion in the South over time, even into the 1870s. So suggest Atack, Bateman, and Weiss in their *Risk, the Rate of Return, and the Pattern of Investment in Nineteenth-Century American Manufacturing*.

The Data Base

The data through which farmers will be observed as demanders and suppliers of loanable funds come from the probate inventories and the administrators' and executors' accounts of 512 decedents in Middlesex County, Massachusetts, between 1730 and 1838.[6] Middlesex County— the agricultural hinterland of Boston, eight hundred square miles stretching from the New Hampshire border to the sea—has a probate archive that is probably unsurpassed for historical coverage, for the quality of its inventories, and most particularly for the completeness of the accounts that accompany the inventories.[7] A study of rural indebtedness depends on the quality of those accounts, for the inventories alone contain nothing of the debts owed *by* the estate and only little of the debts owed *to* it.[8]

One of the more serious obstacles to the use of probate archives is the issue of sample bias. Because the probate process has to do with property—both the intergenerational transfer of property and the orderly settlement of creditors' claims to property—it is likely that decedents with little or no property fall outside the process, and to that extent they are not represented.[9] In addition, the probated tended to be wealthier than the nonprobated simply because a population of decedents is older (and, for that reason alone, wealthier) than a living population. To

---

6. The collection of nationally aggregated data on private capital formation began in 1839.

7. In the Middlesex County Probate Court, e.g., it proved possible to locate 86 percent of the administration accounts accompanying the inventories of sample decedents. Alice Hanson Jones, by contrast, found administration accounts missing for 55 percent of decedents in her sample of New England counties that excluded Middlesex.

8. In addition, one suspects that inventories probably understate wealth both real and personal, for the dying and their heirs have the same incentive to conceal property from appraisers as the living have to conceal it from assessors. One strategy was inter-vivos transfers. To the extent that the intergenerational transfer of property was arranged before death, such property will not appear in inventories of decedents' wealth. Eleven of the 512 in the sample had disposed of their real estate in this way so that it had escaped appraisal. The systematic underreporting of personal property, being easier, must have been more widespread.

The probate process is discussed in the appendix to this chapter. For serious students of probates, the discussion of the probate process in the appendix will be inadequate, and they are referred to Jones, *American Colonial Wealth,* vol. 1.

The complete data base, with colonial currencies converted to dollars, is available on request from the author.

9. At the other extreme, I have come across wills that stipulate that, since all debts have been paid and all legacies settled as therein provided, no inventory be taken. In these cases, the very rich also would not be represented in a sample drawn from probates.

make a sample of probated decedents representative of the universe of
the living from which it was drawn requires either carefully stratifying
the sample or carefully weighting the relevant magnitudes to compensate
for their built-in age and wealth biases.[10]

In the present study, the sample was impressionistically drawn to
constitute, not so much a representative sample, as an "interesting
mix"—drawn principally, but not entirely, from rural towns; principally,
but not entirely, farmers; and selected from across a wide wealth spectrum. Table 9 summarizes some of the sample characteristics.

Can such a sample be called *representative*? In its defense, I make
a distinction between two ways of arguing from sample data. One says,
"There must have been a capital market because these sample decedents
are so like the population from which they were drawn that, if I can
show that the sample engaged in market behavior, then so did everyone
else." The other says, "There must have been a capital market because
these sample decedents engaged in market behavior." The first argument
requires a representative sample; the second does not. The first argument relates to the ubiquity or pervasiveness of a capital market, the
second to its emergence. In this chapter I am making the second kind of
argument. Most conjectures about what might be called *ecological*
transformations of society are, it seems to me, of this second kind; it is
sufficient that a sample behaved as though the transformation had taken
place, for how could they behave that way if it had not?

That said, the wealth distribution of this probate sample does in fact
closely approximate existing estimates of the "true" wealth distribution
of the population. A Gini coefficient calculated for my sample ranked
by total wealth is .675:[11] the top 10 percent of the sample population
held 54 percent of the wealth. This compares well with Jones's estimate
of a Gini of .64 for free wealthholders in the New England colonies in
1774 and with Jeremy Atack and Fred Bateman's Gini of .63 for the
whole rural North in 1860.[12] The sample, then, does not overrepresent

10. This is an issue definitively explored by Jones in *American Colonial Wealth,* 1:1878–
1901. For her purposes it was imperative that the wealth of her sample of probated decedents be
made as nearly as possible a mirror image of the wealth of the living population in America on the
eve of the Revolution.

11. Total wealth = value of real estate + value of portable physical wealth + value of financial assets.

12. Jones, *Wealth of a Nation to Be,* 164, table 6.2. Jones ranked her sample by total physical
wealth = value of real estate + value of portable physical wealth.

Atack and Bateman, "The 'Egalitarian Ideal' and the Distribution of Wealth in the Northern
Agricultural Community," 125. Massachusetts was not included in their sample of the rural North

Table 9   Characteristics of the Sample

	No. of Decedents		
	Period 1, 1730–80	Period 2, 1781–1838	Pooled, 1730–1838
Total	292	220	512
Occupation:			
Known	277	217	494
Farmer	242	167	409
Farmer only	145	87	232
Artisan	78	69	147
Artisan only	10	13	23
Merchant	42	44	86
Professional	18	40	58
Acreage owned:			
Known	229	187	416
0	38	19	57
1–10	15	12	27
11–50	58	47	105
51–99	67	34	101
100–199	33	43	76
200–5224 +	17	33	50
Number of creditors per decedent:			
Known	239	193	432
1–19	122	86	208
20–50	91	81	172
Over 50	14	19	33
Number of debtors per decedent:			
Known	225	186	411
1–19	132	121	253
20–50	7	20	27
Over 50	3	14	17
Number with credits	205	182	387
Number with debts	245	198	443

Source: Probate documents, Middlesex County Probate Court.

the rich. But when their presence might skew the findings, the upper tail (the wealthiest 5 percent) will be removed and separate results produced.[13]

Relevant also to the issue of representativeness is the distribution of sample occupations (table 9). Just over 80 percent of sample decedents

drawn from the 1860 Census, but their Ginis for Connecticut and Vermont are .66 and .67, respectively.

13. Removing the top 5 percent (twenty-three decedents) from the total wealth distribution lowers the Gini coefficient to .53.

were farmers.[14] This accords with the Fourth U.S. Population Census, which estimates that just over 80 percent of the Massachusetts population "engaged in agriculture" in 1820. But of those farmers in the sample, more than 40 percent had by-employments in which they engaged in as many as twenty-two artisan crafts and five professions. The ubiquity of by-employments among these decedents may accurately reflect the fabled versatility of the Yankee farmer,[15] but for the purpose at hand it blurs the distinction between "agriculture" and "nonagriculture" and, later in this chapter, will play havoc with my attempt to specify an occupational variable in regressions explaining portfolio behavior.

That this data base is drawn from probates may bias a study of indebtedness in a still more subtle way and in a direction difficult even to identify, let alone measure. Compared, say, to debts litigated in the Court of Common Pleas, the long-term indebtedness encountered in probate documents suggests that, in the lives of most decedents, there were relations between debtors and creditors that were softened by "some degree of familiarity and trust."[16] That would explain my finding

14. Given the ubiquity of by-employments, occupations are not always easy to identify. In table 9, a decedent was given the occupation "farmer" if his probate inventory showed that he owned both livestock and husbandry implements and produced grain and/or if he was described as "yeoman" or "husbandman" in probate records.

15. An irresistible (although hardly credible) illustration of Yankee versatility and ingenuity is offered by Samuel Blodget: "A New England farmer, having finished his attention to autumnal duties, thought of going to Europe [as captain and owner of his sloop] to dispose of the timber cut from his last new field. His eldest son received the following orders to be observed during his absence. 'John, you may work in the smith's shop till you have iron shod the plow and the cart wheels you have made, after which you may either build a saw or grist mill for yourself, on your own place. If I should not return in three months, you may repair and adjust the old quadrant, and take charge of the old sloop, after you have new decked her. Joseph will help you spin the new rigging the sloop will want, after he has finished the loom for your mother to weave a top-sail on which; after turning the rounds for the spinning wheel, he may plow the old field, and then go on a voyage to Labradore for cod, or a-whaling to Falklands Island, just as he likes. You must take command of the sloop yourself, load her for the West Indies, unless you find that governor Phillips' last price will do for young stock and provisions; if so go to New Holland, and I shall be home, God willing, to welcome your return. My son, Joseph, it is time to leave off making wooden clocks and fiddles, tan the hides and make shoes for the family.' This [Blodget comments] is not beyond the character of the people, however it may agree in the minutiae with any known incidents" (*Economica*, 2n).

16. David Thomas Konig was able to locate on a contemporary map of Lynn the homesteads of a few parties to probated loans in the seventeenth century and found that they lived within two miles of each other and could therefore be presumed to have had face-to-face contact; parties to litigated loans were, however, unlikely to encounter each other in the course of their daily interchanges given the distances or topographical conformations that separated them (see his *Law and Society in Puritan Massachusetts*, 82). This is corroborated by my finding that a large majority of the plaintiffs and defendants in prosecutions for debt at the Middlesex County Court of Common Pleas in the eighteenth century lived in different towns.

that 15 percent of the (dated) notes (even excluding long-term mortgages) held by the richest quartile of probated decedents after 1781 had been outstanding for more than ten years, 2 percent for over twenty years, and some for over thirty years. The New England farmer of legend—shrewd, unforgiving, hard as flint—is to be found not in administration accounts at probate but in the dockets of the Court of Common Pleas. It is there that creditors, immediately on the maturity of a note, initiated collection proceedings, the outcome of which was (more often than not) "to attach the goods or Estate of the debtor to twice the debt" and for want thereof (more often than not) "to take the Body of the said debtor and him safely to keep." [17]

But even if there is a difference in ambiance between litigated debts and debts outstanding at probate, it is not clear whether the probate sample imparts a bias to this study and, if it does, in which direction that bias runs. If the long-term indebtedness in a probate data base overrepresents "personalized" credit transactions, then my sample is biased against my hypothesis, which only strengthens my findings: for we shall see market relations emerging even in a data base protected against the market.

On the other hand, during the period of this study, Massachusetts judges were responding to the transformation of the economy by *softening* the legal remedies that commercial creditors could seek in actions against their debtors. The abolition of imprisonment for debt was only one way in which commercial law, instrumentally conceived, was moving in the direction of making the relations between debtors and creditors at litigation look more and more like the forgiving links between kith and kin at probate. [18]

Periodization

Section II below will discuss a number of alterations in what I am calling the structural or institutional elements of the capital-transfer process. In these respects, at least, the world of the rural wealthholder will be seen to have changed dramatically and in some cases abruptly in the first quinquennium of independence. The balance of the chapter explores the depth and breadth of that transformation. It hypothesizes a breakpoint

---

17. This is the wording used on attachments instructing court officers to collect from a debtor personal property worth twice the value of the debt outstanding or, failing that, to arrest the debtor.

18. See, e.g., Feer, "Imprisonment for Debt in Massachusetts before 1800," esp. 264–66.

at 1781 (the cessation of hostilities in the American Revolution) and
makes cross-sectional comparisons between the first period (1730–80)
and the second (1781–1838). The validity of the periodization is supported not only by the kinds of evidence adduced in section II but also
by significance and chi-square tests of the evidence presented in section
III, by sizable shifts in the quartile analysis of portfolio composition in
section IV, and by Chow tests of the period regressions in section V.

But by Donald McCloskey's "Jewish mother test" the periodization
is best confirmed by asking, "So what else is new?" [19] On that test, the
American Revolution was an extraordinary breakpoint, ushering in "a
new era of shared ideation" [20] affecting a stunning number and variety of
social indicators.

II. CHANGES IN THE STRUCTURAL ELEMENTS OF
CAPITAL TRANSFER
A Widened Menu of Investment Opportunities

There is a sudden alteration at the close of the revolutionary war in the
portfolio holdings of sample decedents. Beginning in 1778, securities
appear in rural inventories for the first time: shares in bridges (the
Charles River, Malden, Chelsea, Andover, Merrimac, Piscataqua, West
Boston, Cayuga), in turnpikes (the Medford and Andover, the Worcester, the Providence), in the Middlesex Canal, and in the Boston Aqua-
duct Company. There are shares in the U.S. Bank, Union Bank, Boston
Bank, Salem Bank, Lowell Bank, Neptune Bank, Bunker Hill Bank,
Farmers' Exchange Bank, and something called the Railroad Bank; in
the New England Marine Life Insurance Company, the Massachusetts
Marine and Fire Insurance Company, the Union Insurance Company, the
Charlestown Fire and Marine Insurance Company, and the Massachusetts Hospital Life Insurance Company. Holdings of Massachusetts State
5 percent notes appear as early as 1778, followed by New Hampshire,
New York, and Rhode Island State notes, U.S. Loan Office certificates,
Continental Loan Office notes, 3 percent and 6 percent deferred stocks,
something called U.S. Stocks, and Treasurers' notes. Sample decedents
died "seized of" shares in the Boston Manufacturing Company, the Boston Hat Manufactory, the Glass Manufactory, Newton Iron Works,

19. McCloskey, "The Loss Function Has Been Mislaid," 201.
20. Nelson, *The Americanization of the Common Law,* 117. Nelson has explored the vast
consequences for the common law alone of "the gradual breakdown of ethical unity in Massachusetts over a thirty-year period beginning in the 1780s" (ibid.).

Hamilton Manufacturing Company, Merrimac Manufacturing Company, Boott Cotton Mills, Lawrence Manufacturing Company, Tremont Mills, Otcheco Manufacturing Company, Nashua Manufacturing Company, several railroads, and the Boston Type and Stenotype Foundry. If "large holdings of securities were common in eastern cities by the late 1840s,"[21] it is clear that they had begun to be important in the Massachusetts countryside sixty years earlier (see fig. 7).

Securities, then, as now, were not widely held. They appear in the accounts of only 13 percent of the second-period decedents (the financial assets of the majority continued to be loans); of that 13 percent, half lived in Cambridge and Charlestown, the urban places in the county.[22] It is therefore all the more interesting that the other half of securities holders lived in the rural communities of Framingham, Dunstable, Stoneham, Wilmington, Stow, Chelmsford, Malden, Weston, Woburn, Concord, Groton, Newton, and Tewksbury.

Why this sudden appearance of securities in the composition of financial assets in the early 1780s? Funding the prosecution of the war in the absence of banks of any kind had placed U.S. and state government bonds in the hands of a wide cross section of the population who had accepted them in payment for army requisitions, in payment for military service, or as an act of patriotism. Independence unleashed a demand for internal improvements and, in turn, for innovative and reliable sources of borrowed capital to finance them—a demand that found expression in the clamor for the free chartering of limited-liability corporations generally and of banks in particular. Those internal improvements may very well have played the same role in mobilizing capital that the turnpike and canal trusts were playing at the same time in England. They tapped into idle savings, "which may not have been made available for more risky direct investment in industry or commerce, and applied them towards the development of a form of social overhead capital essential for industrial and commercial expansion. In this sense they acted as 'conduits' connecting the 'reservoirs of savings' with the 'wheels of industry.' "[23]

It was not until 1830 that limited liability was fully established in Massachusetts corporation law, and it is in the 1830s that the bulk of manufacturing shares show up in sample portfolios. But the securities

---

21. Sturm, "Investing in the United States," 72.

22. Charlestown was then part of Middlesex County. It was annexed to Boston (Suffolk County) in 1873.

23. Albert, *The Turnpike Road System in England*, 119.

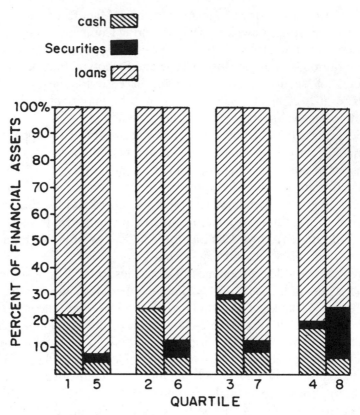

Fig. 7 Shift in the composition of financial assets by quartile and period, 1730–1838.
Source: Administration accounts at probate, Middlesex County.
Note: Financial assets = (loans and mortgages) + securities + cash. Quartiles 1–4 =
first period, 1730–80; quartiles 5–8 = second period, 1781–1838.

of insurance companies are evident as early as 1778 and of banks in
1784, which speaks to the role played by financial intermediaries in
channeling rural savings to industrializing firms. Much of the start-up
capital of the Boston Manufacturing Company, for example, had come
from the Massachusetts Hospital Life Insurance Company, and Massachusetts Hospital Life Insurance securities were held by rural investors.

Interest Rates

During the Revolution, estate administrators suddenly begin to speak of
interest as the "improvement" of money, a metaphor carried over from

land management to portfolio management. With the prospect of "improvement," the lending of money loses the character of "mutual aid among men exposed to the common risks . . . [where] the charitable man comes to the help of distress out of goodwill"[24] and becomes investment, that is, the productive use of a resource the return to which is interest. Also in 1783, there is evidence for the first time of interest being conceived of as the money value of time. Interest begins to be charged by the courts on delayed administration of estates, on delayed payment of court costs, on delays in disbursements of legacies, and even on late payments of rents to the estates of decedent landlords.

Arguably, however, the most important changes between the colonial and the early national periods occurred in the notion of interest as the price of money, and that involves two separable issues: the increased *incidence* of interest charges and market determination of the level of interest *rates*.

From 1781 to 1800, interest was charged on 20 percent of sample administration accounts, increasing to 33 percent from 1800 to 1810 and to 37 percent from 1810 to 1838. This stands in sharp contrast to the years before the Revolution, when interest charges appeared in only about 5 percent of sample probate accounts. What are we to make of that 5 percent? Is it plausible that something like 95 percent of loans in the colonial period were really interest free? Alternatively, was the taking of interest in fact widespread throughout the eighteenth century but concealed from the scrutiny of usury laws?[25]

Because the notion of a price for money is intimately related to the emergence of a market for money, a choice must be made between these two interpretations. It is clear from the dockets of the Court of Common Pleas that "lawful interest" was exacted at least from the beginning of the eighteenth century, but, I have observed, only when the debt arose from the borrowing of money. Debt that stemmed from unpaid account book balances remained customarily interest free. Thus, the marked increase in the frequency with which interest was charged in second-period probates might be explained in one of two ways: either there was in fact an increase in the taking of interest, or there was a shift in the composition of debt away from book accounts (which did not bear interest) and toward the "traffic in money" (which did).

24. Tawney, introduction to Wilson's *Discourse upon Usury*, 23.
25. "I would as much abhorre to lend money for gaine hereafter as I doe abhorre to steale by the high waye, or to murdr any man violentlye for his goods, which god forbyd that ever I shoulde thinke or minde to doe" (Wilson, *Discourse upon Usury*, 379).

The format of administration accounts does permit a test of this distinction because financial obligations are often carefully identified. "Due on book" continued to bulk large enough in the debts of second-period decedents to argue for an increase in the *incidence* of interest taking after 1781, but if this finding is in error, and the apparent increase in the incidence of interest is really a compositional shift from account book credits to notes, mortgages, and bonds,[26] that fact alone would testify to the enhanced liquidity of the rural economy.

In litigation during the colonial period, neither promissory notes nor the attachments issued by the Court of Common Pleas against debtors specified a rate of interest. It was written simply as "Lawful Interest," which was 6 percent. Similarly, in probate documents before 1781, the rate (when it was given or when it could be calculated from information that was given) was also 6 percent—on rare occasions less, but never more. Then, beginning in 1785, interest rates begin to climb to 7, 8, and 9 percent, floating free of their ancient and customary restraints, free enough, presumably, to rise to the level of the returns on physical capital, a phenomenon critical to the historical development of capital markets.[27]

To find rates as high as 9 percent as early as 1785 is worthy of attention because the prohibition of usury, legislated in Massachusetts in 1693 but enforced by the Puritan churches from the very beginning of settlement, was still on the statute books at the outbreak of the Civil War. To be sure, rising rates were not in themselves usurious; usury consisted only in exceeding statutory limits that were themselves free to rise. But with one hand Massachusetts continued until the Civil War to legislate limits on interest rates while with the other hand it began to dismantle, bit by bit, the complex structure of legal remedies that penalized usurious contracts. In doing so the courts were acknowledging mounting pressure from commercial interests to free money from the

26. Apparently, bonds, unlike notes, were protected from the operation of usury laws: "That the issue of negotiability first arose in connection with bonds seems to confirm the suspicion that until the nineteenth century bonds were widely used to prevent judicial interference with commercial transactions . . . [and] almost surely could successfully immunize usurious contracts from legal attack" (Horwitz, *The Transformation of American Law,* 217). This may explain the preponderance of bonds among the credits of the wealthiest decedents.

27. "The capital market in a 'developed' economy successfully monitors the efficiency with which the existing capital stock is deployed by pushing returns on physical and financial assets toward equality, thereby significantly increasing the average return. Economic development so defined is necessary and sufficient to generate high rates of saving and investment (accurately reflecting social and private time preference), the adoption of best-practice technologies, and learning-by-doing" (McKinnon, *Money and Capital in Economic Development,* 9).

notion of "just price" from which the "will theory of contract" had already freed other commodity prices."[28]

Negotiability

That credit instruments be empowered to "pass like currency from debtor to creditor almost indefinitely" took on a special urgency after the Revolution, when the chronic currency shortage that had plagued Massachusetts since its founding was exacerbated by the withdrawal of British bills of exchange.[29] Negotiability is an attribute not so much of the creditworthiness of the instrument as of the evolved state of the capital market within which it moves and of the body of commercial law that guarantees, all the way to the last holder, a right of recovery "against the world." I quote here at some length from Morton J. Horwitz:

> No development had a more shattering effect on American conceptions of the nature of contract than the necessity of forging a body of commercial law during the last decade of the 18th century. At the heart of all commercial problems lay the question of negotiable instruments and of whether the American legal system could assimilate the principle of negotiability into a conception of contract that challenged a whole range of accepted legal notions. . . . How could A, who had given a promissory note to B, be sued by C, to whom B had transferred the note, when nothing passed between A and C? . . . Where C endorsed a note over to D, could D sue B, a prior endorser, if the original promisor defaulted? Could C, a subsequent endorsee, receive a better title to [a defective] instrument than B had . . . so that subsequent innocent purchasers of an instrument might depend on payment regardless of any known defects in the obligation arising out of the original transaction between distant parties?

Most important of all, can C or D, "innocent purchasers," recover against A even if A has already paid B the value of the note? For it is this, "to allow an endorsee to recover against a promisor who had paid the value of the note to his original promisee," that constitutes "full negotiability." On this "crucial" point Massachusetts courts balked until some time after 1809.[30]

28. Horwitz, *The Transformation of American Law,* 237–45.

29. Freyer, "Negotiable Instruments and the Federal Courts in Antebellum American Business," 441; and Horwitz, *The Transformation of American Law,* 215.

30. Horwitz, *The Transformation of American Law,* 212–13 and 338, n. 6.

Even in the absence of "full negotiability," there is evidence in the administration accounts of acceptances, "indorsements," and notes payable "To Bearer," or to "Order" as early as 1754.[31] They attest that IOUs have left the world of face-to-face contacts to travel among strangers, but at that early date the third-party signatures may have been merely sureties, extending face-to-face contact to include "the friend of my friend," and would not constitute evidence of the "personal divorcement in the capital transfer" necessary for a market in these instruments.[32] But when the word *indorsement* appears juxtaposed to scheduled payments of principal and interest, the instrument in question may be truly negotiable (even if falling short of being "fully" negotiable). Each time such an instrument was transferred it was necessary not only to endorse it but also to compute interest at the time of transfer.[33] While evidence of this sort appears in the probate documents of eleven first-period decedents beginning as early as 1764, there are thirty-eight decedents with notes so endorsed in the second period. Again, we cannot know from probates whether these instruments achieved full negotiability in Horwitz's sense—that, he tells us, required nothing less than the transformation of the privity notion of contract—but it is certain that financial institutions to effect their passage were in place by 1785.

III. THE MOBILITY OF CAPITAL: WIDENED AND THICKENED CREDIT NETWORKS

The emergence and proper functioning of a regional capital market will be retarded or much impaired by the combination of risk aversion and high transactions costs traditional in a rural economy. Evidence that can date the weakening of those inhibitions will go a long way toward dating the presence and penetration of the market.[34]

---

31. In a personal communication to the author, John J. McCusker takes issue with Horwitz on the timing of negotiability: "Bills of exchange were negotiable instruments in New England in the 1630s. The colonists knew about the idea because it was an English idea, an English practice, and they were steeped in English mercantile traditions. Bills of exchange circulated, endorsed over to the next party, from the first days of settlement."

32. Davis, "Capital Immobilities and Finance Capitalism," 89.

33. Bruchey, *Robert Oliver, Merchant of Baltimore*, 112.

34. I say *weakening,* not *disappearance.* These inhibitions remain to this day. As recently as 1978, a major factor affecting the household portfolio behavior of even the very wealthy "may be the costs of acquiring and processing the information required to make decisions about how best to allocate resources across different assets. We would expect such costs to vary among households

The evidence that economists typically look for is the convergence of risk-standardized rates of return across a spectrum of investment alternatives. Another approach—one that lies, as rates of return do not, within the purview of probate data—is to find evidence of both the thickening and the widening of credit networks as an operational restatement of "personal divorcement in the capital transfer" and increasing capital mobility. We shall want to know, Is each decedent in the second period linked to *more* credit partners than were decedents in the first? Is each decedent in the second period linked to *more distant* credit partners than were decedents in the first?

From administration accounts at probate the names were taken of 11,956 borrowers and lenders involved in the credit networks of the sample decedents, and with those names three approximations were attempted. The first was merely to compare the first- and second-period frequency distributions. For the period as a whole, each decedent left, on average, seventeen creditors and/or debtors. But there was enormous variance around the mean size of these networks, ranging from those who died free and clear, debtor or creditor to no one, to Newell Bent of Cambridge (1831), creditor to 490 debtors, to Abel Bancroft of Groton (1786), who left a young widow to settle with 166 debtors, to Tilley Merrick, a Concord storekeeper (1768) with 135 debtors, and to Benjamin Blaney of Malden, who died in 1750 in debt to 140 creditors. Table 10 compares the average size, standard deviations, and maximum size of debt and credit networks in five time intervals between 1730 and 1838. The number of creditors of the average decedent increased from under nineteen in the first period to over twenty-six in the last and the number of debtors from under four in the first period to over twenty-six in the last. Even omitting Bent, Bancroft, Merrick, and Blaney, with their exceptionally large networks, the number of individuals with whom decedents had forged credit links increased steadily over time. When it is recalled that administration accounts at probate contain only those credits and debts outstanding at death—only the unpaid balances left over after a lifetime of borrowing, lending, and litigation—the increased size (or thickening) of the networks in table 10 may safely

and, in particular, with observable variables such as the level of educational attainment and occupation" (King and Leape, "Wealth and Portfolio Composition," 34). If transactions costs inhibited optimal portfolio management by the King and Leape sample whose mean net worth in 1978 was a quarter of a million dollars, how much truer it must have been of my sample whose mean net worth, in 1800 dollars, was $3,600.

be characterized as vastly understating the credit networks of the living.

The second approximation is much more difficult: it is to test the hypothesis that credit networks widened in space. To observe changes over time in the distance between borrowers and lenders, one must know the towns both of the decedent and of all his credit partners, but the latter are seldom given in administration accounts. One is forced to make an accommodation: if one cannot locate the partners to whom decedents were linked, one can sometimes locate the decedents to whom partners were linked. That is, 22 percent of the borrowers and lenders who names were recorded in the accounts were found to be involved in credit transactions with at least one other decedent in the sample.[35] Because the towns of the decedents are known, the test consisted of determining whether the decedents to whom these borrowers and lenders were linked were more widely spaced in the second period than in the first. There was dramatic confirmation of some very wide networks in which the same individuals appeared as the debtors or creditors of fifteen, sixteen, even twenty-one different decedents in the sample, scattered in as many as nine different towns across the county. But whether the geographical spread of credit networks had markedly *increased over time* could not be confirmed.

There were, however, over seven hundred instances—468 in the first period, as it happens, and 236 in the second—in which the towns of both parties to each credit transaction were given. For them a third approximation proved possible: to draw two grids with the towns of credit partners across the top, the towns of decedents down the side, and the number of instances of each pairing in each cell. In the first-period grid, the cells with the largest numbers ran along the diagonal; that is, for the subset of cases for which both towns are known, more loans took place between parties in the same town than between parties in different towns.[36]

---

35. Because of the ubiquity of parent naming and Bible naming in Massachusetts in this period, the pool of names was not large, and it would have been a mistake to have assumed that all appearances of the same name referred to the same individual. John Adamses, e.g., abounded. To avoid this problem, various algorithms were tested, but in the end the distinction was made by time: it was assumed that the same name denoted the same individual only if the time interval between appearances of that name was less than twenty years. By holding to this perhaps-too-stringent rule, the 11,956 names that appeared as borrowers or lenders in the accounts of the 512 decedents reduced to 8,515 presumably different individuals, of whom 1,873, or 22 percent, appear as partners of two or more sample decedents and 627 as partners of three or more.

36. It appears that Concord occupied the center of gravity of the grid in the first period. Not only were there more instances of Concord residents transacting with each other than of any other

Table 10   The Average Size of Credit Networks across Five Periods,
1730–1838

Period Dates	Creditors				Debtors			
	N	Mean	SD	Max.	N	Mean	SD	Max.
1730–50	110	18.7	18.2	140	107	3.8	9.8	74
	(109)	(17.5)	(13.9)	(81)				
1751–70	93	22.2	17.4	75	110	6.5	15.8	135
					(109)	(5.1)	(8.4)	
1771–90	56	26.0	19.7	106	57	9.0	24.3	166
					(56)	(6.2)	(11.6)	
1791–1810	116	22.4	17.5	67	124	12.7	17.1	75
1811–38	34	26.1	19.8	73	36	26.2	81.0	490
					(35)	(12.9)	(15.5)	

Source: Probate documents, Middlesex County Probate Court.
Note: The numbers in parentheses are calculated omitting the exceptionally large networks. The mean number of creditors (omitting outliers) is significantly different at the 5 percent level in the five time periods. Mean number of debtors (omitting outliers) is significantly different at the 1 percent level in the five time periods.

After the Revolution this pattern changed. In the second-period grid, the diagonal loses its dominance. It would appear that no special bond linked townspeople to one another in what had once been the intimate business of extending credit. Rather, one senses a widening search for more far-flung credit partners.

To say *far-flung* suggests a measure of distance, a proxy for which appears in table 11. Here the distance between credit partners in this subset of seven hundred networks is measured as the number of "towns apart" they are on a county map held constant at its 1838 conformation. The vanishing diagonal appears in the table as a 42 percent decrease in the second period in the proportion of networks within the same town. Most of the decrease spills over into a 60 percent increase in links to contiguous towns and a near doubling of the proportion of networks reaching out of Middlesex County. Indeed, ties to Worcester County alone nearly tripled (as a percentage of the whole) after 1781.[37] Partners

---

pairing, but more decedents from all over the county were linked to Concord borrowers and lenders than to any other. While it is true that Concord is centrally located in the county and was also a shire town in the colonial period, the centrality of Concord in the county's credit networks may be an artifact of a local tradition of painstaking estate administration. If such were the case, Concord ties would dominate a subset like this one that, in naming the towns of both credit partners, shows unusually painstaking record keeping.

37. Even in the first period, credit flows between Cambridge and Worcester County ran second only to Concord/Concord networks. Thirty decedents owned outlying property in at least one town in Worcester County.

Table 11   The Geographical Spread of Credit Networks

	1730–80		1781–1838	
	No. of Observations	% of Sample	No. of Observations	% of Sample
Total	468	100.0	236	100.0
Same town	155	33.1	45	19.1
Contiguous towns	83	17.7	67	28.4
Two towns apart	74	15.8	26	11.0
Three towns apart	40	8.5	20	8.5
Four towns apart	31	6.6	15	6.4
Five towns apart	20	4.3	11	4.7
Six towns apart	20	4.3	13	5.5
Seven towns apart	3	.6	3	1.3
Out of Middlesex County	34	7.3	32	13.6
Out of Massachusetts	8	1.7	4	1.7

Note: Based on the configuration of towns in Middlesex County as of 1838. Significance level on the chi-square statistic = .0005.

living more than two towns away from each other accounted for one-third of these networks in the first period and for 42 percent in the second. This small subsample—700 out of 11,956 borrowers and lenders—modestly confirms the process of "personal divorcement in the capital transfer" necessary to a functioning capital market.

IV. QUARTILE ANALYSIS OF SHIFTS IN PORTFOLIO COMPOSITION

In table 12, the sample decedents in each period are ranked and sorted by total wealth[38] and presented by quartile in a two-period cross-sectional comparison. The change in each quartile between the first and the second periods (i.e., between cols. 1 and 2) reveals the striking increase over time in borrowing, lending, and the shift of wealth shares from physical to financial assets across the wealth spectrum.

The readers' attention should be drawn at the outset to the finding that the quartile results are sensitive to the wealth measure employed to sort and rank decedents. Using total wealth results in all but the wealthiest second-period decedents emerging as net debtors. But had decedents been sorted instead by, say, portable physical wealth (PPW) rather

38. Total wealth = value of real estate + portable physical wealth (PPW) + financial assets. Financial assets = (loans and mortgages) + securities + cash. Panel A of table 12 defines the wealth magnitudes in current dollars; panel B defines the wealth magnitudes in constant dollars, deflated by my price index (see the note to table 12).

Table 12   Credit Activity by Wealth: Quartile Behavior, 1730–1838

A. Wealth Defined as Undeflated Total Wealth

	First Quartile		Second Quartile		Third Quartile		Fourth Quartile	
	(1) 1730–80	(2) 1781–1838	(1) 1730–80	(2) 1781–1838	(1) 1730–80	(2) 1781–1838	(1) 1730–80	(2) 1781–1838
Total wealth:								
Quartile maximum	318.70	1,694.90	736.90	3,554.60	1,583.20	7,583.10	23,425.10	210,199.10
Number observations	71	54	71	54	71	54	70	53
Mean	173.57	1,049.13	525.77	2,613.61	1,096.62	5,372.30	3,484.79	26,457.55
SD	77.33	413.19	123.98	560.43	245.02	1,139.71	3,517.90	36,009.69
Real estate:								
Maximum	283.30	1,500.00	629.40	3,152.00	1,381.70	6,260.00	18,099.10	76,620.00
Mean	51.45	470.34	302.88	1,688.73	749.62	3,629.75	2,484.56	10,818.28
SD	70.11	424.61	177.57	783.98	292.55	1,289.53	2,884.97	11,719.95
Real estate/wealth:								
Maximum	.99	.95	.99	.99	.94	.97	.96	.96
Mean	.27	.41	.56	.63	.68	.68	.69	.54
PPW:								
Maximum	318.70	1,080.20	522.20	1,100.30	625.20	2,936.60	2,473.10	41,094.00
Mean	80.35	285.35	158.96	471.50	243.56	915.52	536.62	2,731.82
SD	64.27	186.33	104.11	219.39	102.72	593.78	474.27	5,794.87
PPW/wealth:								
Maximum	1.00	1.00	.89	.40	.84	.53	.50	.60
Mean	.48	.33	.31	.18	.23	.17	.17	.12
Financial assets:								
Maximum	264.60	1,455.60	458.30	2,454.50	1,162.00	4,926.10	4,088.30	130,886.60
Mean	41.76	293.44	63.93	453.38	103.44	827.02	463.61	12,907.45

Table 12   (Continued)

A. Wealth Defined as Undeflated Total Wealth

	First Quartile		Second Quartile		Third Quartile		Fourth Quartile	
	(1) 1730–80	(2) 1781–1838	(1) 1730–80	(2) 1781–1838	(1) 1730–80	(2) 1781–1838	(1) 1730–80	(2) 1781–1838
Financial assets/wealth:								
Maximum	1.00	.90	.89	.98	.80	.69	1.00	.96
Mean	.25	.26	.13	.18	.09	.15	.14	.34
Acres:								
Maximum	100.00	399.00	171.00	230.00	505.00	379.00	5,224.50	10,000.00
Mean	16.00	30.00	45.00	80.00	83.50	134.00	267.00	429.00
Debts:								
Maximum	469.60	7,698.50	1,318.90	5,226.20	938.70	7,391.00	4,770.20	188,975.50
Mean	71.92	576.68	135.23	857.35	203.43	1,794.00	650.18	6,268.95
Debts/wealth:								
Maximum	1.99	7.13	3.16	2.89	.75	1.37	1.48	1.18
Mean	.41	.60	.27	.38	.19	.34	.20	.18
Net assets (financial assets − debts):								
Maximum	165.50	1,455.60	448.20	2,189.20	1,122.30	3,112.90	2,804.10	124,904.60
Mean	−31.94	−321.91	−74.26	−423.90	−94.59	−903.64	−168.60	6,960.45
SD	108.19	1,336.54	223.97	1,187.72	326.65	1,990.39	1,058.61	25,026.45
Net worth (wealth − debts):								
Maximum	296.20	1,674.60	687.90	3,467.90	1,519.80	7,530.80	19,894.10	136,785.10
Mean	107.53	441.49	385.63	1,802.36	881.48	3,442.16	2,628.46	20,966.84
SD	104.89	1,266.71	222.67	1,378.94	286.63	1,830.23	2,902.30	25,873.34
FPC/wealth:								
Maximum	.69	.49	.52	.18	.31	.14	.19	.07
Mean	.19	.08	.14	.06	.10	.05	.07	.02

				B. Wealth Defined as Deflated Total Wealth				
NFPC/wealth:								
Maximum	.33	.15	.14	.09	.11	.21	.24	.52
Mean	.01	.01	.01	.01	.01	.01	.01	.02
Total wealth:								
Quartile maximum	397.70	1,679.43	1,372.71	3,649.58	2,713.51	7,067.19	47,095.72	195,898.50
Number observations	71	54	71	54	70	53	71	54
Mean	341.15	1,053.67	998.27	2,663.56	1,978.49	5,229.91	6,188.73	24,407.64
SD	153.42	433.61	245.97	607.97	413.98	1,046.53	7,091.58	32,691.77
Real estate:								
Maximum	481.51	1,382.98	1,182.24	3,062.88	2,290.94	5,864.84	39,099.60	71,407.25
Mean	91.84	497.43	600.55	1,710.61	1,389.62	3,538.23	4,397.89	10,121.96
SD	129.10	434.92	339.58	810.71	526.10	1,395.33	5,881.83	10,805.52
Real estate/wealth:								
Maximum	.94	.95	.99	.99	.94	.97	.96	.96
Mean	.24	.42	.59	.63	.70	.68	.68	.55
PPW:								
Maximum	524.18	975.67	790.27	1,115.92	1,346.29	2,848.31	6,868.77	37,155.52
Mean	159.91	297.13	296.72	468.19	432.20	876.59	943.99	2,540.25
SD	121.83	197.60	168.34	231.94	200.71	546.02	1,039.86	5,237.25
PPW/wealth:								
Maximum	1.00	1.00	.89	.40	.84	.53	.50	.60
Mean	.49	.33	.31	.18	.22	.17	.17	.13
Financial assets:								
Maximum	455.18	1,651.06	1,048.17	2,229.34	1,833.01	6,351.31	6,901.12	121,981.30
Mean	89.40	264.11	101.00	484.75	156.67	815.10	846.85	11,745.43

Table 12 (Continued)

B. Wealth Defined as Deflated Total Wealth

	First Quartile		Second Quartile		Third Quartile		Fourth Quartile	
	(1) 1730–80	(2) 1781–1838	(1) 1730–80	(2) 1781–1838	(1) 1730–80	(2) 1781–1838	(1) 1730–80	(2) 1781–1838
Financial assets/wealth:								
Maximum	1.00	.98	.82	.90	.70	.96	1.00	.95
Mean	.27	.25	.11	.20	.08	.16	.15	.33
Acres:								
Maximum	100.00	399.00	102.00	243.00	505.00	379.00	5,224.00	10,000.00
Mean	14.00	30.50	44.00	79.00	83.00	140.00	265.00	411.00
Debts:								
Maximum	984.54	6,960.67	3,663.11	6,350.18	1,895.44	6,415.80	8,240.98	176,118.80
Mean	140.50	598.19	257.66	928.33	402.35	1,574.42	1,088.17	5,809.85
Debts/wealth:								
Maximum	2.00	7.13	3.16	2.89	.75	1.37	1.48	1.18
Mean	.42	.63	.25	.37	.21	.31	.18	.19
Net assets (financial assets − debts):								
Maximum	448.33	1,324.60	1,048.17	1,988.37	1,797.37	2,784.35	6,036.26	110,731.10
Mean	−49.76	−359.86	−154.50	−468.28	−250.45	−817.97	−212.22	6,110.98
SD	216.76	1,231.79	457.37	1,341.98	499.12	1,809.93	2,016.34	21,827.21

Net worth (wealth − debts):								
Maximum	586.45	1,562.34	1,340.59	3,517.14	2,588.40	6,883.88	32,087.26	121,263.46
Mean	211.56	441.79	755.18	1,792.05	1,563.52	3,487.10	4,576.03	18,948.84
SD	207.22	1,171.25	504.15	1,447.19	530.98	1,713.40	4,602.26	22,778.92
FPC/wealth:								
Maximum	.69	.49	.52	.18	.31	.14	.19	.09
Mean	.19	.08	.14	.06	.09	.05	.07	.02
NFPC/wealth:								
Maximum	.33	.15	.14	.08	.11	.21	.24	.52
Mean	.01	.01	.01	.01	.01	.01	.01	.02

Source: Probate documents, Middlesex County Probate Court.

Note: Definitions of variables: PPW = portable physical wealth; FPC = farm physical capital; NFPC = nonfarm physical capital: wealth = total wealth. See text for definitions of other variables.

Wealth magnitudes in panel A are in current dollars; wealth magnitudes in panel B are in constant dollars. For conversion of colonial currencies, see the appendix to this chapter. The deflator is my Massachusetts farm price index, 1795–1805 = 100, presented in chap. 4, table 8. Its construction is discussed in my "A Price Index for Rural Massachusetts." The index was constructed for the period 1750–1855 and extrapolated backward to 1730 using a nonlinear trend fitted by an OLS regression:

$$INDEX/100.0 = 0.221 + 0.145 \times 10^{-1} \, TIME - 0.51 \times 10^{-4} \, TIME^2.$$

This procedure yields values for observations before 1750 as follows: 1730 = 23.5; 1739 = 36.0; 1742 = 40.0; 1743 = 41.3; 1744 = 42.6; 1745 = 43.9; 1746 = 45.2; 1747 = 46.4; 1748 = 47.7; 1749 = 48.9.

than by total wealth, all quartiles but one (the third) would have emerged as net creditors in the second period—a spurious outcome, as it happens, and one with very different implications. This sensitivity stems from the fact that the share of wealth invested in PPW—in apparel, furniture, husbandry implements, artisanal tools, livestock, and provisions—is itself a decreasing function of wealth (see fig. 8) so that sorting by PPW acts perversely to deposit in the *bottom* quartiles just those wealthy decedents who had invested most heavily in financial assets. Far from handicapping the exercise, however, this very lack of robustness confirms the shift in the composition of wealth away from physical assets and toward financial instruments, the shift on which my argument heavily rests.

But there is more direct evidence of that shift from physical to financial assets in table 12. While the share of total wealth invested in farm physical capital (FPC) decreased sharply between the first and the second periods in every quartile and nonfarm physical capital (principally artisanal tools) maintained, with curious constancy, its 1 percent share of wealth in both periods, mean holdings of financial assets (even in constant 1800 dollars) tripled for the poorest, quadrupled for the second, increased fivefold for the third, and increased nearly thirteenfold for the richest quartile. And financial assets as a *share* of wealth doubled for all but the poorest. Mean debts and debt share, in the meantime, increased in each quartile in a pattern that suggests that debt is a logistically shaped function of wealth.

Although all quartiles (except the wealthiest in the second period) remained, on average, net debtors through both periods, there are decedents in each wealth class who appear to be specialized lenders, whose holdings of financial assets far exceed their debts. That this is true in each quartile and that the variance (standard deviation) of net assets (defined as financial assets minus debts) rises sharply with wealth suggest that wealth is not determining, or is not acting alone to determine, those net outcomes. The regression analysis in the next section tests the hypothetical determinants of the marked increases in financial investments across wealth quartiles and over time.

V. The Determinants of Portfolio Composition: Regression Analysis

Farmers have always extended credit to one another. Farming, with its long production periods, sharp seasonal discontinuities, and periodic

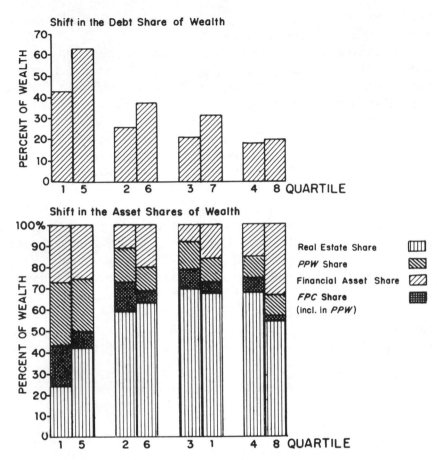

Fig. 8   Shift in the *a*) debt share and *b*) asset shares of wealth, by quartiles and period, 1730–1838.
Source: Administration accounts at probate, Middlesex County.
Note: Quartiles 1–4 = first period, 1730–81; quartiles 5–8 = second period, 1781–1838. PPW = portable physical wealth; FPC = farm physical capital.

disasters, is unimaginable without credit. It is not, then, the presence of promissory notes in rural portfolios that makes a capital market. Rather, it is the displacement of embodied physical capital by financial assets, the shift in the composition of rural assets away from cattle and implements and toward evanescent forms of wealth whose liquidity is enhanced by the collective willingness to make that shift. In the quartile analysis in the previous section, the shift was placed between the first and the second periods and confirmed at all wealth levels. What remains to be explored is the causal path. On what variables did market forces work to explain the observed changes?

In the two panels of regression results shown in table 13, the dependent variable is, in the first, *holdings of financial assets* and, in the second, *debts outstanding*. The specification of the regressions hypothesizes that decedents' portfolio behavior is explained by the following variables: *total wealth, distance from Boston, owned acres,* and *time* (which picks up the development of the regional economy generally).[39] Following the procedure used throughout this chapter, regressions are run on the entire period (pooled) and on the two subperiods, and these in turn are compared both with and without the wealthiest 5 percent of decedents. The strength of the overall specification of both the *financial assets* and the *debt* regressions is confirmed by the high *t*-statistics on most of the coefficients and the high R^2 = .91 on the entire sample pooled across both subperiods (see the first and seventh columns of table 13). The strength of the periodization—indeed, the strength of the hypothesis of this chapter—is abundantly confirmed by the very sizable gains in the R^2's in all second-period equations using the entire sample, and by the Chow-test results which reveal that the structure of explanation of portfolio behavior in the two periods is very different.

The Financial Assets Regressions

The total wealth variable. In the regression results shown in table 13, decedents' wealth is the principal determinant of their financial holdings. Log-log regression equations not presented here confirm that *financial assets* increased more than proportionally with increasing *wealth* and also that *wealth* is the dominant determinant of the share of wealth held in financial instruments. But the most important finding

---

39. There is a danger of multicollinearity—a functional relation between the independent variables—in this specification. *Total wealth* includes the value of real estate, which is obviously related to *acres owned*, and *distance from Boston* will also affect real estate values. Furthermore, *total wealth*, as will be noted later, is inversely related to *distance from Boston*. In cases of multicollinearity, significant *t*-statistics on the coefficients can be used as evidence that there is sufficient independence between the variables to validate the specification.

The variable *acres* in these regressions is carrying added freight as a proxy for that elusive thing, a noncommercial *mentalité*. A simple farmer/nonfarmer occupational dummy would have been preferable, but it is compromised, as was said earlier, by the ubiquity of nonagricultural by-employments among farmers. An alternative specification that attempted to capture this same thing by comparing investment in farm vs. nonfarm physical capital raises simultaneity problems with *total wealth* of which they are components.

Table 13   The Determinants of Liquidity

	A. Financial Assets[a]						B. Debts					
	Pooled, 1730–1838		First Period, 1730–80		Second Period, 1781–1838		Pooled, 1730–1838		First Period, 1730–80		Second Period, 1781–1838	
	Entire Sample	Lowest 95 Percent[b]	Entire Sample	Lowest 95 Percent[b]	Entire Sample	Lowest 95 Percent[b]	Entire Sample	Lowest 95 Percent[b]	Entire Sample	Lowest 95 Percent[b]	Entire Sample	Lowest 95 Percent[b]
Constant	-2,000.6	-192.25	182.33	57.88	-3,219.8	-520.66	-1,234.7	-42.48	-76.86	-16.55	-1,061.9	-198.22
	(-4.84)	(-1.25)	(1.05)	(.38)	(-2.10)	(-.80)	(-1.84)	(-.21)	(-.32)	(-.77)	(-.73)	(-.25)
Total wealth[c]	.83	.30	.05	.19	.85	.34	.17	.11	.25	.08	.0011	.13
	(48.49)	(13.40)	(2.75)	(7.55)	(38.01)	(9.66)	(6.56)	(3.96)	(8.87)	(2.18)	(.053)	(2.94)
Acres	-4.71	-3.53	.61	-.09	-4.60	-4.60	10.87	1.77	-.64	4.20	17.04	.045
	(-12.70)	(-5.21)	(3.11)	(-1.63)	(-8.54)	(-3.92)	(19.21)	(2.06)	(-2.46)	(4.71)	(34.57)	(.03)
Distance from Boston[d]	269.44	20.20	-55.05	-9.13	256.83	27.98	121.46	-40.54	-12.34	-74.86	-183.77	-9.46
	(3.61)	(.71)	(-2.04)	(-.36)	(2.11)	(.53)	(1.00)	(-1.1)	(-.33)	(-2.13)	(-1.57)	(-.14)
Time[e]	-19.31	.54	7.29	-2.34	-6.86	3.36	-2.28	11.37	4.32	12.63	19.46	12.65
	(-3.70)	(.27)	(1.57)	(-.54)	(-.36)	(.42)	(-.27)	(4.30)	(.68)	(2.15)	(1.07)	(1.28)
No. of observations	415	397	228	225	187	172	358	342	190	188	168	154
R²	.91	.38	.32	.29	.94	.38	.91	.21	.44	.31	.95	.09

Sources: See text.

Note: t-statistics are in parentheses. A Chow test of the difference between the first- and the second-period regressions is significant at the 0.1 percent level.

[a] Financial assets = (loans + mortgages) + securities + cash.

[b] Refers to the lowest 95 percent of the sample; i.e., it excludes the top 5 percent, the wealthiest twenty-three estates as measured by total wealth.

[c] Total wealth = value of (real estate + PPW + financial assets).

[d] Distance is measured as the number of towns on a straight line between decedent's town and Boston. See text.

[e] Time is entered as (year - 1729).

in the regression analysis is that there were marked differences between the colonial and the early national periods with respect to the following.

The strong association between *total wealth* and *financial asset* holdings is a post–revolutionary war phenomenon, as is shown by the very large increase between the first and the second periods in both the size and the significance of the coefficient on *total wealth*.

The high wealth elasticity of these holdings (defined as the percentage increase in *financial assets* with a 1 percent increase in *total wealth* and measured as the coefficient on the *total wealth* variable in the logarithmic form of the regressions) is also a second-period phenomenon, shifting from $e = 0.4$ before the Revolution to $e = 2.0$ after.

When the wealthiest 5 percent of the sample is removed and the behavior of the poorest 95 percent is observed separately, the sharp discontinuity between the two periods remains but is muted: true, the coefficient on *total wealth* increases and remains positive and statistically significant, and the elasticity at the mean increases, but these are not dramatic shifts. I see this as revealing the behavioral consequences of the changes in what I earlier called *structural elements of capital transfer*. New types of credit instruments emerged in the postwar period and were taken up by the very rich, whose portfolio behavior was transformed by their appearance, while poorer decedents were making incremental adjustments to patterns of lending traditional to farmers. This reading of the results would suggest that the capital market remained rather thin throughout the period.

Speaking more generally, however, the increasingly close association over time between *financial asset* holdings and *total wealth* must have had important macroeconomic consequences, for it suggests that the rise in wealth (in both current and constant dollars) observed across all wealth quartiles in table 12 itself contributed, through the increasing wealth elasticity of demand for credit instruments, to the enhanced liquidity of these instruments and hence to the emergence and integration of a capital market.

The acres variable. The strongly negative coefficients on farm size in the pooled regressions support the hypothesis of competition between investment in land, on the one hand, and investment in financial assets, on the other. This is true whether the very rich are present or not. But the period breakdowns reveal that the coefficients on *acres* are not all negative. That the sign on *acres* is positive for the full sample in the first period suggests that, in the early years, the income effect of the wealth of the very rich on landholdings overwhelmed the substitution effect between landholdings and financial holdings, until a market emerged in financial holdings. The decision of the wealthy in the second period to substitute ephemeral forms of property for land itself is of enormous consequence for the economic development of Massachusetts, and it appears in the regressions as a shift in sign, an increase in significance, and an increase in the size of the coefficient on *acres*.

The distance variable. Distance from Boston measures the decedents' access to the center of the financial market. Its use as an independent variable in these regressions, like the analysis of the mobility of capital in table 11, treats the capital market as an economic phenomenon with spatial extension. The implicit hypothesis is that the "magnetic field" of an underdeveloped market will extend (geographically) little if at all beyond its center, while the magnetic field of a more developed and integrated market will penetrate (geographically) farther from its center, and that penetration can then be used to testify to the development of that market.

Distance is construed in the regressions as an integer variable that measures, not miles, but the number of towns (on a straight line) between the decedent's town and Boston. *Distance* values run from one, for towns contiguous to Boston, to nine, for Ashby, the westernmost town in the county. Because the unit in which distance is measured is the number of "towns between," that unit is standardized across time by holding the county map constant at its configuration as of 1838 (see fig. 9). Thus, the county's seventeen new towns, carved out of the corners of old ones and incorporated between 1730 and 1838, are assumed for this purpose to have been there throughout the period. Distance, it will be recalled, was measured the same way in table 11. In 1838, the towns were roughly equal in size and configuration, making "towns between in 1838" not a bad unit for measuring distance.

Because the cardinal ordering of the *distance* variable increases as distance from Boston increases, a negative sign on its coefficient would imply a narrow capital market restricted to Boston's immediate hinterland, while a positive sign would imply a wider and thicker capital market penetrating the more distant reaches of the county. The signs in the regression results confirm the hypothesis of market extension. The effect of *distance from Boston* on the holding of *financial assets* shifts from negative in the first period to positive in the second.

There is a provocative lack of transitivity in the relations between the three variables: *total wealth* decreases with *distance from Boston*

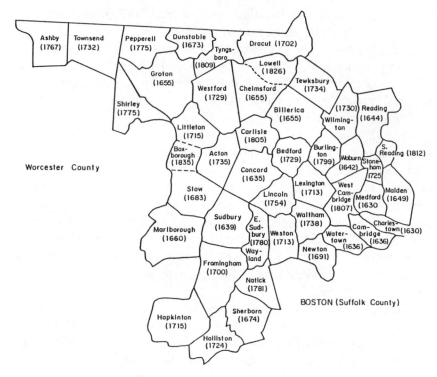

Fig. 9   Map of Middlesex County in 1838.

while *financial assets* increase with *total wealth*. That nevertheless a positive relation emerges in the second period between *distance* and *financial assets* therefore becomes a phenomenon of considerable interest. The decision of more remote decedents to increase their financial holdings was being made in the face of first-order pressures acting to decrease their wealth.

The Debt Regressions

Using the same specification to explain the level of indebtedness as was used to explain the level of financial assets gives the same strong $R^2 = .91$, but only in the sample pooled across both time periods and only when the very rich are included. The hypothesis of a discontinuity between the first and the second periods is amply confirmed, but the very wealthy seem to have experienced the discontinuity differently. For poorer decedents, *total wealth* is a significant (and, notice, positive) determinant of the level of *debts*. For the very rich, *total wealth,* which had been important in the first period, fades into insignificance in the second, and *acres* alone explains their second-period *debts.* In other words, there appears to have been what may be called an *implicit mortgage market,* where acreage set limits on the level of borrowing, even when it was not being used as collateral.

What were the very rich borrowing for? Not for private physical capital formation: that was retreating as a share of wealth.[40] The very rich appear to have been borrowing in order to lend, using their acreage in some as yet undefined way to underwrite their borrowing while at the same time shifting the composition of their assets out of farming and into commercial paper. The very rich were coming into the capital market on both sides. And they alone were emerging as net creditors.

CONCLUSION

Why did industrialization happen first in Massachusetts? Why, once begun, did it take root so successfully? What had prepared the rural economy for such a transformation? In chapter 4, repeated experiments were found to confirm that, within a few years of the Revolution, a network of integrated product markets had emerged in the farm economy of Massachusetts considerably in advance of industrialization. The present chapter confirms that, at about the same time, a regional capital market emerged in Boston's agricultural hinterland. It mobilized the supply of agricultural savings and channeled them toward new investment on the cutting edge of growth.

Using a data base built on the debts and credits of a probate sample of 512 decedents in rural Middlesex County between 1730 and 1838, this chapter has tested three attributes of a capital market: the appearance of developmental financial institutions, the increased mobility (presumptive evidence of decreased transactions costs) of capital transfers, and the enhanced liquidity of asset holdings. It has also explored the determinants of that critical metamorphosis. The very sizable increase, after the Revolution, in the wealth elasticity of demand for financial assets is itself a major clue to the feedback process by which the growth of the regional economy itself enhanced the liquidity of rural portfolios, which then fed back into economic growth.

40. See fig. 8*b* and the magnitudes PPW/wealth, FPC/wealth and NFPC/wealth in table 12.

How is the enhanced liquidity of rural portfolios related to the capitalist transformation of the rural economy? The answer emerges from
the network, quartile, and regression analyses. The enhanced liquidity
of rural portfolios *is* the capitalist transformation of the rural economy.
This phenomenon, it seems to me, must henceforth loom large in whatever is meant by the coming of capitalism to the New England village
economy. Capitalism is necessarily, even if not sufficiently, the creature
of a developed capital market. And that market, in eastern Massachusetts, can be dated to the early years of national independence.

APPENDIX

After death, then as now, an inventory was usually filed in the county probate
court,[41] and the debts and bequests of the deceased were then paid out of the
value of the estate by an executor (if there was a will) or by an administrator
(if there was none) who lodged one or several accounts with the court as debts
were paid and outstanding credits collected. The usual form of the administration account was, first, for the administrator to acknowledge his responsibility
for ("he charges himself with") the value of total personal estate left by the
deceased as per the inventory. To that was added whatever may have been
received since the inventory was taken (revenues from the sale of personal
property, payments of debts owed to the estate) or additional property that may
have been overlooked.

The administrator then "craves allowance" for expenditures he made out
of the estate to pay its debts, and those payments were usually listed in the
accounts by name and amount. It is these, together with the credits, that constitute the data in my analysis. I omit other charges the administrator claimed
such as probate fees, journeys to settle debts, and the cost of legal advice, of
surveying, of advertising for creditors, of medical care for the deceased's last
illness, of mourning clothes for the family, of the funeral, and of digging the
grave.

If there was no will, the first claim on the estate, before debts were paid
and before legacies were distributed, was the widow's portion—her "dower"
was her life claim to one-third of the real estate; her "thirds" was one-third of

---

41. That not all decedents' estates were (or are) subjected to the probate process, coupled
with the obvious age bias of decedents, has led most probate researchers to suspect probates of a
pro-wealth bias and therefore to correct a probate sample for these two sources of bias when using
the sample to comment on the living universe from which it was drawn. Counties differ in the
distribution of wealth of probated estates. This is another respect in which I think Middlesex
County's probates are exemplary. I have seen laborers' estates probated there in which the only
item owned was "one-half a beef creature."

the personal estate. Claims to widows' portions are also omitted from this analysis.

Obligations to creditors were paid, first, out of cash in the hands of the administrator, then, if that was not sufficient, out of court-ordered sales of two-thirds of the personal estate. What remained was distributed according to the will, if there was one, or, if there was none, according to Massachusetts law, which prescribed equal shares to the children. (A double share went to the eldest son by law until 1784.)

If, however, debts still remained, the court ordered the sale of as much real estate as was needed to pay them, again saving out of the sale the widow's dower. There were a very few cases where the widow relinquished her claim to satisfy all creditors of her late husband, but she need not. If claims still remained after two-thirds of the real estate and two-thirds of the personal estate had been sold to pay them, then the estate was declared insolvent and creditors paid off proportionally, so many pence on the pound or cents on the dollar, which, in the judge's words, "is all they can receive until the widow's death," at which time creditors were able once again to attach liens to the property.

The Data Base

Inventories, administrators' accounts, wills, reports of the real estate commissioners, reports of the insolvency commissioners, reports of the sale of personal estate—these are the documents that yielded the data base for this chapter. The 512 individuals came from forty-seven towns (a uniquely New England way of referring to what are in fact mostly rural villages) in Middlesex County, only one of which (Charlestown, now and since 1873 part of Boston) was urban throughout the period 1730–1838. Confirming the rural nature of this sample is the fact that, of the 479 males, 419 were "farmers"; that is, their inventories contained a full complement of husbandry tools and of livestock.

For each individual the following data were obtained: (1) year of inventory, which, because inventories were supposed to be taken within one month of death, is usually the year of death; (2) town in which the homestead is located and other towns in which the deceased owned property; (3) number of acres owned in that town and, coded separately, in outlying towns; (4) the value of all real estate (taken from the inventory unless superseded by a more careful reappraisal by the court-appointed real estate commissioners); (5) occupation(s), ascertained from how he or she was described in the records, or from the kind of tools dominating the inventory, or from the ownership of a shop, store, mill, or wharf (the most frequent occupation was yeoman or husbandman: the terms, although very different in Britain, seem to have been used interchangeably in American parlance); (6) the value of all husbandry tools (carriages and chaises, not being for husbandry, were excluded); (7) the value of all nonfarm tools, raw material inventories, stock in trade: in other words, nonfarm physical capital; (8) the value of all livestock, including bees and barnyard fowl; and (9) the value of all provisions and animal feeds, that is, the output of the farm.

The sum of items 6–9 plus the value of wearing apparel and all household goods constitute the portable physical wealth (PPW) of the deceased. PPW + the financial assets of the deceased = the total personal estate with which the administrator "charges himself" to pay claims on the estate.

Financial assets, if any, included the following: (10) cash on hand, usually paper, but occasionally silver or gold coins, and, rarely, bank deposits (the posthumous payments of soldiers' wages for the several campaigns of this period were also placed here); (11) the payments of accrued rents due to the estate (those rents, viewed as a flow variable, were excluded from financial assets, which I viewed as a stock variable); (12) the value of securities (I used the realized market value that appears in administration accounts, not the par value that appeared in inventories); (13) the value of outstanding notes and book accounts owed to the estate and not on interest; (14) the value of notes and bonds on interest, the interest, and (where it can be calculated) the interest rate; (15) the value of mortgages held by the deceased (when these were interest bearing—and even these were not always so—the interest was placed in the previous column); and (16) the value of notes deemed uncollectable (I included these "bad" notes among the financial assets of the creditor—the loan had in fact been made, after all, and thus testified to the deceased's propensity to hold financial assets—but deducted them from financial assets in the calculation of net worth [net worth = real estate + total personal estate − debts] on the assumption that, if not collected, those funds were not available to the estate for the payment of its debts; but estate administrators often erred: some debts called "bad" were in fact paid, and some considered "good" were not).

Debts included: (17) notes and book accounts owed to others and not on interest; (18) notes and bonds owed to others that were demonstrably on interest; and (19) mortgages held against the deceased and rents owed to others.

In addition, three characteristics were flagged: (20) insolvency; (21) whether the interest rate, if it can be calculated, was equal to, greater than, or less than the 6 percent customary rate; and (22) the presence of endorsements on notes.

Currency Conversions for the Colonial Period

While studies of two or more colonial economies, or studies relating a colony to England, typically convert provincial currencies into pound-sterling equivalents, here it was preferable to render all money values into their U.S. dollar equivalents. Over the period 1730–1838, in addition to Spanish dollars, five currencies circulated at one time or another in Massachusetts: new tenor, old tenor, lawful money, continentals, and U.S. dollars. Excepting the continental, these currencies bore a statutory relation to one another at the time that each redeemed the "sunken" one that went before it. Old tenor equaled 4, or sometimes 4.5, times new tenor (which appears occasionally on inventories from the 1730s) and 7.5 times lawful money, the specie currency that followed it in 1750.[42] One pound lawful money = 3.334 U.S. dollars. Therefore, entries in old tenor were divided by 7.5 to convert to lawful money and then multiplied by 3.334 to convert to dollars. Entries in new tenor were multiplied by 0.533 or by 0.6 (i.e., multiplied by 4 or 4.5 and divided by 7.5) to convert to lawful money and then multiplied by 3.334 to convert to dollars.[43] The continental was almost never used in probate documents as a medium of account. On the two occasions when it was, conversion rates could be ascertained from other values (typically, the price of a bushel of corn) in the document, from other documents in the probate packet, or from the monthly conversion ratios for the continental that were discovered, quite by accident, in the executor's account of Hannah Cordis (Curtis), Probate no. 330, Middlesex County Probate Court.

42. "Early in 1749 the legislature voted that after March 31, 1750, the treasurer should redeem outstanding bills in silver at the following rates: for every 45 shillings in old tenor bills, one piece of eight; and for every 11 shillings 3 pence in middle tenor and new tenor bills, one piece of eight. . . . One year was given for redemption. All subsequent contracts were payable in coined silver. In September, 1749, the Boston colonists witnessed a novel sight. The silver freighted from England arrived in Boston; seventeen trucks laden with 217 chests of Spanish silver coins and ten trucks with 100 casks of copper coin were hauled up King Street and delivered at the office of the provincial treasurer. . . . Approximately the paper currency was redeemed at the rate of 7½ paper to 1 specie" (Hart, *Commonwealth History of Massachusetts,* 2:212–13).

43. For confirmation of these currency conversion ratios, the reader is referred to McCusker, *Money and Exchange in Europe and America.*

6

The Development of Labor Markets and the Growth of Labor Productivity

DOCUMENTING THE EMERGENCE OF RURAL LABOR MARKETS IS AS NEC-
essary to understanding the preindustrial New England economy as their
operation was to its transformation. Like commodity and capital markets, the labor market is not an institution but a process, and as a process
it has evolved in historical time from less to more self-regulating, from
less to more efficient in the allocation of resources and distribution of
factor payments, from less to more integrated in space and time, from
less to more hegemonic over the production relations in an economy.

When the agricultural labor market is viewed as an evolving process, delineating its early forms in the English manorial economy provides a helpful perspective. Elaborately stratified as the feudal hierarchy
was, it is nevertheless possible to discern four broad categories of agricultural workers: tenants, whose labor services (defined by custom with
great specificity but periodically renegotiated) were in lieu of, and could
be commuted by, a cash payment of rent; serfs, born unfree, who la-
bored "at the will of the lord"; villeins, who worked on the lord's demesne year round for annual wages paid in cash, in kind, or sometimes
in land; and occasional laborers, who were hired, with their tools, at
public market-places to work for piece-rate wages paid in cash or in
kind.[1]

Eventually, an increase in domestic commerce and in the quantity of
cash in circulation permitted the monetization of these transactions, but
until then human labor—"that other commodity," in Marc Bloch's significant phrase[2]—was used by all classes, from the knights to "the poorest he," for the payment of rents, taxes, feudal dues, debts, and trade.
In such an economy, fixing the value of a day's labor, either by custom
or by fiat (or, what is the same thing, fixing other values in terms of
labor), was a matter of paramount importance. It maximized landlords'
real rents in times of falling produce prices; it minimized landlords'
labor costs in times of upward pressure on wages; and it acted to stabilize the value of what was, for most transactions, the numeraire.

Even in this prototypically "traditional" economy, the market principle penetrated the barriers that custom had erected against it. Just as
numerous estate-level studies have documented the growing magnitude
of marketing networks in the internal grain trade of the Middle Ages, so

1. For an instance of renegotiated terms, see Harvey, *Westminster Abbey and Its Estates in
the Middle Ages*, table 10, pp. 220–22. Reference has already been made in chap. 1 to Searle,
Lordship and Community, the study of the estates of Battle Abbey, which were worked entirely by
wage labor after 1348.

2. Marc Bloch, *The Growth of Ties of Dependence*, 67.

it has proved possible to identify market processes in the determination
of wages of medieval farm workers. This is demonstrable even before
the plague; after the plague, the brute force required to enforce fixed
wages under the Statute of Labourers (1349) is itself evidence of market
forces lurking in what a leading medievalist has called "wage elasticity
in response to short supply."[3]

In much the same way, the persistence in early Massachusetts of a
variety of allegedly nonmarket mechanisms—such as wage and price
fixing, bookkeeping barter, personalized and kinship exchanges, and
"truck" and other "interlinked, multiplex credit transactions"[4]—may
signify not that the market principle was inapplicable so much as that it
was being held at bay. Far from testifying to the absence of the market,
these features of the so-called moral economy testify like a thumb in the
dike to its presence, to its "latent threat,"[5] if you will, to effect transforming change.

To identify the functioning of a market despite the control mechanisms that societies erected to thwart it may testify to its long history,
but the empirical problem remains: to date its evolution from a lurking,
shadowy, subversive presence to governor of all the production, distribution, allocation, and exchange relations in an economy.

I. THE WAGE CONVERGENCE TEST
OF LABOR MARKET FUNCTION

The emergence of markets, their geographical integration, and their
functional efficiency are typically confirmed by testing for the presence
of their consequences: the tendency of buyers and sellers of a "good" to
arbitrage price differentials to convergence. This methodology, it will be
recalled, was the linchpin of the analysis of farm commodity markets in
chapter 4. It is applied now to farm labor markets, where wage convergence, measured as the decrease over time and space of the coefficient
of variation of wages for the same occupation, is the standard measure
of labor market performance and the diagnostic of labor market function. The extent of any given labor market in space is defined by the
geographical boundaries of the convergence process. Within those regional boundaries wage rates are arbitraged toward uniformity princi-

3. Raftis, *The Estates of Ramsey Abbey,* 201. Some additional estate-level studies of medieval
marketing are cited in chap. 1, nn. 15–20.
   4. Bardhan, "Interlocking Factor Markets and Agrarian Development," 85.
   5. Polanyi, *The Great Transformation,* 162.

pally by labor's supply response to information about wage differentials. The persistence of job-standardized wage differentials is evidence of the presence of insurmountable transactions costs, which, as impediments to labor's mobility, act as barriers to market integration.

It would appear, then, that testing for and dating the emergence of regional labor markets should be fairly straightforward. But it is not. Buyers and sellers of labor services, particularly in a rural setting, are involved in a relationship far more complex than that between buyers and sellers of commodities. If defining *the same good* presented us with problems in the analysis of commodity-price convergence, *the same occupation*, even in the comparatively simple agricultural economy examined here, is considerably more problematical. For hidden in the notion of *occupation* are the many distinctions that farmers themselves made in the wages they paid: distinctions based on task, based on different proportions of complementary inputs, between men and boys,[6] between day workers with board, day workers without board, and live-in workers on monthly contracts. It is also likely that, even before it became customary to measure labor time in hours, day wages varied with seasonal variations in the length of "a day."[7]

Heterogeneities like these among wages do not constitute a defect in market performance and will not be smoothed away by the convergence process, but because they violate the homogeneity assumption they must be eliminated from the raw data so that the unit—a man-day of work at a given occupation—may be defined as uniformly as possible. What are not to be removed or defined away are locational pay differentials that arise when homogeneous labor inputs performing homogeneous tasks are paid unequally because of differences in transactions costs. These barriers to convergence will remain and, indeed, will set the geographical boundaries of the market.

6. The choice of gender-biased wording throughout this study, but particularly here and in chap. 7, is deliberate, corresponding as it does to the gender-specific work roles in late eighteenth- and early nineteenth-century Massachusetts agriculture. Females appear in Massachusetts farm account books only when hired as domestic servants, spinners, or weavers or (rarely) to pick hops, but never as farm laborers. This was not true in England, where about one-third of the servants in husbandry were female (according to Kussmaul, *Servants in Husbandry in Early Modern England,* 4). Nor was it true in Pennsylvania, where Timothy Dwight was shocked to see German women in the fields.

7. Or, to put it another way, seasonal wage differentials confound seasonal task differentials and seasonal differences in the length of the working day. According to the *Farmers' Almanac* published in Boston in 1810, there were fifteen hours and six minutes between sunrise and sunset in late June of that year but only eight hours and fifty-four minutes between sunrise and sunset in late December—a difference of six hours of daylight between a summer and a winter work "day."

For this study we return to farm account books. The data base is 3,285 task-specific daily wage observations for day labor between 1750 and 1855, taken from ninety farmers' account books from sixty-five towns in New England: fifty-two in Massachusetts, four in Connecticut, three in Vermont, three in Maine (part of Massachusetts in the time period covered by those account books), and three in New Hampshire.[8] The wages were coded for year, month (and therefore season), town (and therefore regions East, West, and Central), and the following ten tasks: mowing and raking; haying; hoeing, hilling, and weeding; reaping and cradling; harvesting and gathering; planting and sowing; cutting, hewing, chopping, and scoring wood; building (walls, wells, fences, structures); threshing; and, finally, a portmanteau category labeled *unspecified,* which includes both the labor hired to do what farmers called *work*—the most frequent task in account books—and miscellaneous tasks (which, curiously, are seldom mentioned in account books) such as clearing, draining marsh, manuring, preparing flax, picking apples, and digging potatoes.[9]

That this study is constructed on task-specific wages distinguishes it from other studies of agricultural wages.[10] Yet a hierarchical structure of task differentials constitutes the very architecture of farm wages. This is clearly evident when the ten tasks are partitioned into two groups—low-paying tasks and high-paying tasks. When their annual means are plot-

8. Following the procedure used throughout this book, colonial currencies were converted to U.S. dollars and cents. In colonial Massachusetts, there were two moneys of account in use after 1750, old tenor and lawful money. Old tenor is divided by 7.5 to convert to lawful money, which is multiplied by 0.1667 to convert to U.S. cents. I found no instance in farm account books of wages recorded in continentals during the Revolution.

9. It is important to draw the reader's attention to the fact that wages for hauling and carting and for plowing and harrowing were, reluctantly, omitted from this data base because labor in these jobs was employed jointly with a large and costly capital component—yokes of oxen, a horse, a wagon, plow, or harrow—the presence of which is often inadequately described in the account books and the payment imputed to which is often obscured in a composite "wage" from which the wage to human labor can be extracted only by assuming (or at best estimating) it. Excluding these tasks is one of the compromises undertaken to make the man-day unit homogeneous.

10. Robert Wolfson ("An Econometric Investigation of Regional Differentials in American Agricultural Wages") used monthly wages of contract labor without board. Stanley Lebergott (*Manpower in Economic Growth,* chap. 6) used monthly wages with board. Carville V. Earle and Ronald Hoffman ("The Foundation of the Modern Economy," table 3, p. 1086) used a yearly wage for farm labor based on monthly wages with board. Thurston M. Adams (*Prices Paid by Vermont Farmers . . . and Received by Them for Farm Products*) constructed two weighted indexes, one of monthly and one of day wages, both with board, but without reference to task. The most recent study of farm wages by Donald R. Adams ("Prices and Wages in Maryland") averages daily and monthly wage rates without board for unspecified work.

ted, as in figure 10, it exposes, as early as 1750, a differential that becomes only more pronounced over time. This widening stratification, it should be emphasized, is itself evidence of an increasingly efficient market in which wages respond, with greater sensitivity over time, to tasks with different skill components, to the effect on the elasticity of labor supply of job opportunities off the farm, to seasonal urgencies in the demand for specialized labor,[11] and to the shifts in demand for crop-specific tasks that follow shifts in crop mix. It is because only day wages capture task differentials that they, and not monthly wages, are used throughout this chapter.[12]

For purposes of the analysis of regional wage convergence, the sixty-five New England towns represented by the sample of ninety account books were placed in one of three regions—East, West, and Central—and the ten tasks were combined into three task groups. The coefficients of variation (the standard deviation divided by the annual mean) of day wages by task group and by region were regressed on a polynomial time trend, that is, on year, year squared, year cubed, and so on. Using the same analytic technique as in chap. 4, the emergence of a labor market process is dated from the onset of convergence, that is, from the year the slope coefficient turns negative, which is to say, the year the regression equation reaches a maximum (see n. 17 below).

In the initial trials, however, out of nine possible combinations of three task groups and three regions, the regression coefficients were statistically significant in only three, forcing a reexamination of the definition of *occupation* being employed here. Farm work is wide ranging, varied, and enlists many separate competencies, but, it appears, these competencies are not "occupations." A single farm task is not an occupation. One would not, for example, expect to find markets for hayers

11. Widening seasonal differentials over this period attracted comment from T. M. Adams as well: "Significant changes took place during this period in the pattern of the seasonal differences in day wage rates. The extent of the seasonal changes increased from the last decade of the eighteenth century when July and August payments averaged 18 percent above the annual average, until 1870–79 when they were 38 percent above it" (*Prices Paid by Vermont Farmers . . . and Received by Them for Farm Products*, 85).

The changing crop mix of Massachusetts agriculture in response to western competition is documented in a comparison of the 1801 and 1855 weight bases of my farm-commodity price index (see table 8, pp. 109–10).

12. The increased use of live-in labor hired on monthly contracts, like the emergence of a market for day labor, is an important part of the nineteenth-century transformation of Massachusetts agriculture. It is analyzed in chap. 7.

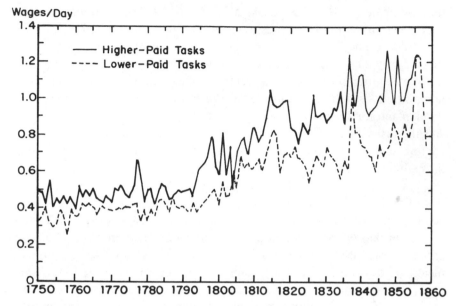

Fig. 10 Mean per day wages by task group, 1750–1855.
Source: Farmers' account books. See text and Appendix B, chap. 6.
Note: For the sake of visual clarity, only two task groups are presented: the higher-paid tasks of mowing, haying and reaping and the lower-paid tasks of hoeing, harvesting, planting, chopping wood, and threshing. Building-related tasks are omitted.

or weeders or potato diggers as such in antebellum New England.[13] The "occupation" is farm laborer, hired by the day to do whatever tasks are dictated by the season and paid according to which task he did.

The polymorphic character of farm work is nowhere more vividly demonstrated than in the extraordinary journal of a farm laborer, Abner Sanger (born 1739, died 1822), of Keene, New Hampshire.[14] In the twenty years between the marriage of his twin brother and his own, Abner worked tirelessly both on his brother's place (until the brother was exiled as a Tory) and for other farmers in Keene. After the Revolution, he moved to Dublin, New Hampshire, and worked for neighbors

13. By the end of the century, however, migratory pickers and traveling work crews on steam-powered farm machinery had become a specialized farm labor force. For a most interesting treatment of the social consequences of such an alteration in the "relations of production" in agriculture, see Rikoon, *Threshing in the Midwest.*

14. The manuscript of Abner Sanger's journal is in the Library of Congress. A microfilm copy is in the Keene (New Hampshire) Public Library. A portion of it was published in Wilber, ed., *The Repertory.* The Sanger journal has now been transcribed, annotated, and edited by Lois K. Stabler and published in full as *Very Poor and of a Lo Make.*

there and on land his sister owned. He raked, heaped, and burned debris in the fall and worked into the night watching the fires from trees burned for the ashes. He hewed logs, peeled bark, chopped wood, and carried it to the house on his back the greater part of every day during the long winters. He planted, hilled, hoed, gathered, husked, shelled, and threshed corn; poled beans; threshed oats and rye; took grain and provender to the mill; planted potatoes and dug them up; winnowed beans; sawed shingles; pulled and swingled flax; shoveled, carted, and spread dung; mowed, raked, and stacked hay, turning it to dry and putting fence up around the stacks because the barn was too small to hold it. He made a hog pen, made a rack for drying pumpkins, and heaped up "chip dung" around the house for winter insulation. He felled brouse for the cattle and horses and trained them to eat it. He built a soap trough and a sugar trough; tapped sugar maples and boiled syrup; made and repaired shoes. He lay floor. He did masonry work on the chimney and helped frame a new house and barn. He cleared the brook of brush and logs. He made brooms. He carted clay. He butchered the hogs. He harrowed and sowed and went all over trying to get someone to come over to plow. He repaired roads and bridges, mortared and plastered, mended tackle, bottomed chairs, and lay up a log fence. He also found time to learn surveying from Batchellor's manual, to keep accounts for his brother, to read *Paradise Lost,* Edmund Burke, John Locke, Bishop Butler's *Analogy,* John Adams's letters, Daniel Leonard's *Massachusettensis,* and Jonathan Edwards's "Careful and Strict Enquiry into the Modern Prevailing Notions of Freedom of the Will," to "spen[d] a while talking about Verses," and to write in his journal every day for all but six of 968 consecutive days. Yet, when he was imprisoned as a Tory in 1777, the Committee of Safety released him without demanding the £500 bond required of Loyalists because he was judged by them to be "very poor and of a lo make." Reading his journal, one cannot help but be reminded of the hired man in Robert Frost's poem: "He never did a thing so very bad. / He don't know why he isn't quite as good / As anybody. Worthless though he is, / He won't be made ashamed to please his brother."[15]

15. Frost, "The Death of the Hired Man," in *Complete Poems of Robert Frost* (New York: Holt, Rinehart & Winston, 1979), 49–55.

Is Abner Sanger representative of wage earners on Massachusetts farms in the late eighteenth and early nineteenth centuries? If not, it is for the very reason that his journal is so valuable to us: he remained a farm laborer and tenant throughout the whole of his very long life. On the two occasions when he came into possession of a farm, he sold the land within months. In his old age he was imprisoned again, this time for debt. On his wife's death his children, still young, were dispersed among relatives rather than allowed to remain with him. It is certain that he eschewed

We will have reason to return to Abner. For the time being he has
served to remind us that the wage-convergence test of labor market function depends for its confirmation on correctly specifying the "occupation" whose wages are arbitraged toward equality in response to widening market integration. When the occupation is so defined—that is,
when the observations used in calculating coefficients of variation are
the wages for "unspecified work"[16]—the results, displayed in panel A
of table 14, do indeed confirm a market process in the determination of
wages and date the onset of that process (i.e., the maxima of the
inverted-U functions) at 1802 for the East region, at 1808 for the West
region, and at 1800 for all regions pooled.[17]

The exception is the Central region, which failed to yield statistically significant coefficients and does not exhibit convergence until
1822. This anomaly presents us with the opportunity to examine the
association between labor market performance and regional economic
development. The Central region started late. King Philip's Indian at-
tacks in 1675 and 1676 had wiped out the four seventeenth-century
white settlements in Worcester County, leaving the region destitute of
population, Indian or white, for forty years thereafter. It was not until
the Peace of Utrecht in 1713 (which, by establishing English dominion
in eastern Canada, ushered in a generation of peace with France and her
Indian allies) that settlement was resumed. Thereafter, formation of
towns was rapid, but one can presume that economic development in
the Central region continued for some time to lag behind the coastal and
river valley towns begun fifty to seventy-five years earlier. For what this

-----

the opportunities wage differentials presented to specialize in the higher-paying farm tasks.
Whether he was atypical in his improvidence, his dependency, or his bad luck must wait until we
know more about how the "agricultural ladder" actually functioned in Massachusetts in the period
covered by this study.

   For new work on the "agricultural ladder," see Atack, "Tenants and Yeomen in the Nineteenth
Century," and "The Agricultural Ladder Revisited." Atack's sample of nearly twelve thousand farm
households is a subset of the Bateman-Foust sample of over twenty-one thousand northern rural
households drawn from the Census of 1860. New Hampshire, Vermont, and Connecticut are the
New England states in the Bateman-Foust sample. Massachusetts is omitted.

   16. Although the task-specific architecture of farm wages did not prove to be useful in dating
the onset of convergence, it will structure the farm wage index developed in sect. III below.

   17. The year in which the coefficient of variation reaches a maximum can be calculated
directly from the regression equations in table 14. In the equation $y = ax^2 + bx + c$, set the first
derivative, $2ax + b$, equal to zero; then $x = b/2a$, where b is the coefficient on *time* and a is the
coefficient on the *time squared* term. In panels A and B of table 14, where *time* is (year $-$ 1749),
the value for x (multiplied by 100) is then added to 1749, to get the year at which the function is
at a maximum.

Table 14 Regressing the Coefficient of Variation on Time: Wages for Unspecified Work by Region, 1750–1855

	A. All Years (1750–1855)				B. Truncated at 1840 (1762–1840)				C. Years of Revolution Omitted (1750–74 and 1782–1855)			
	East	West	Central	All	East	West	Central	All	East	West	Central	All
Constant	12.288	4.581	12.459	13.298	12.479	12.433	9.694	18.073	−19.451[a]	−19.043[a]	−7.443[a]	−14.755[a]
	(2.17)	(1.37)	(2.12)	(5.57)	(2.24)	(3.39)	(2.05)	(5.66)	(2.96)	(4.78)	(.91)	(4.48)
Time[b]	.637	.709	.253	.428	.909	.492	.590	.720	21.647	21.090	8.219	16.414
	(2.78)	(4.97)	(1.13)	(3.38)	(2.93)	(2.37)	(2.23)	(3.91)	(2.97)	(4.77)	(.91)	(4.49)
$(Time)^2 \times 10^{-2}$	−.603	−.598	−.201	−.421	−1.096	−.468	−.617	−.920	−.601	−.583	−.226	−.456
	(2.97)	(4.59)	(.79)	(3.66)	(2.96)	(1.86)	(1.89)	(4.13)	(2.98)	(4.75)	(.90)	(4.49)
R^2	.12	.23	.05	.12	.14	.11	.11	.18	.13	.25	.05	.18
Year at which coefficient of variation reaches a maximum[c]	1802	1808	1822	1800	1790	1802	1797	1788	1800	1808	1817	1801

Source: Farmers' account books. See text and Appendixes A and B.

Note: Absolute values of t-statistics are in parentheses. Regions East, West and Central are defined in Appendix B. "All" is all regions pooled.

[a] All coefficients multiplied by 10^3.

[b] Time is (year − 1749) in panels A and B; time is year in panel C.

[c] Owing to rounding error this may not be exactly equal to the implied year at which a maximum is reached.

gross and casual measure is worth, the mean date of founding for the sample towns in the East region is 1684, in the West region 1739, and in the Central region 1750.[18]

The convergence of wages in the East and West regions for "unspecified work" is particularly persuasive because "unspecified work" is itself a bundle of tasks the relative wages for which, when examined separately as in figure 10, were *diverging* over time. This suggests that the determination of day wages for this portmanteau occupation was a process that pit what may be called an "undertow" of *divergence between tasks* (stratification) against an "incoming tide" of *convergence within tasks*. The rising and then falling coefficient of variation of wages for "unspecified work" or general farm labor can be seen as testifying to a shift over time in the strength of "undertow" relative to "tide"—both, incidentally, consequences of labor market development—that ultimately favored the latter.

That the results in panel A of table 14 confirm the emergence of a market for farm labor by 1800 will be greatly strengthened if it can be shown that other interpretations of the same results will not stand. First, could the inverted-U shape of the regression results be, not a diagnostic of market integration, but an artifact of an unequal distribution of observations over time? Second, could the onset of convergence around 1800 signify only a return to the status quo ante, a tamping down of wartime price shocks that had momentarily disequilibrated customary rural wage patterns? Third, and most important, if convergence indicates market function, then what meaning should we attach to the divergence—the rising coefficient of variation—that precedes the onset of convergence?

The first question, the problem of heteroscedasticity,[19] arises because, as the number of wage observations per year increases (as,

18. I am aware of the appearance of a tautology here. I am using the argument that the Central region's economic development was retarded relative to the East and West regions' to explain its delayed labor market development when, apart from its later settlement, the evidence I present for its retardation *is* its delayed labor market development. But it will be recalled from the analysis of trip destinations in chap. 4 that the "West"—which included Worcester County, this chapter's Central region—exhibited market concentration later than the East and that prices began to converge later in the West than in the East.

19. When the number of observations that enter into the calculation of the coefficient of variation for each year varies, then the error term in the regression (which is picking up that portion of the behavior of the coefficient of variation that is *not* explained by *time*) cannot be assumed to be normally distributed with a mean of zero and a constant variance. Weighting the variance of each year's residuals by the number of observations for that year could have been done to correct for the heteroscedasticity. Instead, I chose to test for the influence of heteroscedasticity by removing those years, early and late in the period, for which there are fewer observations.

roughly speaking, it does in the early years of the period), that fact alone can account for increases in the wage variance observed in the rising coefficient of variation; and if the number of wage observations per year decreases over time (as, roughly speaking, it does in the late years of the period), a parallel but opposite argument could be responsible for the decreased dispersion seen in the falling coefficient of variation.[20] This opens the possibility that the behavior of wage variance may be only an artifact of the distribution of sample observations rather than the working of a market process. I removed the two tails—the early and the late observations—and performed the test for convergence on a truncated sample that omits the years 1750–61 and 1840–55.[21] Removal of the years with fewer observations does not alter the inverted-U pattern of initial divergence followed by convergence, produces an earlier maximum, and does not diminish the significance of the regressions (see panel B of table 14). The appearance of a market process at work in the convergence of farm wages is not an artifact of the temporal distribution of wage observations.

The second question can be stated more generally. How does one distinguish between the narrowing of differentials that is the diagnostic for market integration and the narrowing of differentials that may reflect only the postwar return to customary patterns of wage dispersion? The implication is not only that *wages* move with macro-level price shocks but also that wage *dispersion* so moves.[22] I tested this hypothesis by

20. A prolonged effort to increase the number of observations for the early and late years doubled the sample size but left intact its bell-shaped distribution in time, for the fact is that the keeping of account books by Massachusetts farmers has a history, a time shape of its own. As discussed in chap. 3, there really are relatively few farm account books from the 1750s, and in the mid- to late 1830s they again became fewer, replaced, it has been suggested, by "cash books" that recorded transactions merely as inflows and outflows of cash "rather than [as] components of dyadic relationships between households" (Larkin, "The World of the Account Book," 20).

The decadal frequency distribution of observations is as follows: 1750s, 6.0 percent; 1760s, 10.6 percent; 1770s, 8.7 percent; 1780s, 7.0 percent; 1790s, 13.2 percent; 1800s, 10.1 percent; 1810s, 12.2 percent; 1820s, 12.0 percent; 1830s, 9.0 percent; 1840s, 8.7 percent; and 1850s, 2.5 percent.

21. Regressions were also run with the right tail of the distribution truncated at 1830, which, when compared with the 1840 cutoff, resulted in higher R^2 values, earlier maxima, and higher t-statistics on the *time* variables in the West region and all regions pooled. However, because 9 percent of the observations are from the 1830s, truncating at 1830 would eliminate, from both tails, 27.8 percent of the observations, while truncating at 1840 loses only 18.8 percent of the observations. I therefore chose the 1840 cutoff.

22. The inference that farm wages moved with macro-level price shocks is supported by the finding of a $+ .85$ correlation between my (weighted) farm price index, which—it will be recalled from chap. 4—did exhibit synchronicity with macro-level events, and my (weighted) nominal farm wage index to be discussed in sec. III below.

removing the war years 1775–81 (see panel C of table 14). That the timing of convergence was similar with and without the war years suggests that, whatever else it did, the war had little effect on the underlying pattern of wage variance. This may be due in part to the fact that during the war the sample account books, without exception, recorded transactions, not in continentals, but in old tenor or lawful money. Thus, while the wage data register some price shocks from the wartime inflation, the stability of the unit of account acted to filter out the currency hyperinflation of those years.

The third question remains. What significance is to be attached to the *rising* coefficient of variation that precedes convergence? There are several possible answers. Even when the war years are removed, serious postwar dislocations—the depression of 1784–86, Shays' Rebellion in 1786–87, the war scare of the 1790s—are left to transmit macro-level disequilibria to the patterns of wage dispersion in the farm economy of New England prior to 1800.

Increasing divergence might also have come as account books entering the sample introduced wages from towns at different stages of maturity.[23] Over the period 1750–1855, account books from frontier towns in Maine and New Hampshire joined those of the old settled communities in the East region; the towns in the Central region, as was noted earlier, were settled late; and account books from the hardscrabble hill towns newly settled in the West appear at the end of the eighteenth century to share that region with the "River Gods" of the old Connecticut Valley towns. Some of the frontier towns, severely constrained by labor scarcities, had high wages; some had enlisted the force of custom or command to hold wages down; but all contributed to the greater dispersion. Referring once again to the three panels of table 14, that the coefficients of variation reach a maximum in the West region six, eight, even twelve years later than in the East, and as late as 1822 in the Central region, may thus be explained, at least in part, as a frontier/new town phenomenon.

So far, the arguments I have enlisted to explain increased dispersion in the first half of our period—heteroscedasticity, the persistence of postwar price shocks, and the heterogeneities introduced by wage data

---

23. Philip R. P. Coelho and James F. Shepherd confirm that markets in areas recently settled were less developed. Higher transport costs, the absence of competition, and greater excess demand in frontier areas were some of the factors accounting for impediments to trade and distribution and barriers to market expansion (see their "The Impact of Regional Differences in Prices and Wages on Economic Growth," 73).

from settlements at different stages of maturity—would explain the rising coefficient of variation as a consequence of "noise," of one form or another, in the data. But increasing dispersion may have an important substantive explanation as well. Identifying market forces only in the downward movement of the coefficient of variation ignores a prior process and (in the Puritan commonwealth, at least) one as necessary to the emergence of a market economy. Just as increasing price variance after 1750 told, in chapter 4, of what was called there a *proto-market* process—the gradual abandonment of a social control regime—so increasing wage variance after 1750 tells of the gradual erosion of customary notions of the "just wage" and "just" earnings differentials.[24]

We have already discussed this problem at some length in chapters 2 and 4. The argument here, as there, is that in the transition from Puritan to Yankee, from "market-ouvert" to market economy, wage rates, like all prices, scattered as they left the world of uniformities imposed on covenanted communities by statute, custom, and controls,[25] to enter the radically different world of uniformities that are the result of an equilibrium process. As in chapter 4, the rising coefficient of variation beginning in 1750 points to a centrifugal process marking the prolonged transition from a social control regime to a market economy.

If we can explain farm wages by region, task (which includes season), and time, it would be useful to be able to distinguish among them, to separate—or partition[26]—the region, task, and time effects, particularly in view of the surmise that those effects may have worked in op-

---

24. Examples of customary wage fixing appear in the account book of John Burke of the western Massachusetts hill town of Bernardston. In 1766 Burke charged John Evans the same amount (15/ old tenor = thirty-three cents a day) for reaping, cutting stalks, picking corn, making a fence, mowing, clearing brush, husking corn, digging potatoes, threshing rye, threshing wheat, chopping wood, dressing flax, and haying. The following year Burke paid 20/ old tenor (= 44.4 cents a day) for the mowing, haying, reaping, hoeing, chopping, raking, and clearing that was done for him. And as late as 1774 he again charged 44.4 cents a day (2/8 lawful money) to mow, hay, reap, and hoe. In the tenacity with which he hangs on to the notion of a fixed wage for a day's work—any day's work—Burke is idiosyncratic.

25. Paralleling the effort to fix prices by statute, the effort to fix wage rates by statute began in both Massachusetts Bay and Plymouth in 1630. The legislation was reenacted at lower rates in 1633 with penalties to be levied on both employers and laborers for exceeding the statutory wage rates. By 1635, however, all such efforts on the provincial level were abandoned in favor of giving each town local option to fix wages in accordance with the fall and rise of prices. A brief discussion of wage fixing and some scattered seventeenth-century wage rates in New England agriculture appear in Bureau of Labor Statistics, *The History of Wages in the United States From Colonial Times to 1928;* and in Carroll Wright, *History of Wages and Prices in Massachusetts.*

26. On partitioning, see Rosenbloom, "The Integration of U.S. Labor Markets," and "One Market or Many?"

posite directions. Regressing the log of observed wages on region, task, and decade dummies calculates as coefficients the percentage wage differentials associated with each variable. Table 15 presents the results. The coefficients are all strikingly significant. The steadily increasing coefficients on the decade dummies present evidence (confirmed in sec. III below) that nominal wages for farm labor doubled over the transitional century of this study. Large task differentials (a 39 percent spread between wages for mowing and haying and wages for threshing, and a 45 percent spread between wages for reaping and wages for threshing) exhibit the stratification that I have called *undertow,* and small regional differentials (a 3 percent spread between wages in the East and Central regions and those in the omitted West region) exhibit the convergence in space that I have called *tide.* Not only intraregional but also interregional differences were being extinguished in a process of market integration embracing all the sample farmers.

Dating labor market function from the onset of wage convergence can be confirmed with the so-called Chow test, in which the entire sample of wage observations (actually, log wage observations) is split into two time-period subfiles, experimenting with a number of alternative break-point dates. We then examine the two subperiod regressions of log wages on region, task, and decade dummy variables to determine if the slope and intercept of the regression equations shifted after the hypothesized onset of a market process. The Chow test allows us to make two determinations: to ascertain if there was a transformation over some break point in the structure of explanation governing the behavior of wages, and if so—that is, if the same regression does not explain both subperiods equally well—to date the most decisive shift from among our alternative break points. According to the Chow test, $F(5,3008) = 354$ when the two subperiods are divided at 1790, 594 when divided at 1810, and 274 when divided at 1820. When the "turning point" is set at 1800, however, $F = 643$, with a very low probability (.0001) that that result could have been achieved by chance. Thus, the Chow test robustly confirms both conclusions from the convergence test of labor market function: that between the two subperiods there was indeed a transformation in the specification relating wages, region, task, and time and that the timing of that transformation is best captured at 1800.[27]

27. While the number of observations in the two subperiod groups need not be the same for the Chow test, "the test may not be applicable in case the assumption of homoscedasticity is

Table 15 Partitioning Wages by Region, Task, and Time Effects

	Coefficient	Absolute value of *t*-Statistic
Constant	− 1.209	− 43.06
Region:		
East	− .034	− 3.16
Central	− .027	− 2.24
Task:		
Unspecified work	.187	8.19
Mowing and haying	.389	16.64
Hoeing	.183	7.24
Reaping	.446	16.34
Harvesting corn	.091	3.02
Planting	.085	2.94
Chopping, etc., wood	.120	4.58
Decade:		
1760s	.101	4.29
1770s	.130	5.38
1780s	.153	5.94
1790s	.227	10.01
1800s	.461	19.33
1810s	.694	30.34
1820s	.653	28.30
1830s	.749	31.01
1840s	.818	33.81
1850s	.919	27.45
R^2	.62	
No. of observations = 3,018		

Source: See text.

Note: The dependent variable is the log of the wage. Excluded dummy variables are task threshing. Region West, decade 1750s.

II. Arbitraging Wage Differentials: The Convergence Process

If the convergence of job-specific wage rates is the diagnostic of labor market function, then it is necessary to document the historical process by which wage differentials were arbitraged into convergence.

It is usual in economic historiography to make the rise of a labor market, or any market, depend crucially on the historical moment when labor became free to move. Whether that moment—the transition, as

violated, that is, when there is heteroscedasticity" (Gujarati, *Basic Econometrics,* 445). The presence of heteroscedasticity in the wage data was acknowledged earlier. This may modify the Chow test results, but the *F*-statistics here are so very large that the conclusions to be drawn from the test are not seriously compromised.

Henry Sumner Maine called it, from status to contract[28]—is viewed as the "realization of the agrarian dream"[29] or as having unleashed "an avalanche of social dislocation" that "annihilate[d] all organic forms of existence,"[30] it is the unobstructed movement of people that is given the primary role to play in factor-price equalization.

In 1860, according to Jeremy Atack and Fred Bateman, "at least one-third of the inhabitants of rural townships in the northern United States were living in a state other than that of their birth."[31] Unfortunately, their sample does not include Massachusetts. Massachusetts may have had an out-of-state migration rate as high as Vermont's (34 percent), as low as New Hampshire and Connecticut, where heads of family still residing in their state of birth in 1860 accounted, respectively, for 90 and 85 percent of the whole, or a rate that falls somewhere in between. These numbers are subject to all the misgivings that color migration estimates generally, but interstate migration seriously understates mobility in any case, neglecting just those short-distance moves postulated by the hypothesis of regional wage convergence.

I therefore attempted a small mobility study of my own: using farm account books to link farm workers by name to more than one sample farmer in more than one town. Out of 1,810 names of men doing farm work, there were many who appeared in more than one farmer's book, but only four who appeared in the books of farmers in different towns. While, then, I cannot confirm the mobility of farm laborers from within my data set, neither do I challenge it; instead, I am suggesting that there is another kind of mobility: the flow of information. To arbitrage wage differentials it is not necessary that any workers move; it may be enough that information move. In a labor-scarce farm community, workers can, presumably, effect increases in local wage rates by talking about the higher wages that are paid elsewhere in language understood to carry the implicit threat to leave. Employing farmers will respond more rapidly if matching the higher wage is seen by them to be less costly than undertaking a new search for labor. This will be especially true, of course, in seasons of urgent labor demand when the grain and hay stand ripe under lowering skies or the apples lie moldering on frosty ground.

28. Maine, *Ancient Law,* 182.
29. Atack and Bateman, *To Their Own Soil,* 71.
30. Polanyi, *The Great Transformation,* 40 and 163.
31. Atack and Bateman, *To Their Own Soil,* 73 and table 5.1.

Abner Sanger's journal is perhaps most illuminating in just this respect: he reveals a densely crowded work life embedded in a thick web of face-to-face encounters. He mentions by name well over a thousand people (one editor counted 2,250) with whom he came in contact and with whom conversation could have served as a conduit for information that, presumably, was passed on as he went from door to door looking for work, looking for help, settling accounts, seeking to borrow provisions, a wagon, a plow, or a team of oxen. The moving about between neighbors was incessant; not a single day appears to have been spent alone. This is not the hired man of Robert Frost or of Katherine Ann Porter,[32] men who positioned themselves on the outer rim of family and community. In the era before the mechanization of farming, a farm worker, whether he liked it or not, had to work in a setting teeming with other people:

> August 17, 1775: Mn [morning] looks thick & cloudy; Cohoon [Calhoun], A. Gray and Young Isaac gets up a Ld [load] of Hay early out of 16 acres. D. Stone & I work some in Garding [garden] & Yoake a Hog. Yn [Then] Cohoon & I go to mowing at ye Mosketo Lot; Wm Ellis comes to us; Ol Wright come to work at sd Wymans; D. Stone— A. Gray, Wright & Isaac to Carting Hay; the Guile River Bridge gets break; sd Stone is put to work with a party to mend it; Cloudy— warm; aftn [afternoon] sd Wright & Gray & Ellis to pulling flax; Stone works at sd bridge aftn; Cohoon & I go to Raking ye first mowed Hay and ye Mosketo Lot; young Isaac Wyman comes & helps; ye sun shines hot & thund Clouds go about; we finish ye Raking sd Hay & go & Joine the Flax party till aft. sundown.

In the course of these face-to-face encounters, the following entry, heavy with significance, appears in Sanger's journal as a clue to the role of information flows as surrogates for mobility in labor market formation: "September 13, 1777: Young Isaac [Wyman] come to me . . . he talk of not working any more for his Father till he has a Deed of ye New Farm. Also Young Thos Barker come along by and has talk about it."[33] In Sanger's conversation with young Isaac, young Isaac's with young

---

32. I refer here to Porter's short story "Noon Wine" and Robert Frost's poem "The Death of the Hired Man."

33. Stabler, ed., *Very Poor and of a Lo Make,* 58, 157.

Tom, and, by implication, young Isaac's with his father, there is the suggestion that information about the existence of alternative opportunities for young people off the family farm was acting to reverse the traditional (i.e., child-to-parent) direction of family wealth flows, and inter vivos property transfers were becoming the price sons exacted for not leaving home. Improvising adaptations to the increasing unreliability of sons' labor is a consequence of the emergence of labor markets.[34] That, in a simultaneous development, financial assets came increasingly to substitute for farm physical assets in rural wealthholdings after the Revolution provides additional evidence of the endogeneity of family strategies to the expanding market process.[35]

Ten years of Sanger's journal—December 1782 to December 1791 and April 1792 to March 1793—have disappeared. When the manuscript resumes in 1793, it has lost much of its narrative style and taken on the tone and, in places, the format of an account book. Work time is now closely calculated in hours or small fractions—"⅔rds of ½"—of a day; wages and prices appear for the first time for most transactions; call it a "paradigm shift" or call it just plain orneriness, but several times Abner tries to deduct from the "wages" he owes for borrowed oxen the value of the times that they stood still! When, in April 1794, he is badly injured in a fight over wet hay, the affront is immediately given a cash value.[36] The change in tone, structure, and content of Sanger's diary is itself evidence of a shift in *mentalité* having occurred sometime between 1782 and 1793 in response to a transformation of economic relationships in the culture. When on 5 and 6 August 1794 Sanger reaped for Lieutenant Thomas Hardy at the rate of 3/ a day (50 cents), he was informed— presumably by the other five or six men who were reaping with him— that at the time the prevailing wage for a day's reaping was 4/ (67 cents).[37] The 4/ wage was the work of a market process. That Sanger

34. For a vivid analysis of the direction of intrafamilial wealth flows in traditional societies and of the forces reversing that direction in modernizing societies, see Caldwell, "The Mechanisms of Demographic Change in Historical Perspective." In Sundstrom and David's "Old Age Security Motives, Labor Markets, and Farm Family Fertility in Antebellum America" and David and Sundstrom's "Bargains, Bequests and Births," it is suggested that family limitation in the early nineteenth century was an adaptive strategy pursued by farm families as a consequence of the effect of labor and capital markets.

35. Documenting this shift from farm physical assets to financial assets was the subject of chap. 5.

36. "[He] asalts me & strikes me with a green large Beach Leaver on my Head & wounds me considerable & sheads considerable Blood. I rate ye damage at 40/" (p. 504).

37. "August 6, 1794: Hardy Lieut Thos, Dr. to 3/4 of a day Reaping &c—2/3. Some say Reaping is valued at 4/ per Day this summer" (p. 521).

38. See Griliches, "Agriculture"; and Weiss, "Economic Growth before 1860," esp. 4.

was aware of it but deliberately eschewed it says much about Sanger, but it does not deny that process.

III. Wage Indices for Hired Farm Labor
and Estimates of Productivity Growth

Documenting the emergence and integration of farm commodity, rural capital, and agricultural labor markets is fundamental to understanding the economic transformation that occurred in Massachusetts, but it still remains to forge the link between the increasing hegemony of markets and the growth of the preindustrial economy.

Over the region and time period of this study there was little if any mechanization or technological change in agriculture, no economies of scale, a decreasing share of the labor force in farming, and decreasing farm size only partially offset by cumulative investments in improving land quality. Under these circumstances, an increase in per capita agricultural production can be achieved only by a very great increase in agricultural output per worker. Where is that increase to come from if, as late as the 1840s, there was virtually no capital deepening—technological change—in New England agriculture? From endogenously generated intensification in the use of labor. The major source of the growth of agricultural output must be attributed to increased labor productivity.[38]

One would like to measure the change in labor productivity (the growth of farm output per man-day or manhour) directly—either as the percentage increase of agricultural output plus the percentage decrease of manhour inputs producing that output or as the increase in per acre yields times the increase in acres per man—but New England farmers, as was pointed out in chapter 3, appear to have kept no records of acres, outputs, yields, or total labor inputs (hired help plus family). The calculation of labor productivity has therefore to be indirect.

In competitive labor markets the wage of labor is equal to the value (i.e., the market price) of its marginal product. Having now established the operation of markets in farm labor and in the commodities produced by that labor (markets we can assume to have been competitive or equally imperfect), farm labor's marginal product can be measured by dividing an index of farm wages by an index of farm product prices.[39]

---

39. This measure is called the "dual." Other ways of measuring labor productivity in agriculture are mentioned in Allen, "The Growth of Labor Productivity in Early Modern English Agriculture," 118.

Appendix C presents two new farm wage indexes, one unweighted (UWI) and one weighted (WWI); my weighted farm commodity price index (PI);[40] and two "real cost of labor" indexes, one constructed on the unweighted wage index (UWI/PI) and one constructed on the weighted index (WWI/PI) (see also fig. 11). In the calculation of these indexes we are now able to make use of the task structure of farm wages, an insight we had to abandon earlier in order to define a standardized "occupation" for the study of convergence. The weighting procedure is described in Appendix B. Briefly, daily wage rates for tasks associated with a particular crop were combined into *crop-specific task clusters,* averaged annually, relative to a 1795–1805 reference base, and weighted by the percentage that that crop was of the aggregate value of output produced in 1801 in the sample Massachusetts (and Maine) towns. This magnitude, in turn, was calculated from the 1801 Massachusetts town valuations.

It is therefore clear why there must also be an unweighted index: it is constructed of annual wage relatives for those tasks that are not crop specific, such as building, miscellaneous tasks, and "unspecified work." (It will be recalled that wages for some tasks that should fall into this category—ploughing and harrowing, hauling and carting—have been omitted altogether because of the difficulty of extracting the wage to labor from the composite wage to labor and capital used jointly in those tasks.)

To facilitate an evaluation of this index, figure 12 plots my weighted "real cost of labor" index (WWI/PI) along with three other deflated day-wage indexes: Thurston M. Adams's Vermont farm wage index, the Margo-Villaflor index of civilian wages paid at Army forts, and the David-Solar index of wages of common unskilled labor (see the notes to fig. 12).[41] Because each of these indexes, as constructed, has a different base, I shifted all to 1825 = 100 to facilitate comparisons not only of their slopes and inflection points but also of their levels.

If labor's productivity can be measured by an index that is the ratio

40. From table 8, 1800 weights, pp. 109–10.
41. Kenneth Sokoloff has compared my weighted farm wage index with the Margo-Villaflor index and with his own index of manufacturing wages in the Northeast. For his purposes he deflated all three by the David-Solar consumer price index and finds such substantial (and reassuring) agreement between the three as to constitute "a formidable body of evidence pointing to significant gains in the rate of compensation to labor in the Northeast between 1820 and 1860" ("The Puzzling Record of Real Wage Growth in Early Industrial America," 23).

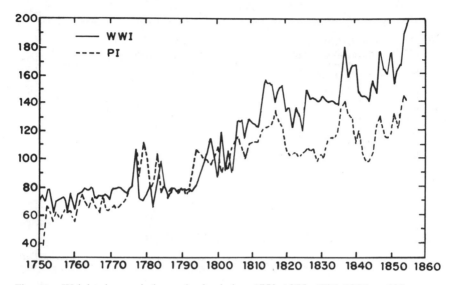

Fig. 11   Weighted wage index and price index, 1750–1855, 1795–1805 = 100.
Source: Farmers' account books. See text and Appendix C, chap. 6. Price index from
Rothenberg, "A Price Index for Rural Massachusetts."
Note: WWI = weighted wage index of crop-related tasks; PI = Rothenberg farm com-
modity price index.

of wage and price indexes, then the change over time in labor's productivity can be traced by regressing that index on a polynomial (i.e., nonlinear) time trend. This is done in table 16 and figure 13. It is in the
behavior of the "real" indexes (both the crop weighted and the unweighted) over time that the link is established in the agricultural sector
between the emergence of product and labor markets, on the one hand,
and the growth of output per man, on the other. Constructed from farmers' own wages and farm-gate prices, figure 13 tells the story, first, of
declining productivity until 1780[42] (the turning point comes a bit later in

42. The cubic regression line that best fits the whole period does decline between 1750 and
1780. But this regression line (fig. 13) may be unduly influenced by the sudden fall in the index
during the revolutionary war years due to wage "stickiness" in the numerator and inflationary price
rises in the denominator of the ratio. (It will be recalled from chap. 1 that the Price Revolution of
the sixteenth century had the same asymmetric effects on wages and prices in Florence, England,
Alsace, and France.)
    "Eyeballing" fig. 13 suggests that a better sense of the early years might have been achieved
by fitting two separate trends: one would have held steady between 1750 and 1774, and the other
would have risen from 1779 to the mid-1840s.
    But if the decline is "true," there are two possible explanations. One would accept that farm
labor productivity in Massachusetts was genuinely low and becoming more so, until the emergence

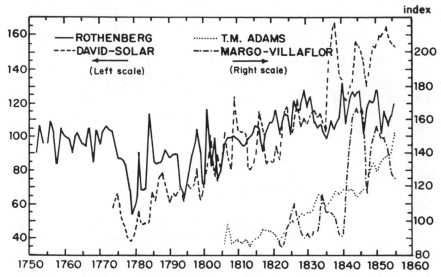

Fig. 12   Comparison of deflated daily wage rate indexes, 1825 = 100.
Sources: Margo-Villaflor: 1856 = 100 (Margo and Villaflor, "The Growth of Wages in
Antebellum America," table 7, p. 895). T. M. Adams: 1910–14 = 100 (Adams,
"Wages of Vermont Farm Labor," table 47, p. 97). David-Solar: 1860 = 100 (David
and Solar, "A Bicentenary Contribution to the History of the Cost of Living in Amer-
ica," table B.1, p. 59). Rothenberg: 1795–1805 = 100 (see text, sec. III).
Note: The bases of all indexes have been shifted to 1825 = 100.

the unweighted index), followed, after a pause, by the steady growth of
labor productivity at about 5 percent per decade until the 1840s.[43]

The behavior of the index in its early years seems to reflect the
familiar story Jared Eliot told about this agriculture: the waste of ma-

---

of integrated markets shortly after the Revolution. The second explanation finds farm practices
improving but asserts that, at least at the outset, the improvements consisted largely of *intensifying*
the use of labor inputs, which would have increased the output per unit of complementary inputs
but decreased the output per man-day of labor inputs.

In the text I am suggesting that both explanations can be combined to understand the
downward-sloping portion of the regression line.

43. My estimate of 0.5 percent annual labor productivity growth in Massachusetts agriculture
from 1780 to 1840 is, curiously, the same annual growth rate that Kuznets estimated for these
years. (See the introduction to this volume.) But it exceeds Robert Gallman's national estimate of
0.3 percent per annum growth in grain and cotton agriculture, the magnitude John Komlos cites as
evidence for his argument that American nutrition between 1840 and 1860 suffered a decrease in
protein and caloric intake that he attributes to the failure of agricultural labor productivity growth
to offset the exodus of labor from farming (see Komlos, "The Height and Weight of West Point
Cadets," in particular, n. 35, p. 910).

Table 16   Regressing Rothenberg Wage-Rate Indexes on a Time Trend, 1752–1855

	UWI	WWI	PI	UWI/PI	WWI/PI
Constant	74.239	61.808	54.034	127.332	128.443
	(14.94)	(15.61)	(15.35)	(25.31)	(23.66)
Year	.102	.644	1.112	−1.056	−2.253
	(.469)	(3.702)	(7.182)	(4.772)	(5.057)
(Year)^2 × 10^{-2}	1.038	.463	−.424	1.332	4.869
	(5.15)	(2.88)	(2.97)	(6.52)	(4.95)
(Year)^3 × 10^{-3}					−.255
					(4.13)
R^2	.84	.87	.75	.45	.51

Source: See text, sec. III. Weighting procedure is discussed in Appendix C.
Note: UWI = index of wages for non–crop–related tasks and therefore unweighted; WWI = weighted index of crop-related tasks; PI = Rothenberg farm price index; UWI/PI = "real" unweighted wage indexes; WWI/PI = "real" weighted wage index. Absolute values of *t*-statistics are in parentheses.

nure, the neglect of livestock, the export of potash, the failure to rotate tillage crops or to cultivate and fertilize meadow, the absence of fencing, desultory ploughing, and so on.[44]

But, I would argue, low and sharply falling "real labor costs" during the Revolution, together with the rationalizing, allocational consequences of market orientation, led to increased labor inputs, and farming, which had been wastefully extensive, became increasingly intensive. One such alteration was the greater use of contract labor (see chap. 7). Another was the shift to the cultivation of outputs valued more highly in the market; another was the stabling and stall feeding of cattle, a labor-intensive technique that at a stroke forced better clover hays, pro duced better manure, improved breeding, fattened the stock, introduced leguminous feed supplements that were nitrogen fixing in rotation, shortened or eliminated fallow, and upgraded land use to release unimproved to pasture, pasture to meadow, and meadow to tillage (see chap.

But Gallman's annual growth estimate is built on data *beginning in 1839*. In this respect we do not disagree, for my indexes show the rate of labor productivity growth declining after 1840. "The downturn in 1840 was one of the worst in American history. Evidently the brunt of the contraction fell most heavily on unskilled wages" (Margo and Villaflor, "The Growth of Wages in Antebellum America," 885).

Incidentally, Komlos enlists early unpublished work of mine in support of his argument. The labor productivity measures in the present chapter supercede those he cites.

44. Carman and Tugwell, eds., *Jared Eliot's Essays upon Field Husbandry in New England.* For an excellent summary statement of these farming practices and their ecological consequences, see Cronon, *Changes in the Land,* 150–51.

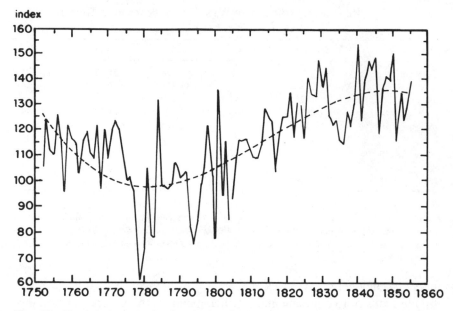

Fig. 13　Tracing the growth of agricultural labor productivity: the real cost of labor index, WWI/PI, 1752–1855.
Source: See text, sec. III.
Note: 1750 and 1751 were omitted as outliers. The dotted line is the plot of the regression equation for (WWI/PI) in table 15, where WWI = weighted wage index of crop-related tasks, and PI = Rothenberg farm commodity price index.

8).[45] Those Massachusetts farmers who had pursued a policy of increasingly labor-intensive farming were then in a position to survive the opening of the Erie Canal and the competition of western produce and of Cincinnati hog markets by specializing in the cultivation of upland hays, dairying, and truck farming.

The increased labor inputs during this first phase of intensive growth will register first as decreasing marginal product of labor. The investment of effort in the enhanced fertility of the soil will show up initially as increased yields—a land productivity measure. But by 1785, as is apparent in figure 13, the farmers in this sample were beginning to experience growth of output per worker as well as output per acre, an

45. For a summary of the ecological consequences of these "improved" farming practices, see Cronon, *Changes in the Land,* 159–60.

increase in labor productivity that long predated the diffusion of new farm machinery.[46]

Increased labor productivity on Massachusetts farms was achieved under the discipline of producing for an expanding market with a fixed technology, a more or less fixed land input, and a steadily decreasing labor force. The process bears this resemblance to the productivity growth in early manufacturing: that there too significant gains were achieved, not with the application of more or better capital, but by learning by doing and by improvements in the organization of manufacturing processes in response to the expansion of markets. The thirteen manufacturing industries studied by Sokoloff achieved total factor productivity growth rates of 1.8 percent per annum between 1820 and 1860, rates of growth as high as between 1869 and 1953, with only "trivial" differences between the performances of the more and the less capital-intensive industries.[47]

Paul Paskoff's detailed analysis of the Hopewell Iron Forge in the late eighteenth century gives us insight into an analogous process in that industry. Constrained by a static, labor-intensive technology and fixed plant size, between 1768 and 1774 the management of the forge raised output per man over 62 percent and reduced the consumption of charcoal per ton 46 percent, with a 21 percent decline in the labor force. As Paskoff sees it, the iron firms that survived within these constraints did so by what we earlier called an endogenous process, achieving productivity gains through organizational efficiency—a kind of managerial learning by doing—"long before the time when the pulse of economic

46. Although there are advertisements for cast-iron ploughs in agricultural journals as early as 1823, I have found only three cast-iron ploughs in eastern Massachusetts probate inventories, and none before 1844 (see chap. 3, n. 27). This late timing is supported by the application of one John Wilson of Deerfield for a patent for a cast-iron plough in 1836 that enjoyed a modest local success (see Garrison, "Surviving Strategies," chap. 3).

That there was little or no technological change in Massachusetts agriculture is confirmed in Kenneth Sokoloff's analysis of patent rates by sector and by region between 1791 and 1846. With the exception of the period 1836–42 (which is an unusual period for other reasons as well), southern New England, Sokoloff finds, lagged far behind New York in agricultural inventions, whether measured per capita or as a percentage of total inventions. It also lagged behind northern New England for much of the period ("Inventive Activity in Early Industrial America," esp. table 1, pp. 824–25.

47. See Sokoloff, "Productivity Growth in Manufacturing during Early Industrialization," 718, 721, and 724.

activity is thought to have quickened in response to the capital-induced productivity surges of the putative industrial revolution."[48]

CONCLUSION

It is important, in concluding this chapter, to emphasize what it has *not* been about. It has made no assertions about the conditions of work or the standard of living of the farm laboring population; it has made no attempt to translate wage rates for work that is in fact highly seasonal into annualized earnings; it has made no attempt to assess the effect of developments in the industrial sector on wages or the level of employment in agriculture; and, finally, the deflator of nominal wage rates is a producer price index, not a cost-of-living index, so that my so-called real indexes measure real costs, not welfare. Rather, I have attempted here to examine farm wage rates only with respect to their twin capacities to serve as a diagnostic of labor market integration and as a measure of labor productivity growth.

The focus of this chapter has been on *day* labor and its wages. Laborers hired on monthly contracts, usually to live with the farm family, were also to be found on many Massachusetts farms. It would appear from the analysis in chapter 7 that the increasing incidence of monthly contracts after 1800 represented a structural change in the farm labor force, one that raises many interesting issues.

APPENDIX A: TOWNS, BY REGION, AND TASKS[49]

Region East. Acton, Biddeford (Maine), Billerica, Braintree, Bridgewater, Bridgton (Maine), Cape Elizabeth (Maine), Danvers, Epping (New Hampshire), Framingham, Haverhill, Hingham, Holliston, Hopkinton, Ipswich, Kingston, Marlborough, Milton, New Bedford, Newbury, Newburyport, Pepperell, Plymouth, Rowley, Wenham, Wrentham.

Region Central. Bolton, Charlton, Douglas, Grafton, Harvard, Leicester, Leominster, Northborough, Oakham, Sturbridge, Woodstock (Connecticut).

Region West. Amherst, Bernardston, Blandford, Buckland, Conway, Deerfield, Durham (Connecticut), Gill, Greenfield, Hadley, Hinsdale (Ver-

---

48. Paskoff, "Labor Productivity and Managerial Efficiency against a Static Technology," 135. See also his *Industrial Evolution*, chap. 2.

49. Unless otherwise noted, all towns are in Massachusetts.

mont), Keene (New Hampshire), Lee, Longmeadow, Newtown (Connecticut), Northampton, Northfield, Rutland (Vermont), Shutesbury, Springfield, Stockbridge, Vernon (Vermont), Westfield, Westhampton, West Springfield, Windsor (Connecticut).

Farm Tasks are coded as follows: 1 = unspecified work and miscellaneous; 2 = mowing and raking; 3 = haying; 4 = hoeing, hilling, weeding; 5 = reaping and cradling; 6 = harvesting and gathering; 7 = planting, sowing; 8 = chopping, hewing, cutting, scoring and sawing wood; 9 = building walls, wells, fences, structures; 10 = threshing.

APPENDIX B: THE WEIGHTING OF THE WAGE INDEXES

The weighted wage index (WWI) is constructed to reflect the fact that some tasks are bound up with the production of more value than others. The components of my index are the cluster of tasks associated with the production of each of the major farm commodities. Hay production enlists the tasks of mowing, raking, and haying, the wages for which have been combined and annual means taken. Corn production enlists the tasks of planting, hoeing, hilling, weeding, harvesting, and husking, the wages for which have been combined and annual means taken. Wages for the tasks involved in small grain production—sowing, reaping, cradling, threshing—have been similarly averaged, as have the wages for the tasks involved in processing wood: hewing, cutting, chopping, sawing.

As noted in the text, wages for the large category of "unspecified work" and miscellaneous tasks were combined with building wages. Because they cannot be associated with any one output, these are presented as the unweighted index, UWI.

The value weights for each output-specific task cluster are calculated from data in the Massachusetts tax valuations of 1801, which give, for each of the Massachusetts and Maine towns in the study sample, the outputs of small grains (wheat, rye, oats, barley), corn, and hays (upland, fresh meadow, salt marsh). The magnitudes for each town, summed over all sample towns and multiplied by the 1795–1805 mean price of each crop—as calculated for my price index—give the value of aggregate output of these crops produced in the sample towns in 1801.

Wood is not assessed in the 1801 valuations, yet the cluster of tasks associated with its processing must be included among the components of the wage index because it accounted for a very large share of hired farm labor effort. Its weight is estimated from the 1801 town valuations by assuming that the value of wood bore to the value of total output (including wood) the same relation that the value of woodland acreage bore to the value of total improved acreage (including woodlands).[50]

The value of all grains, hays, and corn (Q) is $1,147,554; that of all improved acreage (IA) is $367,086, of which the value of woodland acreage (WA) is $20,778, or 5.7 percent. To get the value of wood (W), assume $W/(Q + W) = WA/IA$. Then W is $69,364, and total output (Q + W) is $1,216,918.

The weights on the crop-specific task clusters, by crop, are as follows: wood, 5.7; corn, 27.0; grains, 12.2; hays, 55.2. The formula for the weighted wage index is

$$I = \Sigma \left[(w_{ia}/w_{ib}) \times (p_{i0}q_{i0})\right]/\Sigma \, p_{i0}q_{i0},$$

where for each year (*a*) the mean wage (*w*) of each crop-specific task cluster (*i*) relative to its level in the reference-base period 1795–1805 (*b*) is weighted (multiplied) by the proportion the value of the *i*th task-related crop (p_iq_i) in the weight-base year 1801 (0) was of the total value of all *i* task-related crops in year 0, multiplied by 100. These weighted relatives are then summed across all *i*'s and divided by the sum of the weights (= 100, except in cases of missing values).

APPENDIX C: INDEXES OF WAGES, PRICES, AND PRODUCTIVITY (1795–1805 = 100)

Year	UWI	WWI	PI	UWI/PI	WWI/PI
1750	72.8	70.1	42.7	170.5	164.2
1751	63.8	74.4	37.8	168.8	196.8
1752	62.3	69.8	66.5	93.7	105.0
1753	100.0	79.2	63.7	157.0	124.3
1754	65.3	59.6	53.6	121.8	111.2
1755	63.4	69.9	63.6	99.7	109.9
1756	72.5	71.5	56.6	128.1	126.3
1757	71.9	73.0	62.6	114.9	116.6
1758	73.2	59.7	62.7	116.7	95.2
1759	76.6	76.1	62.4	122.8	122.0
1760	71.9	63.3	54.4	132.2	116.4
1761	80.6	75.0	65.6	122.9	114.3
1762	87.5	75.7	74.1	118.1	102.2
1763	78.5	79.1	68.4	114.8	115.6

50. The 1801 tax valuations include acreages and per acre values of the following categories of land use: tillage, English and upland mowing, fresh meadow, salt marsh, pasture, woodland exclusive of pasture land enclosed, unimproved, unimprovable, owned by the town, owned by any other proprietors, used for roads, covered with water.

APPENDIX C (*Continued*)

Year	UWI	WWI	PI	UWI/PI	WWI/PI
1764	82.1	76.5	63.8	128.7	119.9
1765	93.4	80.4	72.2	129.4	111.4
1766	75.8	70.8	65.5	115.7	108.1
1767	76.4	74.5	60.8	125.7	122.5
1768	88.3	71.6	74.0	119.3	96.8
1769	70.0	75.0	62.0	112.9	121.0
1770	68.3	69.1	63.8	107.1	108.3
1771	89.4	79.0	66.9	133.6	118.1
1772	83.2	78.9	63.6	130.8	124.1
1773	75.1	80.2	66.6	112.8	120.4
1774	70.0	77.0	68.7	101.9	112.1
1775	80.9	74.6	74.8	108.2	99.7
1776	79.4	81.5	80.6	98.5	101.1
1777	86.0	104.8	108.2	79.5	96.9
1778	119.2	71.2	86.3	138.1	82.5
1779	75.7	68.6	112.7	67.2	60.9
1780	98.1	73.3	100.6	97.5	72.9
1781	83.0	81.4	77.4	107.2	105.2
1782	99.8	63.7	81.3	122.8	78.4
1783	74.2	81.9	104.6	70.9	78.3
1784	87.4	98.6	74.5	117.3	132.3
1785	86.0	80.8	82.3	104.5	98.2
1786	93.0	70.9	72.7	127.9	97.5
1787	77.9	77.3	79.9	97.5	96.7
1788	97.2	77.8	79.1	122.9	98.4
1789	83.4	79.4	73.9	112.9	107.4
1790	89.4	78.7	78.4	114.0	100.4
1791	88.5	77.7	75.7	118.1	102.6
1792	90.8	78.3	75.0	121.1	104.4
1793	82.8	76.0	92.3	89.7	82.3
1794	91.7	79.3	106.8	85.9	74.3
1795	82.3	87.2	103.9	79.2	83.9
1796	86.0	95.8	98.6	87.2	97.2
1797	91.1	103.1	99.0	92.0	104.1
1798	99.2	115.3	94.8	104.6	121.6
1799	86.2	103.6	98.7	87.3	105.0
1800	96.4	85.0	109.1	88.4	77.9
1801	113.8	120.2	88.4	128.7	136.0
1802	113.6	90.2	97.1	117.0	92.9
1803	93.4	105.7	91.1	102.5	116.0
1804	116.0	90.0	107.3	108.1	83.9
1805	120.9	104.4	111.2	108.7	93.9

APPENDIX C (*Continued*)

Year	UWI	WWI	PI	UWI/PI	WWI/PI
1806	115.8	126.9	116.4	99.5	109.0
1807	129.8	128.1	110.6	117.4	115.8
1808	136.2	114.0	98.6	138.1	115.6
1809	144.5	128.6	110.1	131.2	116.8
1810	122.8	126.4	111.8	109.8	113.1
1811	137.9	122.8	112.5	122.6	109.2
1812	130.0	121.2	111.5	116.6	108.7
1813	124.9	135.9	120.0	104.1	113.3
1814	150.6	156.7	121.9	123.5	128.5
1815	136.6	153.7	123.6	110.5	124.4
1816	124.3	153.5	124.8	99.6	123.0
1817	129.6	138.6	134.3	96.5	103.2
1818	133.8	150.1	126.2	106.0	118.9
1819	136.2	152.4	121.4	112.2	125.5
1820	140.6	132.0	105.3	133.5	125.4
1821	101.1	136.9	101.4	99.7	135.0
1822	149.6	121.2	104.1	143.7	116.4
1823	126.0	136.5	104.0	121.2	131.3
1824	121.7	130.4	100.3	121.3	130.0
1825	153.6	119.6	103.2	148.8	115.9
1826	132.3	149.9	106.3	124.5	141.0
1827	142.3	141.2	105.6	134.8	133.7
1828	141.7	141.9	106.4	133.2	133.4
1829	118.1	142.0	95.8	123.3	148.2
1830	153.2	139.7	103.1	148.6	135.5
1831	158.7	145.3	100.3	158.2	144.9
1832	146.8	141.4	112.8	130.1	125.4
1833	141.1	139.9	115.2	122.5	121.4
1834	124.0	140.8	113.0	109.7	124.6
1835	152.3	137.2	118.1	129.0	116.2
1836	169.4	155.5	136.6	124.0	113.8
1837	163.8	178.9	140.1	116.9	127.7
1838	169.8	157.0	130.4	130.2	120.4
1839	154.2	166.8	128.6	119.9	129.7
1840	173.2	167.8	108.6	159.5	154.5
1841	167.7	147.5	120.1	139.6	122.8
1842	164.0	143.1	102.4	160.2	139.7
1843	127.7	142.7	96.8	131.9	147.4
1844	168.5	139.8	97.4	173.0	143.5
1845	167.4	155.7	104.3	160.5	149.3
1846	160.0	145.1	123.4	129.7	117.6
1847	204.9	177.4	130.5	157.0	135.9

APPENDIX C (*Continued*)

Year	UWI	WWI	PI	UWI/PI	WWI/PI
1848	191.9	164.0	115.7	165.9	141.7
1849	174.3	159.0	114.0	152.9	139.5
1850	141.5	176.0	117.0	120.9	150.4
1851	157.4	151.7	132.1	119.2	114.8
1852	188.7	161.5	119.3	158.2	135.4
1853	185.7	165.4	134.9	137.7	122.6
1854	220.2	188.2	145.2	151.7	129.6
1855	283.0	197.9	141.7	199.7	139.7

Note: UWI = unweighted wage index of unspecified tasks; WWI = weighted wage index of crop-related tasks; PI = Rothenberg farm commodity price index; UWI/PI = "real" unweighted wage index; WWI/PI = "real" weighted wage index. For weighting procedure, see Appendix B.

7

Contract Labor in Massachusetts
Agriculture

THE PREVIOUS CHAPTER USED THE BEHAVIOR OF WAGES TO STUDY day labor on Massachusetts farms: defining the heterogeneous character of it, dating the emergence of a market for it, identifying the task stratification of it, partitioning the effects operating on wages paid to it, and measuring the productivity gains captured by it. But complementing day workers on Massachusetts farms, and becoming increasingly important in the early nineteenth century, were live-in laborers on monthly contract. What role they may have played in the productivity growth of the region's farm labor force is not entirely clear, but the increasing frequency with which contract labor appears in farm account books after 1800 raises a great many interesting issues.

First and by no means least of these issues is the absence of coercion in the enforcement of these contracts. America's genuinely "peculiar institution" may not have been plantation slavery at all but free labor on the farms of New England. After all, varieties of bondage—slavery, serfdom, truck, peonage, the *encomienda,* indentured servitude, forced labor interlinked to ill-functioning land and credit markets, foreign workers sold to padrones, *partidaros,* and labor bosses, and the more subtle but no less coercive tyranny of familial production—have characterized agrarian labor systems throughout the world since time immemorial.[1] There is nothing "peculiar" about them. But an agricultural labor force, unconstrained and free to move, may well be a New England innovation.[2]

1 On the tyranny of familial production in traditional societies, see Caldwell, "The Mechanisms of Demographic Change in Historical Perspective." On the tyranny of familial production in the United States, see Parker, "Agriculture," esp. 395. On bound labor on the American frontier, see Lamar, "From Bondage to Contract"; and Hallagan, "Labor Contracting in Turn-of-the-Century California Agriculture." On forms of interlinked labor, credit, and tenurial contracts in developing economies, see Binswanger and Rosenzweig, eds., *Contractual Arrangements, Employment, and Wages in Rural Labor Markets in Asia*; and Bardhan, "Interlinking Factor Markets and Agrarian Development." On truck, see Ommer, ed., *Merchant Credit and Labour Strategies in Historical Perspective.*

2. Free, even, to quit in breach of contract *without penalty.* I find it a matter of considerable significance that the farmers in my sample paid the wages earned by workers who quit in breach of contract, although the state courts had held that express labor contracts bar recovery in *quantum meruit.*

With the "solitary" (Horwitz, *The Transformation of American Law,* 332) exception of *Britton v. Turner,* 6 N.H. 481 (1834), "if [the worker] left his employment before the end of the term, jurists reasoned, the employee could receive nothing for the labor he had already expended. The contract, they maintained, was an 'entire' one, and therefore it could not be conceived of as a series of smaller agreements. Since the breach of any part was therefore a breach of the whole, there was no basis for allowing the employee to recover 'on the contract' . . . it would be an act of usurpation to 'rewrite' the contract and allow the employee to recover in quantum meruit for the 'reasonable' value of his labor." This was true "whether the wages are estimated at a gross sum, or are to be

Contract labor came to Massachusetts from England, where much of the farm labor from the sixteenth century onward had been done by "servants in husbandry" on twelve-month contracts. The institution had evolved in England in response, on the one hand, to the desperate labor shortages that followed each visitation of plague and, on the other, to the increasingly urgent demand for labor on the larger, enclosed, pastoral farms. Servants in husbandry were unmarried young people usually between the ages of fifteen and twenty-four, the sons and daughters[3] of farmers who, for a variety of reasons, shed their own adolescent children and took on someone else's. Servants were hired every Michaelmas at job fairs to live with and in the family (i.e., as a member of the household) of the master and to do all manner of farm work for twelve months from harvest to harvest. Until the eighteenth century, the wage was set by fiat; thereafter, it was set in the open market. The annual contracts, while not always written, were made public, were constrained by custom and law, and were enforceable in the courts.[4]

It is likely that most of the early settlers of Massachusetts had had servants in husbandry in England and expected to have them here, for it has been estimated that nearly three-quarters of the yeomen, nearly half the husbandmen, and nearly one-quarter of the tradesmen in early modern England had at least one live-in laborer. But soon after the initial "peopling" of Massachusetts Bay, farm laborers as a class disappeared. Estimates put the proportion of servants in seventeenth-century Essex County at no more than 4 percent, and in Dedham at less then 5 percent, of the farm population. That first generation of settlers faced not only a

---

calculated according to a certain rate per week or month, or are payable at certain stipulated times, provided the servant agree for a definite and whole term" (Horwitz, *The Transformation of American Law,* 186). The curious thing, then, is why the farmers in my sample did not withhold wages from contract workers who quit in advance of the expiration of their contracts.

Peter Karsten has taken Horwitz to task. In "'Bottomed on Justice,'" Karsten traces the eventual adoption of the *Britton v. Turner* rule by the courts in ten states (although Massachusetts was not one of them). Its influence was also felt in nine more states (including Massachusetts) where penalties against laborers for breach of farm labor contracts were softened. The point I am making here is that my sample of contract workers was paid in *quantum meruit* in fact.

3. In England, adolescent females were servants-in-husbandry because adult females worked in the fields as farm laborers. The ratio of male to female servants was approximately 2:1 in the mid-nineteenth century (see Kussmaul, *Servants in Husbandry in Early Modern England,* 4). This was not true in New England. Females appear in Massachusetts farm account books only as domestic servants, spinners, and weavers and, very occasionally (and very locally), to pick hops.

4. The fifty-two-week residency in the parish required for a settlement under the English Poor Law deterred servants from running away in breach of contract, but employing farmers were all too often able to impose the infamous fifty-one-week contracts that left servants disqualified for a settlement (ibid., 127.)

dearth of live-in help but a "withering" of day labor as well.[5] Farmers breaking a wilderness to grain agriculture could count only on the field labor of their sons or, if sufficiently prosperous, of their tenants.

While Massachusetts farmers may have had little if any live-in help in the seventeenth century, farm account books document the appearance of labor contracts by the mid-eighteenth century and their increased frequency after 1800. Measuring the magnitude of that increase will prove problematical, but what increase there was directs our attention to the functions served by labor contracts, functions that continue to this day to make contractual arrangements the dominant mode of organizing agricultural labor throughout the developing world.

The analysis of labor contracts poses a challenge to labor market theory. Whereas conventional micro-analysis puts the wage bargain at the center of the market process, labor contracts "tend to insulate contracting parties from short-run external shocks" and in so doing "take current wage rates 'out of competition' in allocating labor resources." Where in conventional theory labor inputs adjust to the market wage in a perpetual equilibrium process, in contract theory all options that existed ex ante are closed ex post: renegotiating the wage requires reopening the contract. In brief, where competitive markets are governed by the invisible hand, contract markets are governed by "the invisible handshake."[6] But what is the handshake about? What has been agreed to if wages are not at the heart of the bargain?

Several motivations for labor contracts have been identified in the theory of contracts literature. First, *the insurance motive,* in which the worker—who is assumed to be more risk averse than the employer—is the primary beneficiary of a labor contract. In adjusting output to falling seasonal demand the employer may be indifferent between either lowering wage rates and keeping employment constant or keeping wage rates constant and laying off workers, but the worker is not. Where both contract and day labor are used, the brunt of periodic layoffs is borne by the day workers, while the contract workers accept a wage below their marginal revenue product and considerably below the spot wage of the day worker in return for employment security for the duration of the contract. Sherwin Rosen calls this bargain struck by the contracting parties "implicit payments of insurance premiums by workers in favorable states of nature and receipt of indemnities in unfavorable states."[7]

5. Vickers, "Working the Fields in a Developing Economy," 55; 55, n. 13; and 60.
6. Rosen, "Implicit Contracts," 1145, 1149.
7. Ibid., 1145.

Another motivation concerns the *hoarding of labor.* If the local supply of labor cannot be counted on to satisfy peak seasonal demands, the
employer may have an incentive to secure "downstream" labor in the
off-season, at off-season wages, even if it means hoarding wage labor
for many months. As a corollary, the employer-farmer will have an incentive to restructure the farm enterprise so that the labor he is "storing"
at considerable expense can be gainfully employed in the off-season.
Diversifying the crop mix, home manufacturing, hiring out "my hand"
to neighboring farmers, shifting to dairying and animal husbandry
which use labor throughout the year, can all be understood as responses
to the need to provide continuous, long-term employment for workers
on long-term contracts.[8]

It is difficult to understand the ubiquity of long-term wage and tenancy contracts in labor-surplus economies where the marginal productivity of rural labor approaches zero and the probability of recruiting
harvest workers on the spot is very high. Yet the major incidence of
agricultural labor contracts today is in just such economies.[9] It would
appear that contracts under these conditions disguise as labor recruit-
ment strategies what are primarily arrangements for workers to obtain
access to credit and land in the absence of well-functioning credit and
land markets. Thus, a third motivation concerns *access to interlinked
markets.* The interlinking of labor, land, and credit transactions is facil-
itated by the sunk investment both parties have made in the relationship,
that is, by what Oliver Hart and Bengt Holmstrom have called a "lock-
in effect."[10] The long-term contract acts in lieu of collateral for the

8. See, e.g., Anderson and Gallman, "Slaves as Fixed Capital." It is to the extent that the
hoarding motive generates these incentives to reorganize ("rationalize") the farm enterprise that
contract labor may have contributed to the productivity growth of Massachusetts agriculture. Of
course, not all farmers will be willing to absorb the costs of hoarding labor, together with the
related costs of restructuring the farm calendar. They would be particularly reluctant if "worker
opportunism," i.e., quitting in breach of contract, is not heavily penalized by custom as well as by
law: "Contracts break down if workers accept insurance payments opportunistically in bad times
and renege on premium payments by skipping out in good times" (Rosen, "Implicit Contracts,"
1170). It is for this reason that I attach considerable importance to the finding in farm account
books that wages in *quantum meruit* were in fact paid on incomplete contracts.

9. See Binswanger and Rosenzweig, eds., *Contractual Arrangements, Employment, and
Wages in Rural Labor Markets in Asia.*

10. Hart and Holmstrom, "The Theory of Contracts." The term *lock-in* as used by Hart and
Holmstrom refers to "situations where a small number of parties make investments which are to
some extent relationship-specific; that is, once made, they have a much higher value inside the
relationship than outside. Given this 'lock-in' effect, each party will have some monopoly power
ex post, although there may be plenty of competition ex ante before investments are sunk" (p. 72).

Although Hart and Holmstrom did not have farm labor contracts in mind, Hart has suggested
in private conversation with the author that among the "investments which are to some extent

debtor borrowing against his wages and acts as a screening device for the creditor.[11]

Finally, long-term contracts are, above all else, a means by which both sides seek to *minimize transactions costs,* to save the costs of time spent in negotiation, in matching, in monitoring and enforcement, and in search.[12] While it is well known that a wage contract provides less incentive than a land tenure contract for a worker to perform at maximum effort, the notion of *lock-in* as Hart and Holmstrom use the term— that is, of a relationship-specific investment that has a higher value to both parties inside the relationship than outside it—provides what incentives there were.

Presumably all these factors played a role in motivating the use of monthly contracts on Massachusetts farms between 1750 and 1865. In this chapter, the role of farm labor contracts is explored with respect to (*a*) their frequency and incidence over time, (*b*) their relation to the seasonality of employment in agriculture, (*c*) the place of monthly wages in the pattern of seasonal and structural wage differentials, and (*d*) the relation of contract labor to segmentation in the farm labor force. Together with chapter 6, this chapter is intended as a contribution to the unfinished task of understanding America's "peculiar institution," free farm labor.

I. The Quantitative Significance of Labor Contracts

The data base for this study is a sample of 692 monthly contracts that I have drawn from thirty-six account books of farmers who used contract

---

relationship-specific" (i.e., among "lock-in" situations) may indeed be the mutual commitments made by farmer and monthly worker by the worker's having forgone alternatives, left home and family, and traveled perhaps a considerable distance to move into a quid pro quo relationship where "a considerable amount of time may elapse between the quid and the quo" (p. 71).

Clearly, the term *lock-in* is being used in the theory-of-contract literature in quite a different sense from the way the term has been used by economic historians of the postbellum South, for whom it refers to "debt peonage and the power of the merchant to force farmers into overproduction of cotton" (Ransom and Sutch, *One Kind of Freedom,* 164).

11. It is in this connection that changes in the quality of the farm labor force after 1830, to be discussed in sec. IV below, may have been most telling. Monthly workers hired "off the road" had not been screened.

12. "As I have now little or no Hope of recovering Enoch, I mounted for Hopkinton P.M. to hire a man," wrote Ebenezer Parkman on 14 July 1768, after Enoch, his hired hand, quit. He scoured the countryside again the following March and April, riding from Westborough to Hopkinton, Grafton, Mansfield, Brookfield, Paxton, Needham, and Upton in search of a young man to live in and work for the season (Walett, ed., *The Diary of Ebenezer Parkman,* pt. 2).

labor during the period 1750–1865, containing name of farmer, town of farmer, name of hired "hand," year and month of starting work, duration of contract in months, the wage in dollars per month, and any additional information including, where known, age and town of laborer, sudden quits or terminations, special characteristics of the arrangement, and so on. The sample of workers employed by these thirty-six farmers is augmented on occasion by a data base of 227 contract workers and 181 day workers hired to work on the Ward farm in Shrewsbury, Massachusetts, between 1787 and 1865.[13]

The first set of questions to address with the data is what they tell us about the quantitative importance of contract labor on Massachusetts farms in the period 1750–1865. Was there an increase in the number of farmers hiring contract workers? Did individual farmers increase the number of contract workers they hired per year? Did they attempt to increase the length of the contract term? Is there evidence of a shift, a substitution, away from day labor to monthly live-in labor?

Table 17 presents several alternative ways of calculating the incidence of contract labor on Massachusetts farms. Column 1 indicates the number of farm account books that appear in the sample for each five-year period. Column 2 counts the number of individual farmers with one or more contracts in each period.[14] The number of contracts in each quinquennium is given in column 3. But number of contracts is an unreliable indicator of changes in the importance of contract labor for two reasons. First, column 3 is drawn from a sample—see column 1— whose size is itself changing, as account books varying in time span enter and leave the sample. Second, because it does not acknowledge variations in the length of contracts, the number of contracts misrepresents their importance. Twelve one-month contracts will loom large but may have less significance than one twelve-month contract in terms of the insurance, hoarding, interlinking, screening, and cost-saving motives for hiring labor by the month.

Once the number of man-months under contract in each period is known (col. 4), then we can compensate for shifting sample size by

13. The Ward Family Farm Laborers' File, compiled by Holly Izard under the supervision of Jack Larkin, chief historian, Research Department, Old Sturbridge Village, was generously made available to me by Mr. Larkin. See his discussion based on these data in " 'Labor Is the Great Thing in Farming.' " Two additional studies of farm laborers are Beales, "The Reverend Ebenezer Parkman's Farm Workers"; and Lyman, " 'What Is Done in My Absence?' "

14. For example, in the first period, two farmers accounted for the eighteen contracts, totaling ninety-six man-months; the other four books whose coverage spanned this period used no monthly labor in this quinquennium.

Table 17 The Incidence of Monthly Farm Labor Contracts, 1763–1865

Period	No. of Books Covering This Period (1)	No. of Farmers with Contracts (2)	No. of Contracts Specifying Length (3)	Total Man-Months of Contract Labor (4)	Average Man-Months of Contract Labor:		
					Per Contract ([4]/[3]) (5)	Per Farmer ([4]/[1]) (6)	Per Farmer with Contracts ([4]/[2]) (7)
1763–69	6	2	18	96.0	5.3	16.0	48.0
1770–74	6	5	7	38.2	5.5	6.4	7.6
1775–79	6	3	7	22.2	3.2	3.7	7.4
1780–84	9	5	6	34.5	5.8	3.8	6.9
1785–89	11	4	14	80.2	5.7	7.3	20.1
1790–94	12	8	22	110.0	5.0	9.2	13.8
1795–99	12	6	23	114.5	5.0	9.5	19.1
1800–1804	15	7	34	179.2	5.3	11.9	25.6
1805–9	15	9	53	326.1	6.2	21.7	36.2
1810–14	14	10	69	374.7	5.4	26.8	37.5
1815–19	15	10	36	168.8	4.7	11.3	16.9
1820–24	14	12	63	283.3	4.5	20.2	23.6
1825–29	12	8	36	185.8	5.2	15.5	23.2
1830–34	13	9	38	188.6	5.0	14.5	20.9
1835–39	13	8	29	160.4	5.5	12.3	20.1
1840–44	15	11	47	277.3	5.9	18.5	25.2
1845–49	16	15	58	354.4	6.1	22.2	23.6
1850–54	13	7	34	168.2	4.9	12.9	24.0
1855–59	11	3	8	44.8	5.6	4.1	14.9
1860–65	5	2	15	68.8	4.6	13.8	34.4

Source: Rothenberg sample of farm account books.

Note: Contracts that extend beyond a calendar year are assigned to the year in which they began. The contracts are drawn from a sample of thirty-six account books (= thirty-six farmers), all of whom hired contract labor, but not necessarily in every year covered by their books. 620 of the contracts in the sample specified length. Three are omitted from this table: one from 1713, one from 1752, and one from 1753.

calculating man-months per contract (col. 5), man-months per account book or per sample farmer (col. 6), and man-months per contracting farmer (col. 7).

As noted above, not all sample farmers hired contract labor in every five-year period. It is the presence in any period of farmers without monthly workers (i.e., the difference between col. 1 and col. 2) that accounts for the difference between column 6 and column 7. Both measures are given because table 17 is, in effect, charting the diffusion of an innovation, and in a diffusion measure zero entries are relevant.

The finding, in column 5, that for one hundred years farm labor contracts, on the average, did not lengthen much beyond five months is supported by table 18, a frequency distribution of contracts by length. There is no discernible shift to more frequent use of nine- to twelve-month contracts, no marked increase in the proportion of annual as opposed to seasonal commitments. Between 60 and 75 percent of contracts, depending on decade, ran six months or less.[15] This finding was unanticipated. It suggests that the motives for long commitments discussed above—particularly the insurance motive, which is closely related in the theoretical literature to the Hart-Holmstrom notion of *lock-in*—were overwhelmed by other factors, principally by the inexorable seasonality of New England agriculture.[16]

II. Contract Labor and the Seasonality of Agricultural Employment

A decade ago, Carville V. Earle and Ronald Hoffman published a study in which America's early and successful industrialization was attributed to a surplus, not a scarcity, of unskilled labor made cheap by long periods of seasonal layoffs in agriculture.[17] While recent research indicates that there is much to fault in their analysis,[18] their contribution should be recognized for having put the seasonality of agriculture at the very center of a model of American industrialization.

15. Man-months per contract averaged 5.2 across quinquennia, 4.9 when averaged annually.

16. What I am suggesting here is that there is a difference between one long contract and two sequential short contracts. It will be recalled that the theory of labor contracts "is based on the idea that a firm offers its risk-averse workers wage and employment insurance via a long-term contract. . . . If the lock-in effect that is responsible for the long-term relationship in the first place is small . . . the insurance element of the contract will be put under severe pressure" (Hart and Holmstrom, "The Theory of Contracts," 106, 110).

17. Earle and Hoffman, "The Foundation of the Modern Economy."

18. First, recent research based on harvest wage premia finds considerably *less* seasonality, not more, in American grain agriculture than in British, a result that undermines the Earle-Hoffman

Table 18   Frequency Distribution of Monthly Contracts by Length in
Months, by Decade, 1763–1865

Years	Total No.	Percentage Distribution			
		0–3 Months	Over 3–6 Months	Over 6–9 Months	Over 9–12 Months
1763–69	18	39	22	22	17
1770–79	14	43	43	7	7
1780–89	20	40	20	10	30
1790–99	45	36	36	18	11
1800–1809	87	31	30	21	17
1810–19	105	34	36	22	7
1820–29	99	36	34	23	6
1830–39	67	22	43	28	6
1840–49	105	20	46	23	12
1850–65	57	42	33	12	12

Source: Rothenberg sample of farm account books.
Note: 620 of the contracts in the sample specified length. Three, dated 1713, 1752, and 1753, are omitted from the table.

The issue is revisited in a 1991 study by Stanley Engerman and Claudia Goldin that begins by calculating the heavy cost—in terms of national income forgone—the American economy has paid for seasonal unemployment in both agriculture and manufacturing and, consequently, the "fillip" added to economic growth when seasonality is "surmounted" late in the nineteenth century.[19] The principal credit for reduc-

---

explanation for the greater capital deepening in American than in British industrial technology (Sokoloff and Dollar, "Agricultural Seasonality and the Organization of Manufacturing during Early Industrialization"). Second, seasonally unemployed farm hands in the Midwest—in the very grain-growing regions Earle and Hoffman target—sought winter jobs not in manufacturing but in logging, teamstering, and droving, or they traveled downriver looking for work as itinerant farm workers. If they could not land one of those jobs, they wintered in town, dissipating all their savings on room and board, or stayed on a farm all winter, even for no pay but with free room and board (see Schob, *Hired Hands and Plowboys*, 255–56). Finally, the Earle-Hoffman story depends on the degree to which there was sufficient "meshing" between the seasonal patterns of agriculture and those of manufacturing in the early stages of industrial development. A recent study of seasonality in the late nineteenth century concludes, "After weighing all the evidence, we believe [seasonal unemployment] was not reduced by a movement of laborers across sectors having seasons that meshed" (Engerman and Goldin, "Seasonality in Nineteenth Century Labor Markets," 21). If there was little meshing at the end of the century, there is likely to have been still less in the antebellum decades, when labor markets were a good deal less integrated.

19. Engerman and Goldin, "Seasonality in Nineteenth Century Labor Markets." That seasonality was being "surmounted" is confirmed from the decline of the seasonal wage premium between 1880 and 1900 (p. 3).

ing seasonal unemployment goes to macro-level phenomena: the shift out of agriculture, structural changes within agriculture (mechanization and changes in crop mix), and the seasonal migration of workers between those sectors whose seasonal demands for labor "meshed." But Engerman and Goldin do acknowledge that annual labor contracts may have played a role in diminishing seasonal layoffs within agriculture by 1900.[20]

To posit some correlation between the diffusion of long-term labor contracts and reduced seasonality in agricultural employment is not to posit a direction of causation. Strategies to employ labor on long-term and off-season contracts may have been a response to longer crop years. Or strategies to lengthen the crop year may have been a response to conditions in the labor market (heightened risk aversion, e.g.) that favored long-term and off-season contracts. Or both the extended use of contracts and the shift in crop mix may have been the result of some third factor, say, the growth and spread of the market. While choosing among these causal scenarios is beyond the scope of this chapter, it raises three related questions that can be addressed with the data at hand. Did the length of labor contracts increase over time to provide more off-season employment? Did the frequency of off-season (winter) contracts, regardless of their length, increase over time? Did farmers alter their crop mix to produce outputs that lengthened the crop year?

It has already been remarked that man-months per contract did not lengthen over time (table 17, col. 5), nor did the frequency of long contracts increase over time (table 18). There are seventy-seven nine- to twelve-month contracts in my sample—over 12 percent of the 620 contracts in which length was specified—but that number failed to increase over a period in which, as will be discussed below, contract workers accounted for a far larger proportion of man-days of hired farm labor than did day workers.

But even short-term monthly contracts can have worked to smooth seasonal discontinuities in agricultural employment if it can be shown

20. "About 25 percent of all nonfamily farm workers in 1900 were unemployed sometime during the year and . . . most of these workers experienced 3 to 4 months of unemployment. Whether or not many of the 75 percent who did not report unemployment during the year were involved in a meshing of the sectors through migration, depends on the proportion of farm laborers who found yearly employment in agriculture. Reliable sources indicate that about 25 to 35 percent of all farm laborers were hired on annual contract, although some additional fraction may have found yearly employment in the agricultural sector on monthly, seasonal, and daily bases" (ibid., 20–21).

that an increasing proportion of them began in or extended into the winter months. Overall, over 24 percent of the man-months under contract were for winter work.[21] The number of man-months of off-season (winter) work increased markedly from twenty-one in the 1760s to 151 in the 1840s, but as a percentage of total man-months there is no evidence of a rising time trend (see table 19).

Table 20, a calendar of farm activities drawn from several unusually detailed farm diaries, daybooks, and account books, identifies those tasks reserved for the winter months of November through March. The hewing, drawing, and scoring of timber and the chopping, cutting, and carting of wood took up so much of every winter day that it alone might have kept a hired hand occupied. Market trips were sometimes left to winter because sledding loads of produce or livestock on snow and ice was much faster than hauling it in wagons over rutted or muddy roads. Threshing was typically done in the winter: one hundred bushels of small grains (wheat, rye, oats, and barley), flailed at the rate of five bushels a day, would have occupied one man full-time for nearly a month, and several of my sample farmers produced considerably more than one hundred bushels of small grains.[22] Corn did not suffer, as did the small grains and hays, from being left late in the field and could be harvested, cut, stacked, and husked in winter. The first snow each winter was believed to impart special nutrients to the soil, and that, presumably, accounts for the many instances of plowing in December. And there were always hogs to butcher, sugar maples to tap, brooms to make, shoes to repair, fields to manure, cider to press, and winter rye and wheat to sow.

While the incidence of long-term and off-season contracts did not increase, there was a marked shift in the composition of output that worked to extend the crop year. Plant species cannot, of course, be "deseasonalized." They carry their seasonality in their genetic codes:

21. *Winter* is defined here as the five months from November through March, so 24 percent of the man-months under contract were for 42 percent of the months.

22. "New England farmers hailed mainly from England and Scotland and brought with them the strong preference for flailing that dominated pre-mechanical threshing systems throughout the British Isles. . . . The slower and more individualistic flailing technique suited regional needs and became a common task carried out during the long New England winters" (Rikoon, *Threshing in the Midwest,* 2). Rikoon's estimate of five bushels a day appears on p. 7. Outputs of up to four hundred bushels of small grains are reported for some of my sample farmers in U.S. Census Office, *Seventh Census (1850), Manuscript Census of Population: Massachusetts,* Productions of Agriculture.

Table 19   Winter Work Done on Monthly Contracts, 1763–1865

Date	No. of Man-Months of Winter Work (1)	Total Man-Months Worked (2)	Winter Months Worked as Percentage of Total Man-Months Worked ([2]/[1]) (3)
1763–69	21	96	22
1770–79	11	60	18
1780–89	37	115	33
1790–99	64	147	44
1800–1809	143	500	29
1810–19	104	544	19
1820–29	82	477	17
1830–39	66	349	19
1840–49	151	636	24
1850–59	72	213	34
1860–65	22	69	31
Total	777	3,210	24

Source: Rothenberg sample of farm account books.
Note: Winter is defined as November through March.

corn matures in two thousand growing-degree days, and no reorganization of labor on the farm will alter that.[23] But in the interest of distributing labor inputs and farm income more evenly across the year, the plant mix can be diversified. An important example was the cultivation of broomcorn in the Connecticut River Valley. The home manufacture of brooms for urban markets not only linked farmers to industrial outwork (as palm-leaf braiding linked their wives) but provided remunerative (and very labor-intensive) winter work for males.[24]

When the broomcorn bonanza faded, tobacco took its place in the valley. As early as September 1738, and hardly aware that it was a har-

23. Growing-degree days are calculated as "the cumulative number of degrees Fahrenheit above the base temperatures at which individual crops begin to grow" (Baron, "A Comparative Study of Climate Fluctuation and Agricultural Practices in Southern New England," 5). Corn begins to grow at fifty degrees Fahrenheit. To calculate the number of summer days it takes for corn to mature, divide two thousand by the difference between the actual summer temperature and fifty degrees.

Corn hybridization has produced phenomenal increases in yields (over 400 percent between 1930 and 1980) and advances in pest resistance but has, apparently, not affected the number of growing-degree days required for its maturity, i.e., its "seasonality" (see Kloppenburg, *First the Seed,* 5, 120, 168).

24. Broomcorn cultivation apparently required two to three times as much labor as corn (Bidwell and Falconer, *History of Agriculture in the Northern United States,* 245).

Table 20   A Calendar of Farm Work

Farm Chore	Jan.	Feb.	Mar.	Apr.	May	June	July	Aug.	Sep.	Oct.	Nov.	Dec.
Altering animals				X	X							
Berrying								X				
Birthing calves, lambs, piglets	X	X	X	X								
Breaking up soil					X							
Bringing in cattle for winter									X	X		
Burning over and clearing new land						X		X				
Butchering	X	X	X	X			X		X	X	X	X
Carding wool	X											X
Carting hay to markets		X	X	X			X		X	X	X	X
Carting wheat to markets								X				
Carting and spreading dung				X	X		X			X		
Chopping wood	X	X	X	X	X	X					X	X
Cutting ice	X	X									X	X
Cutting and hanging tobacco								X	X			
Destroying caterpillars					X							
Digging carrots, turnips, etc.											X	
Digging potatoes									X	X	X	
Digging stones				X							X	X
Drawing logs to sawmill	X	X	X									X
Dressing flax	X		X									
Gathering chicken and turkey egs												
Getting in stalks and rowen				X	X				X	X		
Grafting fruit trees				X		X			X			
Harrowing tillage ground				X	X		X		X	X		X
Harvesting corn, beans				X	X		X	X	X	X	X	X
Haying					X		X	X	X	X		

Table 20 (Continued)

Farm Chore	Jan.	Feb.	Mar.	Apr.	May	June	July	Aug.	Sep.	Oct.	Nov.	Dec.
Hewing timber and drawing logs out of the woods	×											×
Highway and road work		×	×	×	×					×	×	
Hilling and half-hilling corn			×	×								
Hoeing corn, potatoes, beans				×	×	×	×					
Husking and shelling corn									×	×	×	
Making brooms from broomcorn	×											
Making cider	×								×	×	×	
Mending dams, walls, fences				×	×			×	×	×	×	
Milling wheat												×
Mowing bushes				×		×		×	×			
Mowing meadow hay						×	×	×	×	×		
Picking hops									×			
Planting broomcorn, cranberries					×							
Planting cabbages, sweet corn, squash				×								
Planting peas, beets, carrots, parsnips				×								
Planting watermelon, cucumbers					×							
Planting corn				×	×							
Planting potatoes, beans					×							
Planting tobacco						×						
Plowing tillage, meadow, kitchen garden				×	×	×	×	×	×	×	×	×
Pruning and trimming fruit trees				×								

Pulling bark for tanning

Reaping or cradling oats, rye, wheat

Shaking or picking apple trees

Shearing sheep

Shoemaking

Shoot wild geese

Shoot wild pigeons

Sledding wood

Sowing clover seed

Sowing flaxseed

Sowing oats

Sowing rye (winter and summer varieties)

Sowing wheat (winter and summer varieties)

Bringing in cattle to stall feed and fatten

Stripping tobacco

Taking calves from cows

Taking cattle to outpastures

Tapping maple trees

Threshing barley, oats, rye

Washing sheep

Winnowing grains

Sources: Account and day books of William Hosmer of Westfield, Julian Robbins of Deerfield, David Hoyt of Deerfield, and Harrison Howard of North Bridgewater.

binger of momentous things to come, Ebenezer Parkman noted in his diary a shipment of five hundred hogsheads of tobacco being sent downriver en route to the West Indies. In 1850, Massachusetts farmers were growing 138,000 pounds of the stuff and, by 1860, 3.2 million pounds. Shade-grown tobacco (for cigar wrappers) had become the region's major agricultural staple, cultivated specifically for the New York market, and remained so for a hundred years. What makes tobacco singularly important for a study of farm labor is that its cultivation, picking, smoke drying, leaf selection, and packing are highly labor intensive. Given the heavy labor requirements of the crop, the case has been made that its success is inextricably linked to the creation of a "permanent agricultural proletariat" in Massachusetts by the mid-nineteenth century.[25]

The making of brooms and the packing of tobacco provided off-season employment, but their growing seasons competed for labor with all other crops grown in the regular season. On the other hand, the double-cropping of rye and (to a lesser extent) of wheat allowed cultivation to be spread across the year: the winter crop was sown in August and September (one farmer even sowed Black Sea wheat in December) and was brought in in March and April; the spring crop was sown in May and was brought in in July. Grass seed, usually sown in the spring, could just as well be sown in August, one farmer noted, just after haying.

In addition, with the expansion and integration of markets, New England farm families were expanding their traditional diet of baked beans, cheese, rye-n'-injun bread, Indian pudding, potatoes, salt pork, salt beef, and cider by growing, eating, and marketing poultry, winter wheat, winter rye, fluid milk, fresh butter, green herbs, celery, rutabagas, beets, winter squashes, pumpkins, mangel wurtzels, carrots, parsnips, turnips, cabbages, onions, tomatoes, asparagus, string beans, and green peas; peaches, pears, rhubarb, strawberries, cherries, damson plums, quinces, cranberries, and wine grapes; and salmon, smelts, alewives, clams, haddock, shad, and mackerel. The cultivation of some of these crops did expand the growing season: turnips could be planted in August and pulled in November; asparagus was picked in May, cranberries in September, apples in October.[26]

The increased emphasis on dairy products alone—on fluid milk and

25. On tobacco cultivation in the Connecticut River Valley, see Clark, *The Roots of Rural Capitalism*, 295–303 and 304.

26. See McMahon, "A Comfortable Subsistence," "Laying Foods By," and "'All Things in Their Proper Season.'"

butter for nearby urban markets and on cheese for local cheese factories—meant that more cows were wintered, fattened, kept in milk for
most of the year, and stall fed, a year-round commitment of labor time.
So commonplace that it was rarely mentioned in farm account books,
milking was nonetheless "the most time-consuming chore."[27] There has
been much confusion as to who actually did the milking on Massachusetts farms—wives and daughters or sons and hired hands. But the
heaviest demands dairying made on hired hands must have been in the
related nonmilking activities of cleaning stalls and barns, washing milk
cans, delivering milk, and, most of all, in restructuring farm space—
mending fences, year-round stabling and stall feeding of cattle, plowing
and seeding and cultivating meadow, upgrading pasture, growing and
preparing better feeds, collecting and spreading dung, and so on—
which activities were spread across the year.[28]

Despite a variety of techniques for mitigating seasonality, its persistence can be read in the persistence of seasonal wage differentials
written, on occasion, into annual contracts. In 1771, Joseph Barnard of
Deerfield agreed to pay Daniel Rider 24*s.* a month ($4.00) from January
to mid-March, 36*s.* a month ($6.00) from April to October, and 24*s.*
($4.00) a month from December to March. In 1788, John Hill's contract
with David Hoyt of Deerfield fixed his monthly wages at $11.67 in
spring and summer, $6.67 in fall, and $5.00 in winter. James Bean, Jr.,
worked for Samuel Plumer of Epping, New Hampshire, for $10.00 a
month from April to December of 1805 and for $6.00 a month from

27. Atack and Bateman, *To Their Own Soil,* 153.
28. See Bateman, "Labor Inputs and Productivity in American Dairy Agriculture." There is
some question about gender roles in dairy farming. Didwell and Falconer, in *History of Agriculture,*
quote the following passage from a tract published by the Western Reserve Historical Society:
"Except in a Yankee family, no man or boy could be induced to milk the cows, it being regarded
as woman's work. But wherever a New Englander was found he and the boys did the 'pailing' of
the cows" (p. 163). On the other hand, I have found only two references in Massachusetts farm
account books to men milking (although it may be the case that "chores," of which milking was
one, were sufficiently taken for granted not to be entered in account books). Schob quotes *The
Prairie Farmer:* "If the hands had worked hard and well [at harvesting] they were not expected to
milk the cows prior to dinner" (*Hired Hands and Plowboys,* 93). Then men in the Midwest *did* do
the milking.
     The following passage, written by Henry Colman in 1839, suggests that the confusion we
find in the sources may be due to a *change over time in gender roles:* "Thirty years ago it would
have been almost as difficult to find a man milking as to find a woman mowing, excepting in cases
of very large dairies. In this respect matters are greatly changed; and any hope, for aught we see,
of getting back to the old practice, would be vain. Half of the young girls now-a-days hardly know,
at least they would pretend that it would be immodest and not at all lady-like to be presumed to
know, whether milk comes from the udder or the horns" (*New England Farmer* 18 [14 August
1839]: 50, quoted in Kelsey, ed., *Farming in the New Nation,* 18).

December to the following April. William Till worked for Charles Phelps, Jr., of Hadley for $6.00 a month between January and April of 1811 and $11.50 a month from May to November. William Rice worked a year for Phelps in 1814 for $14.00 a month from April to November, $10.00 a month from November to January, and $12.00 a month from January to March. In Plymouth, Michael Jacobs in 1847 agreed to pay Henry Barns $8.00 for the month of October and $6.00 for each of the following five winter months. William Dowd, who worked faithfully for William Odiorne of Billerica twelve months a year from 1848 to 1853, was paid $14.00 a month from April to November and $8.00 a month from December to March.

Long-term contracts like these, which wrote season-specific wages into their very terms, appear to have been rare: 90 percent of the seventy-seven nine- to twelve-month contracts in my sample stipulated a flat monthly rate across the year.[29] But it is clear that some of the most interesting issues raised by monthly contracts are to be found in the way they impinge on the complex structure of wage differentials.

III. Wage Differentials Between Contract and Day Labor

The structure of day wages in antebellum Massachusetts agriculture rested, I argued in chapter 6, on stratification by task. The connection between task and season in farming is so intimate that it may be difficult to disentangle them, but that there is a distinction worth making between them is seen by comparing July/August day wages for nonharvest work with July/August day wages for harvest work (i.e., mowing, haying, and reaping). Holding season constant in this way, wages for harvest work were on the average 30 percent higher.[30]

---

29. But a seasonal differential may be implicit even in a flat monthly rate: workers earn a wage below their marginal revenue product ("the insurance premium") in season and above it ("the indemnity") off-season.

Engerman and Goldin assume that the flat monthly wage is a weighted average of the seasonal wage and the off-season wage. Assuming the season to be six months, then "$M_A = .5M_S + .5M_{NS}$, where M_A is the average monthly wage on an annual contract, M_S is the average monthly wage for seasonal labor, and M_{NS} is the implicit average monthly wage during the off season" ("Seasonality in Nineteenth Century Labor Markets," p. 7 and table 2, pt. B).

From the seasonal premia expressly written into annual contracts, however, it is clear that farmers often thought in terms of three seasons, not two, the length of which varied from season to season and from farmer to farmer.

30. A further illustration of the need to distinguish between season and task concerns wages for the month of June. June is of course a summer month, but the dominant tasks done in June

Overlaying the season- and task-specific structure of farm wages was still a third pattern: the differentials between day wages and monthly per diem wages. It is to this that we now turn our attention.

That the per diem wage of workers on monthly contracts was considerably below the daily wage of day workers is well known, and much—though not all—of the gap is easily explained. Since as a rule contract workers lived with the farm family, it was understood that they received part of their wages in room, board, washing, and mending (and, on occasion, clothing, boots, militia training days and election days off, and the use of a horse for a visit home), while day workers "found" for themselves.[31] To make day wages and live-in wages comparable, researchers have valued the income in kind that contract workers receive at approximately 50 percent of their money wages.[32]

But multiplying monthly wages by a factor of 1.50 hardly closes the gap between contract and day wages. The actual differential between (nonharvest) day wages and monthly per diems was on average 1.80 (see table 22 col. 4), suggesting that more than the imputed cost of room and board separated the per day wages of day labor and contract labor.

---

were all low-paying—hoeing, half-hilling, weeding, and picking corn. For the purpose of calculating the harvest premium, to include June with July and August will bias the differential downward.

31. Schob gives this staggering description of a day's food consumed by hired hands on a midwestern farm: "For Breakfast—Coffee or tea, with cream and sugar, just as much as is desired. Fried bacon, and in the season, eggs always. Cold beef or hash, or perhaps fish, and often fresh meat. Irish or sweet potatoes, good butter and plenty of it; cheese, ditto; pickles, stewed dried fruit, light and white flour bread, cornbread, or hot cakes, hot biscuit, often pies or cakes. For Dinner Coffee, sweet milk, or sour, or buttermilk, as may be preferred. Boiled pork, beef, potatoes, turnips, cabbages, beets, &c. White loaf bread and butter, cheese, pickles, stewed fruit, and almost always pie or pastry. Supper—The cold meats and vegetables from dinner, or perhaps a hot dish of meats or fish, or some broiled chickens, and coffee or tea, or course, with bread, as before, to which add a little 'tea cake'. At each meal, all the condiments and provocatives of appetite, such as mustard, catchup vinegar, pepper, salt, pickles, &c, are usually on the table. During harvest time, a lunch in the forenoon and afternoon, of cold meats or fowls, with fresh wheaten loaves or biscuits, cakes or pies, and often accompanied by hot coffee, with cream and sugar, always as a matter of course" (quoted from the *American Agriculturist* in Schob, *Hired Hands and Plowboys,* 97).

32. In the data base for his study of the Ward Farm laborers ("'Labor Is the Great Thing in Farming'"), Larkin multiplied monthly wages by a factor of 1.5 to account for the imputed value of room and board. Earle and Hoffman adjusted monthly live-in wages by a factor of 1.33–1.45 ("The Foundation of the Modern Economy," 1069). The Department of Agriculture series on farm wages per month, 1866–1927, showed a slight but steady decline in the difference between with and without board, from 54 to 41 percent and averaging 44 percent over the period (Bureau of Labor Statistics, *History of Wages in the United States From Colonial Times to 1928,* table D-2, p. 227).

Tables 21 and 22 will suggest that part of the unexplained differential is a seasonal premium, part is a harvest premium—neither of which is fully captured by monthly wages—and, I will suggest, part reflects the working of a dual labor market in Massachusetts agriculture.

Table 21 aggregates to the level of decadal averages two sets of wage data that I have collected from farm account books: monthly per diems (i.e., monthly wages divided by twenty-six working days per month) from the sample of labor contracts and over thirty-two hundred day wages that formed the data base for the study of day labor in chapter 6.[33] Day wages for the tasks of mowing, reaping, and haying were averaged together and entered as "harvest wages" in July and August of the year in which they were observed. Nonharvest day wages are the day wages for all other tasks and were entered in the month and year in which they were observed (see table 21).

In table 22, the monthly data from table 21 are aggregated, and the ratios are calculated that define the overlying pattern of wage differentials. The ratio of day wages (for nonharvest tasks) to monthly per diems (which might be called the day-labor premium) averaged 1.8; the ratio of harvest day wages to nonharvest day wages (the harvest premium) averaged 1.3; the ratio of harvest day wages to monthly per diems (which might be called the spot-market premium) average 2.3. And the seasonal premium—the ratio of peak-season wages to trough-season wages—averaged 1.3 for contract workers and 1.6 for day labor doing nonharvest tasks. Of all these, the only differential that narrowed during the antebellum period was the seasonal differential for contract workers, from 1.5 in the 1770s to 1.1 in the 1840s (see table 22).

If decomposing the differential into its several components explains its magnitude, it does not explain its persistence. Why did wage differentials so lavishly favoring day workers persist for ten decades? Was it more difficult to recruit day workers than contract workers? Did day workers, residing off the farm, have to be compensated for travel costs? for the costs of job search? for leaving their own farms? for bearing the brunt of seasonal unemployment? Or does the persistence of the differential owe something to group characteristics that distinguish between

33. Of the sample of 692 monthly contracts, 553 were fully described; i.e., the account books gave monthly wage, year, starting month, and duration of the contract. In preparing table 21, the monthly per diems were entered for each month for the duration of each of the 553 contracts. In the few cases where wage and starting month were given but duration was not, the wage was applied to the starting month only. In cases of sudden quits, the monthly per diems were entered for the duration of the contract since it is the intentions of the parties to the process of setting wage differentials that interest us here.

Table 21 The Seasonality of Farm Wages, Massachusetts, 1760s–1850s: Day Wages of Contract Workers, Day Workers, and Harvest Workers (decadal averages, in dollars)

Years and Category	Jan.	Feb.	Mar.	Apr.	May	June	July	Aug.	Sep.	Oct.	Nov.	Dec.
1764–69 (N = 17):												
Monthly per diem	.199	.199	.207	.208	.209	.205	.205	.205	.205	.203	.195	.188
Day work	.360	.338	.330	.385	.412	.418	.415	.424	.367	.380	.434	.468
Harvest							.455	.455				
1770–79 (N = 10):												
Monthly per diem	.158	.161	.151	.224	.241	.238	.238	.238	.234	.217	.187	.187
Day work	.330	.365	.358	.398	.393	.396	.436	.388	.411	.384	n.a.	.388
Harvest							.484	.484				
1780–89 (N = 16):												
Monthly per diem	.187	.197	.251	.245	.246	.249	.255	.262	.238	.231	.205	.188
Day work	.330	.290	.383	.499	.437	.404	.423	.417	.330	.260	.520	.415
Harvest							.493	.493				
1790–99 (N = 36):												
Monthly per diem	.208	.208	.243	.241	.250	.246	.272	.263	.258	.241	.200	.216
Day work	.323	.375	.427	.439	.437	.460	.504	.538	.531	.386	.476	.382
Harvest							.589	.589				
1800–1809 (N = 77):												
Monthly per diem	.273	.270	.302	.351	.351	.369	.365	.357	.351	.342	.318	.295
Day work	.432	.531	.532	.569	.531	.571	.653	.572	.611	.490	.464	.528
Harvest							.700	.700				
1810–19 (N = 95):												
Monthly per diem	.332	.341	.328	.366	.391	.395	.403	.401	.397	.371	.383	.360
Day work	.606	.594	.658	.633	.678	.731	.796	.828	.711	.687	.645	.621
Harvest							.919	.919				

Table 21 (Continued)

Years and Category	Jan.	Feb.	Mar.	Apr.	May	June	July	Aug.	Sep.	Oct.	Nov.	Dec.
1820–29 (N = 89):												
Monthly per diem	.303	.319	.331	.362	.370	.361	.356	.359	.355	.344	.317	.328
Day work	.700	.563	.655	.684	.667	.625	.718	.698	.593	.610	.624	.666
Harvest							.867	.867				
1830–39 (N = 63):												
Monthly per diem	.354	.382	.379	.407	.429	.443	.445	.455	.436	.453	.383	.368
Day work	.681	.635	.563	.704	.716	.762	.880	.695	.701	.678	.746	.730
Harvest							.991	.991				
1840–49 (N = 102):												
Monthly per diem	.457	.463	.462	.483	.491	.501	.507	.498	.493	.503	.505	.453
Day work	.604	.612	.767	.750	.762	.802	.901	1.00	.859	.778	.760	.695
Harvest							1.03	1.03				
1850–59 (N = 48):												
Monthly per diem	.360	.348	.383	.490	.502	.502	.501	.502	.487	.478	.424	.375
Day work	.645	.700	.855	1.25	.855	.830	.950	1.06	1.08	.821	.500	.835
Harvest							1.15	1.15				

Sources: Day wages and monthly contract wages are from Rothenberg sample farm account books. (see chap. 3, Appendix A).

Note: "Monthly per diem" is a decadal average of contract wages per month, divided by twenty-six, which have been entered for every month of each contract. "Day work" is a decadal average of the wages paid to day workers for all tasks other than haying, reaping, and mowing, for the month in which it appears in this table. "Harvest" is a decadal average of the wages for the tasks of mowing, haying, and reaping only and performed by day workers in July and August. *N* is the number of fully specified contracts stipulating year, starting month, duration, and wage. The total number of such contracts is 553.

Table 22 Measuring Harvest, Seasonal, and Day Wage Differentials 1760s–1850s, by Decade (wages in dollars per day)

				Harvest Premium		Seasonal Premium	
Years	Average Monthly per Diem (1)	Average Nonharvest Day Wage (2)	Average Harvest Day Wage (3)	Day Wage Premium over Monthly per Diems [2]/[11] (4)	Harvest Wages over Nonharvest Day Wages [3]/[2] (5)	Harvest Wages over Monthly per diems [3]/[11] (6)	High Month/Low Month: Nonharvest Day Wages (7)	High Month/Low Month: Monthly per diems (8)
1764–69	.202	.394	.455	1.95	1.15	2.25	1.42	1.11
1770–79	.207	.387	.484	1.87	1.25	2.34	1.32	1.53
1780–89	.230	.392	.493	1.70	1.26	2.14	1.92	1.40
1790–99	.237	.440	.589	1.86	1.34	2.49	1.67	1.36
1800–1809	.329	.540	.700	1.64	1.30	2.13	1.51	1.37
1810–19	.372	.682	.919	1.83	1.35	2.47	1.39	1.23
1820–29	.342	.650	.867	1.90	1.33	2.54	1.28	1.22
1830–39	.411	.708	.991	1.72	1.40	2.41	1.56	1.29
1840–49	.485	.774	1.03	1.60	1.33	2.12	1.63	1.12
1850–59	.446	.866	1.15	1.94	1.32	2.57	2.50	1.44
Means				1.80	1.30	2.35	1.62	1.31

Source: Table 21.

Note: Column 1 is based on per month wages for contract labor divided by twenty-six. Monthly per diems were entered for every month for the anticipated duration of each contract, even in the case of sudden quits. Column 2 is based on day wages for all tasks except haying, mowing, and reaping. Column 3 is based on day wages for haying, mowing, and reaping.

the populations of day and monthly workers and are relevant to their respective productivities?

In the next section, a case study will cast light on the proposition that the persistence of wage differentials not otherwise explained between day and monthly workers testifies to a considerable degree of segmentation in the farm labor market.

IV. THE COMPARATIVE DEMOGRAPHICS OF FARM LABORERS: THE CASE OF THE WARD FARM

The Ward Farm in Shrewsbury, Massachusetts, used a great deal of both day and contract labor over the period 1787 to 1890. Each of those workers has been identified at Old Sturbridge Village by linking them to tax, census, and genealogical records. Table 23 summarizes personal characteristics of the two groups by decade, from 1787 to 1866.[34] Comparisons with respect to age, marital status, and place of birth strongly support the conclusion that these two segments of the farm labor force were being drawn from two quite different populations, in which case some of the differential, or at any rate its persistence, may be explained as the working of a dual labor market.[35]

When observations for the whole period are pooled, half the day laborers, but only one-quarter of the contract laborers, were born in Shrewsbury. The proportion of foreign born among the contract workers was twice that of day workers. The average age of day workers was 41.6 years (several men were in their seventies), while the average age

---

34. Property holdings may be as important as place of birth, marital status, and age in describing these two populations. In fact, the Wards' day laborers were poor: one-third were without property in the 1790s, over half in the 1800s, over two-thirds in the 1810s, and all were propertyless in the 1820s and again in the 1850s (Larkin, "'Labor Is the Great Thing in Farming,'" 205).

In this respect, too, the day laborers' status was as ambiguous in nineteenth-century Shrewsbury as in early modern England, where day laborers were at the very bottom of the agricultural ladder, were not trusted with the master's horses, seldom climbed out of laborer status, and yet were looked to for special skills. According to Kussmaul, in *Servants in Husbandry in Early Modern England*, "The hierarchy of farmworkers ran from the farmer's sons down to servants [in husbandry] and finally to [day] labourers. . . . To be a servant was to be a potential farmer, but to be a labourer was to be a realized failure" (p. 80). On the other hand, she notes elsewhere that "skilled . . . work continued to be done by day-labourers" (p. 101).

35. I do not intend, by the use of the term *dual labor market*, to engage in a political controversy over whether the market for rural labor "worked," in the neoclassical sense. After all, unlike race, ethnicity, gender, and educational deficits, the contract workers who were too young, too single, too uprooted, and too Irish or Acadian would in time become as old, as married, and as "American" as better-paid workers. Nevertheless, in the short run they were identifiable as having more limited options.

Table 23 Comparative Demographics of Contract and Day Workers on the Ward Farm, 1787–1866

Decade	No. of Observations	Age	Married	Single	Place of Birth				
					Shrewsbury	Within 15 miles of Shrewsbury	Mass.	Native Born, Out of Mass.	Foreign Born
Contract workers:									
1787–96	18	23.0	0	13	9	3	3	0	0
1797–1806	14	27.5	2	6	1	7	3	0	1
1807–16	36	25.9	4	16	14	9	4	0	0
1817–26	66	21.4	2	38	23	18	8	2	4
1827–36	49	23.4	4	25	3	5	16	3	14
1837–46	20	28.7	2	5	0	1	12	0	4
1847–56	26	31.1	3	15	0	2	6	6	5
1857–66	29	30.6	5	13	1	3	2	5	13
Day workers:									
1787–96	59	37.5	47	6	34	2	7	1	6
1797–1806	71	38.5	66	3	27	12	10	1	18
1807–16	67	36.6	42	22	37	14	13	0	1
1817–26	138	42.4	54	43	76	17	29	2	3
1827–36	144	40.0	109	30	69	16	35	4	5
1837–46	74	42.4	62	6	19	9	30	3	6
1847–56	56	45.2	44	6	17	5	17	7	7
1857–66	59	50.5	40	6	12	2	3	20	11

Source: Ward Farm Laborers' File, Old Sturbridge Village. Courtesy of Jack Larkin.
Note: Summing across marital status, or across place of birth, often does not equal the number of observations because of missing information.

of contract workers was only 26.5 years.[36] Over 80 percent of the day
workers were married, while over 86 percent of the contract workers
were unmarried.

But the period should not be treated as a whole, for the distinctions
between these two groups of farm workers changed over time, and 1830
was a turning point. Before 1830, nearly 70 percent of contract workers
came from within twenty miles of Shrewsbury; after 1830, less than 10
percent did. Before 1830, whatever foreign born there were came from
England and Scotland; after 1830, the foreign born came from Ireland
and French Canada. After 1830, the rate of sudden quits rose from 16
to 33 percent. After 1830, we see not only segmentation but perverse
segmentation, by which I mean that irregular day work was being done
by men born and rooted in the community, while the steady, live-in work
was being done, increasingly over time, by "travel-weathered men from
much further away, most of them culturally alien, more migratory but
less hopeful," transients, migrants, passersby who "come here to work,"
hired in the case of the Wards, quite literally, off the road.[37]

Arrangements with such men frequently began cautiously, condi-

---

36. Seven contract workers and eight day workers were boys under sixteen years of age; the
youngest, a day worker, was eleven. The reasons in 1836 for "putting out" young George Homer,
age twelve, to work for the Wards for thirty-five months may have been the same as those in
Plymouth two centuries earlier: to teach him to read and write and an artisan skill, "to bring him
up in his imploymt of husbandry," to remove him from an impoverished home, or to be his guardian
if he had been orphaned (see Demos, *A Little Commonwealth;* the quote is from p. 71).

While I do not know how George Homer fared in the Ward household, there are some hints
about the effectiveness of such apprenticeships to be gleaned from the day book of Jabez B. Low,
a farmer and comb maker of Leominster, Massachusetts, in the manuscript collection at Old Sturbridge Village.

"1813 November the 19: Phineas Prowty come to live with me and will be 15 years in february Next the 15 day. 1815, Febr 4: the above Phineas went from School. and I know not whare.

"1815 June 21: Elize Chandler Come to live with me and was 8 years old th 12 of April Last.
1818 Decr 16: Elize Chandler Left my house & hath not Returned.

"1820 June 19: Persis Warner come to live with me & was 13 years old the 24 of Febr Last.
November 18: Carried Persis to hir Fathers & Left hir.

"1830 Septr 7th: Andrew Low Left my house when I was gone to Albany and without a
justifiable cause."

37. Larkin, " 'Labor Is the Great Thing in Farming,' " 218. Dual labor market theory distinguishes between primary and secondary labor markets, the primary composed of better jobs, the
secondary composed of low-paying jobs "held by workers who have unstable working patterns"
(Cain, "The Challenge of Segmented Labor Market Theories to Orthodox Theory," 1222). "There
are distinctions between workers in the two sectors which *parallel* those between jobs" (Doeringer
and Piore, *Internal Labor Markets and Manpower Analysis,* 65; emphasis added). In calling the
market for rural labor after 1830 *perversely segmented,* I wish to make the point that the distinctions between workers' characteristics in the two sectors (i.e., between daily and monthly laborers)
after 1830 did *not* parallel those between the jobs.

tionally, "as long as I want him," "no stated time agreed upon to stay," with the first month a probationary period at a lower wage, to be regularized "if he live with me a year," "if I want so long," "if we like," "if he is faithful and learns to work well."[38] Many of them did not. In my sample, there are sixty-eight instances of sudden quits, just about 10 percent of total contracts. In August 1820, Samuel Plumer of Epping, New Hampshire, hired one worker on contract who quit after eight days, another in September who quit after two weeks, another in November who quit after four days, and another the following January to work through the winter who left before the month was out.

From a broad perspective one might well ask, "How much of observed, voluntary turnover [i.e., quitting] reflects opportunism and how much of it is the rational outcome of moving workers from lower to higher valued uses?"[39] Merely to raise the question, even if it cannot be answered, suggests that, with "higher-valued" opportunities opening up outside farming, there was a pronounced change in the quality of those who remained.[40] The deterioration would be particularly pronounced in the pool of full-time farm workers.

If day workers and monthly farm laborers were indeed drawn from two increasingly different populations, it might be possible, even in the socially fluid society of antebellum America, to confirm that fact in their subsequent careers. What follows is an admittedly preliminary attempt to discover what became of them by linking some of the contract workers in my sample and in the Ward file to the 1850 federal Manuscript Census.[41]

38. Back-end loading—"the worker gets less than his marginal product at date 0 and at least his marginal product at date 1"—was clearly a defense against worker quits. "One may ask why the contract cannot specify either that a worker cannot quit at all, or (less extremely) that a quitting worker must compensate the firm by paying an 'exit fee' " (Hart and Holmstrom, "The Theory of Contracts," 111). Instead, as has been said repeatedly in this chapter, quitting workers were apparently paid in *quantum meruit*.

39. Rosen, "Implicit Contracts," 1170.

40. Whaling, too, suffered after 1820 from the deterioration in the quality of crews when alternatives ashore became more attractive. It is estimated that productivity in whaling fell 0.3 points between 1820 and 1860 as a consequence of a fifty two-point increase in wages ashore (see Davis, Gallman, and Hutchins, "Productivity in Whaling," 136).

41. The effort to link names in Massachusetts records is always subject to error because the long tradition of necronyms, patronyms, and Bible-naming patterns seriously limited the pool of first names and because two hundred years of very little immigration or in-migration seriously limited the pool of last names. There are not only a large number of John Hunts and William Johnsons but several Ithamar Wards (see Smith, "Child-Naming Patterns and Family Structure Change"). Second, tracing individuals to the 1850 Manuscript Census requires truncating the sample on both ends. Farm workers who appeared as adults in the sample before 1800 are unlikely to be alive in 1850, and those who first appear in the sample around 1850 are beside the point.

Table 24 traces some of the monthly laborers of several major employers of contract labor: the Wards of Shrewsbury, a group of several
farmers in Deerfield, Charles Phelps of Hadley, David Goodale of Marlborough, and an anonymous "market gardener" in West Cambridge
(now Arlington). By 1850, 92 percent of the contract workers who had
worked on the Ward farm in the four or five preceding decades had left
Shrewsbury; 88 percent of Phelps's monthly workers had left Hadley;
96 percent of the men who worked on contract for Deerfield farmers had
left Deerfield; and 68 percent of David Goodale's monthly workers had
left Marlborough. Perhaps because of its access to major urban places,
only 43 percent of the men who worked on contract for the market
gardener in West Cambridge had left town by 1850, and some of these
were found nearby in Cambridge, Brookline, and Boston. Nearly half
the men who had worked on contract in Deerfield and Shrewsbury not
only had left town and county but could not be found in Massachusetts
by 1850.

Segmentation in the farm labor force, then, may have played a role
in explaining the persistence of pay differentials between day and
monthly workers.

V. CONCLUSION: EVIDENCE OF STRUCTURAL CHANGE IN THE FARM LABOR FORCE

Is there evidence of a shift to contract labor—what I term here *structural
change*—in the proportions of day and monthly labor used on Massachusetts farms? How much contract labor was used? How much day
labor? How did this change over time? To argue from a small sample of
account books to the farm population as a whole may raise the issues of
sample bias we discussed briefly in chapter 5, but the experiences
of individual farmers are instructive.

Charles Phelps, Jr., of Hadley, David Goodale of Marlborough, and
the Ward family of Shrewsbury all used large amounts of hired labor. In
the case of Phelps and Goodale, it is possible to count man-days of
monthly labor (number of contract months multiplied by twenty-six
working days per month) and man-days of day labor recorded in their
books. In the case of the Ward farm, the number of men hired (both by
the day and by the month) is in the data base compiled at Old Sturbridge
Village, as is the number of man-months worked by contract labor, but
unfortunately the number of days worked by day labor is not. However,
with the Ward data it is possible to infer the relative magnitudes of day

Table 24 Tracing Monthly Contract Workers to 1850

	Source, Town, and County				
	Ward File, Shrewsbury, Worcester Cty.	Deerfield Farmers, Deerfield, Hamps./Franklin Cty.	Charles Phelps, Hadley, Hampshire Cty.	David Goodale, Marlborough, Middlesex Cty.	Anonymous Market Gardener, West Cambridge, Middlesex Cty.
No. of names searched	50	80	34	31	21
Period of their contracts	1825–50	1800–1849	1805–30	1820–47	1836–43
No. who left Mass.	22	39	9	5	2
% who left Mass.	44	49	26	16	9.5
No. in Mass. but left county	9	16	14	13	3
No. in county but left town	15	22	7	3	4
% who left town	92	96	88	68	43
No. remaining in town	4	3	4	10	12
No. in town with no real estate	3	2	0	3	3

Sources: Ward Family Farm Laborers' File (Old Sturbridge Village, courtesy of Jack Larkin), Rothenberg sample of farm account books, and 1850 Manuscript Census.

and monthly labor from the share of each in the farm's total wage bill (see table 25).

For all three farmers, day workers exceeded contract workers in terms of the number of laborers hired, but contract labor quite overwhelmed day labor in terms of man-days hired. In most of the years between 1787 and 1890, the Ward farm expended more than 75 percent of its total wage bill on monthly labor. In most of the twenty-one years for which I have Phelps's records, he employed at least four times—and in 1815 eighteen times—as many man-days of contract labor as of day labor. Goodale relied even more heavily on contracts, using over ten times as many man-days of monthly as of daily labor in ten of the twenty-eight years covered by his accounts, climaxing in 1835 when he hired 143 man-days of monthly labor and only one day of day labor.

Persuasive as these numbers may be, day labor, although relatively expensive,never disappeared. Every farm account book bears witness to the use of labor hired by the day either to do unspecified "work" or for specified farm tasks. And every farmer relied on gangs of day laborers to bring in his hay. William Odiorne of Billerica, for example, had two workers on annual contract but in 1848 hired ninety man-days of day labor for the haying. Although the mix on individual farms was erratic, day labor remained important even as late as 1890.

The introduction of contract labor roughly coincided with the upturn in agricultural labor productivity that I have dated, in chapter 6, to the late 1780s. That there may have been a relation between productivity growth and the introduction of contract labor cannot be established with certainty, but contract labor may at least be understood as a way of restructuring the farm enterprise in time, analogous to restructuring the farm in space that became central to the agricultural reform movement of the antebellum years.[42] Contract workers do to time what connected farm buildings do to space: they bridge the diverse activities of mixed farming, dairying, home manufactures, and artisanal by-employments and shelter the coming and going between them from inclemencies of market as from inclemencies of weather. "Connected farm buildings were the manifestation of a powerful will to succeed by farming,"[43] and the commitment a farmer makes when he hires a young man to live and

42. For new research on the relation between the reform impulse and changes in farm space, see Synenki, ed., *Archeological Investigations of Minute Man National Historical Park,* vol. 1; and Larkin, "From 'Country Mediocrity' to 'Rural Improvement.' "

43. Hubka, *Big House, Little House, Back House, Barn,* 180.

Table 25   Monthly Labor as a Share of Total Labor on Three Massachusetts Farms

Years	Ward Farm, Shrewsbury, Share of Total Wage Bill Expended Annually for Contract Labor
1790–94	.82
1795–99	.74
1800–1804	.47
1805–9	.92
1810–14	.88
1815–19	.76
1820–24	.71
1825–29	.68
1830–34	.78
1835–39	.88
1840–44	.45
1845–49	.79
1850–54	.81
1855–60	.54

Years	Phelps Farm, Hadley, Man-Days of Contract Labor Hired Annually, as Share of Total Man-Days Hired
1805	416/463 = .90
1806	728/781 = .93
1807	364/431 = .84
1808	572/609 = .94
1809	728/789 = .92
1810	676/780 = .87
1811	832/916 = .91
1812	936/1,023 = .91
1813	572/678 = .84
1814	286/457 = .63
1815	468/494 = .95
1829	0/96 = .00
1830	307/372 = .83
1831	226/285 = .79
1836	0/90 = .00
1837	130/498 = .26
1838	224/284 = .79
1851	130/344 = .38
1852	260/448 = .58
1853	442/668 = .66
1854	234/352 = .66

Years	Goodale Farm, Marlborough, Man-Days of Contract Labor Hired Annually, as Share of Total Man-Days Hired
1819	0/2 = .00
1821	0/1 = .00
1822	0/9 = .00
1823	0/24 = .00
1824	52/107 = .49
1825	104/127 = .82
1826	227/246 = .92
1827	234/244 = .96
1828	117/136 = .86
1829	156/165 = .95
1830	299/312 = .96
1831	390/405 = .96
1832	370/386 = .96
1833	208/219 = .95
1834	357/368 = .97
1835	143/144 = .99
1836	188/191 = .98
1837	0/10 = .00
1838	139/160 = .87
1839	130/244 = .53
1840	182/341 = .53
1841	182/298 = .61

Sources: Ward Family Farm Laborers' File (Old Sturbridge Village, courtesy of Jack Larkin). Account books of Phelps and Goodale.

Note: Share of wage bill was used for the Ward farm because man-days of day labor are not available. The wage bill for monthly contract labor was adjusted (by Jack Larkin) by multiplying by 1.5 to include the imputed cost of room and board.

work with him for five or six months a year is likewise a "manifestation of a powerful will to succeed by farming." The live-in worker is likewise a connection, available "at the will of the lord," "to take and do one sort of Business as well as another, whether Husbandry or Carpenters, or whatever I have to be done, that he is able to do; and to be as handy and helpfull as he can in the Family also."[44]

44. From Walett, ed., *The Diary of Ebenezer Parkman*, 26 March 1736.

8

Productivity Growth in Massachusetts Agriculture: The Testimony of the Tax Valuations of 1771–1801

IN THIS STUDY THE EMERGENCE OF A MARKET ECONOMY HAS BEEN examined both for its own sake and because it lies at the origins of the capitalist transformation of rural Massachusetts. In this context, *capitalist transformation* means a reallocation of resources to achieve, within agriculture, a rate of productivity growth sufficient to sustain the exodus of resources from it in pursuit of higher returns elsewhere. Having devoted most of the preceding pages to developing the diagnostics with which to date the onset of market function, this chapter looks to a new archive, town tax valuations, to seek evidence that the market integration thus achieved was indeed related to the transformation of the rural economy.

I

Two decades ago, Peter Temin proposed a simple two-sector model to expose a logical fallacy in the labor-scarcity thesis.[1] If land is "free," he wrote, then "farmers will find themselves with more land than before, which they will use to produce agricultural products. As their workers will have more land to work, their productivity will rise. If their wages do not rise, it will pay the farmers to hire more workers. If their wages do rise, more workers will be attracted to agriculture. These new agricultural workers will come from the only other sector of the economy: manufacturing."[2] But if land is "free," then capital—no less than labor—will also be attracted to agriculture, where its productivity is enhanced by the abundance of a complementary resource. Thus, free land in American agriculture "explains" capital scarcity as well as it "explains" labor scarcity and therefore cannot motivate the capital-using bias in American manufacturing.

Implicit in Temin's argument was the assumption that the agricultural and manufacturing sectors are sufficiently alike to be treated alike, that labor and capital will shift between sectors in either direction. Useful as this model was for Temin's purpose, it ignored the central paradox of agriculture and, by ignoring it, alerts us: in the development process resources do not flow symmetrically between sectors; they do not flow

---

1. The labor-scarcity thesis holds that the capital-using, labor-saving bias in American manufacturing technology (relative to British) was driven by the high opportunity cost of labor in American agriculture, i.e., "was fundamentally because the remuneration of American industrial labour was measured by the rewards and advantages of independent agriculture" (Habakkuk, *American and British Technology in the Nineteenth Century*, 11).

2. Temin, "Labor Scarcity in America," 255, n. 5.

into agriculture in response to the rising labor productivity achieved there. The response of a developing economy to rising productivity in agriculture—and uniquely in agriculture—is an *exodus* of resources from it. It is the paradox of the development process—but no less true for being a paradox—that, while rising productivity in agriculture has been (and with the exception of oil- and mineral-rich countries still remains) the key to successful economic development, its function is to make possible the sector's declining output share.[3] Only growing productivity in agriculture can release the resources invested in it to still-more productive sectors whose growth relative to agriculture is what we mean by *economic development*. And only growing productivity within agriculture can offset the deleterious health and standard-of-living consequences of its sectoral decline.[4]

The sectoral decline of agriculture in the development process is necessary because, alone among the producing sectors in a market economy, the products of agriculture face implacable price and income inelasticities of demand. Expanded agricultural output, whatever its source, causes farm prices to fall disproportionately and the earnings of farmers to lag further and further behind the growth of output and earnings in the rest of the economy. But should agricultural prices remain high because of a failure to achieve the very productivity growth that dooms it to falling prices, the short-run advantage the sector would experience in its terms of trade would lower real incomes and impede real growth in the rest of the economy. It is the combination of productivity growth, remorselessly low price and income elasticities of demand, falling prices, worsening terms of trade, and no-better-than-constant returns to scale that drives resources out of agriculture—a sector that grows, in effect, by feeding on its own tail![5]

That process in less developed countries today is driven, for better or worse, by deliberate government policy in the areas of commodity

3. Three-quarters of the twenty-three countries that in the 1970s experienced GDP growth of over 5 percent per annum had achieved growth rates in their agricultural sectors of over 3 percent per annum. With the exception of the oil-rich and mineral-based economies, no more than 2 percentage points separated the rates of agricultural and GDP growth in the successfully developing countries in the 1970s (World Bank, *World Development Report*, 44–45, cited in Timmer, "The Agricultural Transformation," 277).

4. The quantity and quality of nutrients (especially proteins) in the diet is being discovered to be a good predictor of height, of life expectancy at age ten, of the capacity to work hard and protractedly, and of resistance to epidemic diseases. Maternal nutrition also plays a major role in the birth weight and health of infants (Fogel, "The Conquest of High Mortality and Hunger in Europe and America"; and Goldin and Margo, "The Poor at Birth," esp. 370–77).

5. I owe these very useful insights to Timmer's "The Agricultural Transformation."

pricing, manpower training, relocation, housing, tariffs and trade, taxation, and subsidization, but in Massachusetts in the late eighteenth century the arbiter of that complex process was the market. It was the market that energized the farm sector to achieve labor's first productivity
gains. It was the market that presided over the shift of resources into the
nation's first industrial sector.

The process of initiating the transformation, of "getting agriculture
moving,"[6] of kicking the system off its suboptimal equilibrium, is not
easy to observe; but once it does begin, the "Smithian" process that
relates the extent of the market to the division of labor generates a feedback process that intensifies the use of inputs, increases output, expands
markets, and—most relevant of all in premechanized agriculture—enhances what Moses Abramovitz has called "the effectiveness of labor
hours."[7] The total factor productivity growth[8] that this feedback process
made possible may well have "got agriculture moving" in Massachusetts. But how did it *begin*?

The trigger may well have been a shift in relative prices: in the late
1770s, crop prices, buoyed by wartime demand and inflation, appear to
have risen more rapidly than farm wages for the first time in nearly three
decades (see fig. 11). Perhaps in this environment of rising prices for
their products and falling "real" wages, farmers could afford to increase
their use of underemployed labor services, "calling forth and enlisting
for development purposes resources and abilities that [had lain] hidden,
scattered or badly utilized."[9] They could afford to. The question is, Did
they? Did Massachusetts farmers respond to these market signals, and
if so, how and when?

The motive and the cue for growth are first to be discovered in evidence that market outcomes informed the decisions respecting land use,
output pricing, employment, the investment of rural savings, livestock
holdings, and crop mix made individually by the approximately fifty

6. "Getting agriculture moving" is a phrase that Timmer adopts from Mosher, *Getting Agriculture Moving*.

7. Abramovitz, *Thinking About Growth*, 15.

8. The growth rate of output can be "decomposed into a portion contributed by 'total factor
input,' which was the joint contribution of labor and capital (including land), and a portion contributed by 'total factor productivity.' The first was the sum of the growth rates of the factor inputs,
each weighted by the share of its earnings in national income. The second was the difference
between the growth rate of output and that of total factor input" (ibid., 14). Depending on how this
second, "residual" portion is measured, it can be made to account for 99, 70, or 51 percent of the
growth of output per worker or for 36 (Edward Denison's estimates for the United States, 1948–
79) or 24 percent (Dale Jorgenson's estimates) of the growth of total output (ibid., 15–19).

9. Hirschman, *Rival Views of Market Society*, 56.

thousand farm households in Massachusetts in the late eighteenth century.[10] Thereafter, one looks to find a way to measure the productivity consequences of that market penetration. The studies in chapters 4, 5, 6, and 7 found evidence in micro-level sources—farm account books, day books, and probates—that the end of the revolutionary war ushered in the transition to a market economy in rural Massachusetts. Expanding market orientation was not only documented from the behavior of the relevant prices but also linked to an upturn in the time trend of labor productivity as measured—not directly (by, say, output per man-day), because data of that kind for our period are lacking, but indirectly—by the dual, an index of the "real cost of labor" to employing farmers, constructed as a ratio of a Massachusetts farm wage index to a Massachusetts farm commodity price index (see chap. 6, fig. 13).[11]

But the inquiry should not be left there. For one thing, it matters to the interpretation of the "real cost of labor index" whether its rise after 1785 is due to a rise of the productivity wage in the numerator or to a decline of the commodity price index in the denominator. Even in highly evolved markets, structural changes—for example, lower transport costs—may have asymmetrical effects (at least in the short run): a significant effect on farm prices but little if any on farm wages. This would compromise our interpretation of movements in the ratio between them. But even more to the point, the question—the timing of the productivity upturn in preindustrial Massachusetts—is of such critical importance to estimates of the pace of early American economic growth that it should not be left to hang on a dual. If it really happened, if Massachusetts farmers—presumably for the first time—experienced increasing output per worker, that fact (or its observable correlates) should show up in the behavior of farmers.

10. I arrive at this estimate of fifty thousand as follows: the surviving records of thirty-eight thousand ratable polls (nonexempt males age sixteen and over) in 1771 are estimated by Bettye Hobbs Pruitt, editor of the 1771 tax valuation list, to constitute two-thirds of the taxable adult males, of which approximately 90 percent were "engaged in agriculture." I am deeply indebted to Dr. Pruitt for sharing with me the data for her pioneering analysis of the 1771 valuation list.

11. "Movements of real wages—defining real wages as money wage rates divided by a cost-of-living index—are not, of course an appropriate indicator of the trend in the marginal physical productivity of labor employed in a particular sector or industry. What is relevant, assuming competitive or consistently imperfect product and labor market conditions, is the real cost of labor to employers in the industry under consideration; real wages received by farm workers could change merely as a result of changes in the farmer-employers' terms of trade with the rest of the economy, without any alteration in marginal labor productivity having taken place. Thus, for the present purpose, the relevant wage-deflator is an index of the prices received by farmers for those commodities in whose production hired labor was used" (David, "The Growth of Real Product in the United States before 1840," 179–80).

The studies in this chapter experiment with the use of *macro*-level sources that we have not heretofore exploited to confirm the turning point observed in the labor productivity index (fig. 13 in chap. 6) and to make more robust the case for the onset of productivity growth in Massachusetts agriculture before 1800. Aggregate data from town tax valuations of 1771, 1786, 1792, and 1801 will be used to test the following propositions.[12] (1) A significant improvement in Massachusetts agriculture can be confirmed from expanded output, diversification of crop mix, shift in land use, improved per acre yields, and increased emphasis on animal husbandry, all by 1800. (2) Growth in this agriculture was accompanied by the intersectoral shift of capital into commerce, banking, and infrastructure investments as required by the development process. (3) Widening differences in rates of productivity growth exacerbate income inequalities within the rural economy, with serious political consequences. The 1786 tax valuations allow us to understand Shays' Rebellion in these terms.

II

The case for increased output and improved yields is made in table 26, where aggregate magnitudes are compared across tax valuations from 1771 to 1801. It should be acknowledged at the outset that intertemporal comparisons of tax lists are as problematic as intercensal comparisons. Much of the 1771 list has not survived, and part of what has survived is illegible. Many of the categories of taxable wealth are incommensurable across time: in 1786, no outputs (except cider) were taxed, and consequently no outputs (except cider) were enumerated; sheep and goats (of which over 115,000 were counted in 1771) were counted but not taxed in 1786, and not counted in 1792 and 1801, so that total livestock holdings cannot be compared across time; the age at which animals became taxable (and therefore enumerated) and the categories into which they were grouped changed from valuation to valuation; and the fact that valuations differed respecting the month in which property was assessed much affects the number of animals found on farms.[13] "Dooming"—that is, underreporting, tax evasion, and the systematic downgrading of land quality—although heavily penalized at the time, was extensive, particularly in the valuation for 1786, a depression year. The ubiquity of out-pasturing from valley farms to hill towns renders town pasture

12. The data are available on request from the author.
13. Garrison, "Farm Dynamics and Regional Exchange," 5.

Table 26   Improvements in Agriculture, 1771–1801

	Date of Tax Valuation			1771–1801, % Change
	1771	1792	1801	
No. of towns[a]	122	239	263	
Polls, ratable and unratable[b]	34,648	79,949	87,842	+154
Tillage, acres	99,280	191,802	208,822	+110
Combined grains (bushels)[c]	1,044,588	2,432,802	2,505,338	+140
Bushels of grain per acre tillage	10.5	12.7	12.0	+14
English/upland mowing (acres)	94,121	195,429	257,214	+173
English/upland hay (tons)	65,148	139,707	190,412	+192
No. of grazing animals	98,216	219,167	251,165	+156
Tons of English hay per grazing animal	.66	.64	.76	+15
Tons of English hay per acre mowing	.69	.71	.74	+7
Fresh meadow and salt marsh (acres)	99,445	169,899	220,657	+122
Fresh meadow (acres)	82,896	140,609	190,149	+129
Salt marsh (acres)	16,534	29,190	30,508	+85
Fresh and salt hay (tons)	53,168	147,279	167,531	+215
Tons fresh/salt hay per grazing animal	.54	.67	.67	+24
Tons fresh/salt hay per acre meadow	.53	.87	.76	+43
Pasture (acres)	200,934	568,534	751,128	+274
No. of cows pasture will "keep"	76,174	275,862	236,700	+211
No. of cows one acre pasture can keep	.38	.49	.32	−17
No. of neat cattle[d]	81,473	185,820	205,140	+152
No. of horses	16,743	33,447	46,025	+175
No. of swine	46,176	80,248	84,949	+84
No. of sheep and goats	115,079	N.A.	N.A.	. . .
No. of total livestock[e]	144,392	299,515	336,114	+133

[a] In addition to the 1771 town valuations that did not survive or are illegible, the towns in Maine, Cape Cod, Nantucket, and Martha's Vineyard are omitted from this table, as they are from this study as a whole.

[b] Includes taxable males sixteen to twenty-one years of age, taxable males twenty-one years of age and older, male polls exempt from tax but not supported by the town (the governor and lieutenant governor of Massachusetts, settled ministers, grammar school masters, and officers, faculty, and students at Harvard), and male polls exempt because supported by the town (paupers). Population is conventionally estimated by multiplying the number of polls by four: "Computing the polls in the ratio of 4½ [is] larger than usual" (Felt, *Statistics of Towns in Massachusetts,* 165n).

[c] The grains are wheat, rye, oats, corn, and barley.

[d] *Neat,* from an Anglo-Saxon root meaning "to use," includes oxen, cows, steers, and bulls. However, several of the valuations distinguish between oxen, cows, and neat cattle. In this table *neat* is used to mean all bovine animals.

[e] Because the valuations of 1792 and 1801 did not count sheep and goats, I have, for the sake of comparability, omitted them from this total in 1771. In 1786, sheep and goats were enumerated but were not taxed.

acreage an understatement and therefore overstates its "efficiency." The reconfigured map of Massachusetts—town boundaries redrawn, lands annexed, new counties carved out of old, new towns "hived off" from old—makes intertemporal comparisons of town outputs, town acreages, and therefore town yields hazardous.[14] Nevertheless, the finding in table 26 that there was considerable improvement in all the magnitudes by 1801 appears robust enough to withstand problems in the data.

The output of grains by 1801 was nearly two and a half times what it had been only thirty years before. Corn was by far the principal grain, accounting for more than 50 percent of grain output.[15] "Rye-n'-injun"— corn mixed with rye—was the staple bread of farm family consumption, but as much as 60 percent of the corn output in 1800, by my estimate, was used as feed to fatten swine and as a supplement for cows in milk.[16]

While grain yields rose over 20 percent between 1771 and 1792, it will be observed in table 26 that they then fell back about 5 percent between 1792 and 1801. That drop in grain yields in the 1790s may testify to the predatory "mining" of the soil that foreign observers and agricultural reformers were fond of deploring, but less grain per acre of tillage may testify also to a diversification of output away from grains. It will be recalled from chapter 7 that, by the turn of the nineteenth century, Massachusetts farmers had found many noncereal crops to grow on their arable lands: potatoes, hops, flax, green herbs, celery, rutabaga, beets, winter squashes, pumpkins, carrots, parsnips, turnips, cabbages, onions, tomatoes, asparagus, string beans, and green peas; and peaches, pears, rhubarb, new kinds of apples, strawberries, cherries, damson plums, quinces, cranberries, and wine grapes.[17] Broomcorn (for brooms) and tobacco (for cigar wrappers) became the major agricultural exports of the Connecticut River Valley.[18] Because none of these outputs (with the exception of peas and beans) is enumerated in

14. Indeed, it is just because working with these valuations is so perilous that data sets built from farm account books and probate inventories are so valuable.

15. Wheat, by contrast, accounted for only 4 percent. Black stem-rust, a fungus, parasitic in one of its stages on the barberry bush, had appeared in 1660 and had virtually eliminated wheat cultivation in Massachusetts except in the western county of Berkshire, where it made up 20 percent of grain output.

16. My estimate of the proportion of corn used up for seed, to fatten swine, and as feed for cows in milk is discussed in Rothenberg, "A Price Index for Rural Massachusetts," 989–90.

17. The diversification of crop mix was discussed in chap. 7 as a strategy to extend the crop year. A source cited there, as here, is McMahon, "A Comfortable Subsistence."

18. "The growing of broomcorn dated from about the year 1800. In 1825 it had become a staple in the river towns; in the town of Hadley alone 1,000 acres were annually planted . . . . 'The mode of culture, in the towns on Connecticut river, is very similar to that of Indian corn, but it is said to require two or three times as much labour' " (Bidwell and Falconer, *History of Agricul-*

the tax valuations for the period, their quantitative importance remains in doubt, but in view of this diversification away from grains it would be an error to make the case for declining *crop* yields on the basis of declining *grain* yields.

The improvement between 1771 and 1801 in aggregate grain output in table 26 should not be allowed to obscure the high variance among towns in both outputs and yields. While aggregate grain *output* expanded 140 percent, the experiences of individual towns varied between a more than fivefold increase in Blandford and a more than 50 percent decrease in Springfield. And while grain *yields* statewide increased 14 percent between 1771 and 1801, there were fifty towns where they increased far more than that—in four of them yields more than doubled—but thirty-three towns where they actually fell, in one case to nearly half the 1771 level. Some of that heterogeneity is caught in table 27, in the differences between counties with respect to yields.

Differential access to urban places, to waterways, to turnpikes, in short, to markets, may have played a role in the uneven pace of diversification away from grains and—by increasing the variance—in moderating the overall improvement of grain agriculture.[19]

But more important than new tillage crops in the transformation of Massachusetts agriculture was the shift from tillage crops to grasses. Massachusetts farmers were moving away from cereals to specialize in hay, and this restructuring was happening in advance of significant western competition: long before through-rail service between Boston and the Midwest (1853), long before competition from the Cincinnati hog markets (1840s), and even long before the Erie Canal (1825). In fact, the shift, visible in table 26, from grains to grasses, and between grasses from the natural to the cultivated, can be observed in the act of happening, as it were, by 1801. While tillage acreage increased 110 percent over the period and fresh-meadow and salt-marsh[20] acreage (both natural

---

ture, 245). Tobacco, having become important to the region when the broom corn bonanza petered out, soon replaced it as the major agricultural staple of the antebellum period.

19. The reader will notice from table 26, e.g., that the increase in grain output did not quite keep up with the increase in population (estimated as four times the number of polls).

20. Salt-marsh hay, with phenomenal yields cited of up to ten tons per acre (more typically, two tons per acre), is the salt-tolerant grass that grows in coastal wetlands wherever a tidal rise and fall occurs. The fact that acreage in salt marsh was always taxed at a higher rate than fresh meadow suggests that it produces more hay, or perhaps a more valuable hay, although I have been unable to discover its nutritional properties. Animals grazing in the marshes or drawing the hay out were fitted with large flat "bog shoes." The hay was thrown into "staddles" to dry and then brought in when the marsh iced over in the winter (see Smith, et al., "Salt Marshes as a Factor in the Agriculture of Northeastern North America").

Table 27 Yields

County and Date	Bushels of Grains per Acre Tillage	Tons of English Hay per Acre Mowing	Tons of Fresh/Salt Hay per Acre Meadow/Marsh	Cows Supportable per Acre Pasture
All towns:				
1771	11.8	.7	.9	.38
	(3.9)			
1801	13.4	.8	.8	.30
	(4.0)	(.4)		
Suffolk/Norfolk:				
1771	14.5	.5	.8	.33
	(2.7)			
1801	14.4	.5	.7	.28
	(3.2)	(.1)		
Essex:				
1771	14.7	.7	1.0	.28
	(2.6)			
1801	16.6	.9	.8	.23
	(3.5)	(1.3)		
Middlesex:				
1771	13.7	.6	.8	.38
	(3.5)			
1801	13.6	.7	.7	.28
	(3.6)	(.1)		
Hampshire:				
1771	7.7	.9	1.0	.59
	(2.3)			
1801	11.1	1.0	.8	.43
	(3.9)	(.2)		
Plymouth:				
1771	11.0	N.A.	N.A.	.34
	(2.6)			
1801	11.6	.6	.8	.21
	(2.0)	(.1)		
Bristol:				
1771	10.0	.6	.8	.31
	(1.6)			
1801	11.1	.5	.7	.24
	(2.1)	(.1)		
Worcester:				
1771	14.1	.8	1.1	.18
	(2.4)			
1801	16.7	.8	.8	.30
	(2.8)	(.1)		
Berkshire:				
1771	8.4	.6	.3	.45
	(1.6)			

Table 27   (*Continued*)

County and Date	Bushels of Grains per Acre Tillage	Tons of English Hay per Acre Mowing	Tons of Fresh/Salt Hay per Acre Meadow/Marsh	Cows Supportable per Acre Pasture
Berkshire:				
1801	10.7	.9	.8	.42
	(3.0)	(.1)		

Note: The 1771 valuations are disaggregated by name of poll. Town totals for 1771 come from summing page totals where given in the original list; where those are missing, the totals are taken from the calculations made by Bettye Hobbs Pruitt for her compilation of the original data. Pruitt did not, however, calculate yields for English hay, salt hay, and meadow hay separately but rather summed all three. The hay yields shown in this table are based on the towns for which there were totals in the original document. Because only five Plymouth County town valuations survive from 1771, there were too few English and meadow hay totals to enter. Standard deviations are in parentheses.

grasses) increased 122 percent, the acreage in cultivated grasses (English and upland mowing) expanded by 173 percent. And English hay, which accounted for 46 percent of total hay tonnage in 1771, accounted for 53 percent thirty years later.

Hay was always of great significance to the New England economy in three respects: as primary input in the production of dairy products, meat, hides, urban livery services, and manure; as primary input in the production of livestock; and as a locally traded output protected from distant competition by its bulk and low value relative to bulk. But the grasses native to New England offered such poor nutrition that they constrained the expansion of the animal stock and—as the principal constituent of manure—failed to enrich the soil. The most outstanding agricultural reform between 1750 and 1800 in the northern colonies was the diffusion of English grasses, which were probably brought to this shore accidentally, "the seeds buried in the fodder and bedding shipped across the Atlantic with the colonists' cherished livestock.[21] The English grass—called *herdsgrass* in New England after John Herds and *timothy* in New York, Maryland, and the Piedmont after Timothy Hansen—was mixed with red-top clover, and broadcast on upland meadows (called *mowing*), which careful farmers kept plowed and dressed with manure. In farm account books English hay was always twice as valuable as

21. Stilgoe, *Common Landscape of America*, 183.

native hay[22]—selling for $10.00 a ton when fresh meadow hay sold for $5.00—and it diffused so rapidly that acreage in English and upland mowing hay came close to tripling in Massachusetts in the thirty years between 1771 and 1801: "Long after the first frost turned the native grasses brown . . . the English grasses remained true to their old climate and stayed green, providing pasturage into December . . . everywhere man shaped the land was green and everywhere he left it untouched it was brown. Herd's grass or timothy announced the coming of civilization, of shaped land."[23]

If the specialization in cultivated grasses was in fact occurring among the generality of Massachusetts farmers, we should see it in a shifting pattern of land use: a retreat from tillage and fresh meadow in favor of an increasing proportion of farm acreage devoted to mowing.[24] From the valuations of 1786 and 1801, table 28 aggregates to the county level the town data on land use as a proportion of total acreage.[25] Tillage and fresh meadow decreased as a percentage of improved acreage in all counties, and mowing increased as a percentage of total.

That the shift in the crop mix and land use from grains to hay, from tillage to grasslands, and from fresh meadows to upland mowing was a shift in the direction of higher-valued uses of land is confirmed in a comparison of tax rates on the several forms of taxable property (see table 29).[26] While the tax rate on tillage in all towns declined between

22. According to Stilgoe, so valuable was the English hay that farmers put their fresh meadow hay in the barn and kept the stacks of English hay out in the meadow where they would be protected from a greater hazard than rain: barn fires lit by lightning (ibid., 184).

23. Ibid., 184.

24. Changes in land use are measured in terms of *proportion* of acreage, not acreage itself, because of the constant redrawing of town boundaries and establishing of new towns from parts of the old that characterized this period. Between the valuations of 1786 and 1801, 116 towns gained or lost land, and some did both.

25. Aggregating to the county level not only is a compact way to handle this large data set but also makes good economic sense. In many respects, the counties are more different from one another than are the towns within them, suggesting that they are good proxies for regions. Counties differed markedly in the proportions of wheat, rye, corn, oats, and barley in their grain output; in indexes of commercialization; and, of course, in the presence of salt marsh.

The year 1771 had to be omitted from table 28 because the 1771 valuation did not count "woodland and unimproved" or "unimprovable" acres. "Unimproved" and "unimprovable" acres were counted in both 1786 and 1801. In table 28, I have not included "unimprovable" lands—much of which is land under water—in the total acres, and hence the rows do not sum to 100 percent. Thus, in table 28, "total" = tillage + English and upland mowing + fresh meadow + salt marsh + pasture + woodland and unimproved.

26. The year 1771 had to be omitted from table 29 because the 1771 valuation contains no tax rates.

Table 28 Acreage by Land Use as a Proportion of Total Acres

County and Date	Tillage	Mowing	Meadows	Pasture	Woodlands
All towns:					
1786	.06	.06	.06	.18	.53
1801	.06	.08	.06	.22	.46
Hampshire:					
1786	.05	.03	.03	.05	.70
1801	.07	.06	.04	.12	.57
Worcester:					
1786	.04	.05	.06	.13	.61
1801	.04	.06	.07	.22	.51
Berkshire:					
1786	.08	.07	.01	.11	.58
1801	.07	.07	.02	.15	.47
Suffolk/Norfolk:					
1786	.05	.10	.11	.32	.34
1801	.05	.11	.09	.29	.35
Essex:					
1786	.09	.11	.11	.45	.18
1801	.08	.11	.11	.44	.20
Middlesex:					
1786	.07	.07	.10	.21	.47
1801	.07	.09	.09	.28	.42
Plymouth:					
1786	.06	.04	.06	.19	.48
1801	.05	.06	.06	.19	.51
Bristol:					
1786	.08	.08	.06	.20	.50
1801	.05	.09	.05	.21	.48

Note: The rows do not sum to one hundred because of the omission of "unimproveable" acreage from this table. Meadows include fresh meadow and salt marsh.

The absolute level of tax rates bears no obvious relation to land values, but their levels relative to one another are suggestive. According to Harold H. Burbank, the procedure for determining how the state direct tax should be apportioned among the towns was first to calculate the poll tax at one penny or ha'penny (1*d*. or ½*d*). per ratable poll, and then each town was compared to other towns with regard to real and personal property to determine how much should be added to each town's poll tax to fill its equitable share of the revenue sought from the tax. A town judged to be poor would derive more of its quota from the tax on polls than from the tax on property. Assessors in each town were instructed to come up with the full quota, but there was considerable room for discretion, for not all property was taxed and rates were seldom if ever assessed on full value. Even during the period 1777–81, when the law required full valuation, the practice of 30–40 percent underassessing continued. The authority on this is still Burbank's, "The General Property Tax in Massachusetts" (pp. 90–235 of which are available in typescript in the Massachusetts State Library, State House, Boston).

Table 29   Tax Rates on Land Usage, by County, 1786 and 1801
(in dollars per acre)

County and Date	Tillage	Mowing	Meadows	Pasture
All towns:				
1786	1.41	1.67	.99	.50
1801	1.18	1.85	1.12	.58
Suffolk/Norfolk:				
1786	1.86	2.11	1.05	.72
1801	1.54	2.25	1.17	.73
Essex:				
1786	1.61	1.90	.99	.55
1801	1.57	2.33	1.11	.63
Middlesex:				
1786	1.48	1.70	1.03	.51
1801	1.27	2.11	1.36	.68
Hampshire:				
1786	1.21	1.55	.94	.45
1801	1.04	1.75	1.07	.50
Plymouth:				
1786	1.26	1.52	.96	.38
1801	1.06	1.67	1.01	.49
Bristol:				
1786	1.39	1.60	.99	.45
1801	1.05	1.73	1.00	.52
Worcester:				
1786	1.39	1.64	.83	.49
1801	1.12	1.69	1.01	.56
Berkshire:				
1786	1.30	1.53	.88	.47
1801	.94	1.39	1.00	.50

1786 and 1801, the rates on all grasslands—on mowing, meadow, marsh, and pasture—rose, and mowing was taxed in each town as the most highly valued use of land.[27]

If agricultural improvement dictated a shift from native to cultivated grasses, we should also see a retreat from pasture—of all cleared acreage on Massachusetts farms, the most hilly, rocky, swampy, over-

27. "Woodland and unimproved lands" paid increased taxes as well. It was the only land use taxed on an ad valorem basis—at 2 percent of market value. The increased burden of taxes on woodland came from a dramatic 37 percent rise in the market value of woodlands between 1786 and 1801.

Of course, to measure the real burden of rising per acre tax rates over time, comparisons should be made in constant dollars. According to my farm price index, there was a 21 percent increase in the level of farm-gate prices between 1786 and 1801; thus, many of these tax rates increased less than the rate of inflation.

grown, "impoverished and skinned."[28] Yet, for the state as a whole, acreage in pasture between 1771 and 1801 increased more than any of the other barometers we have been tracking and increased as a proportion of both improved and total farm acreage in most counties. There are several possible explanations for the expansion of pasture. First, keeping land in pasture for anywhere from three to seven years was a way to fallow tillage in rotation after two or three crops had been taken off, and to the extent that this was true, the increase in pasture acres would signal *more* careful husbandry—that is, more land in rotation— not less. Second, by 1801 the number of grazing animals (cattle, oxen, and horses) was more than two and a half times what it had been in 1771, and larger herds required more summer pasture even if considerable efforts were being made to stable and stall feed animals for the rest of the year.

But these benign explanations for the expansion of pasture fall before the farmers' own judgments concerning the quality of their pasture lands. Between 1771 and 1801 there was a 17 percent decline in the number of cows *per acre* that farmers reckoned their pasture "will keep"—a subjective, but important measure. Whatever improvement in the "carrying capacity" of an acre of pasture had been realized between 1771 and 1792 was more than offset by the decline in its carrying capacity between 1792 and 1801 (see table 26). Pasture acreage had increased because pasture quality had unquestionably deteriorated, so that by 1800 more land was required to support each grazing animal.[29]

For the average farmer to have attempted to reclaim this, the uncultivated, overgrazed, exhausted 20–40 percent of his land,[30] would have required, at the very least, intensive manuring. Cattle can be viewed as curious machines. "They are the best machine for turning herbage into money,"[31] yes, but, even more important, they turn herbage into manure. Each cow or ox that is stabled all winter consumes in that time two tons of hay, from which it produces two loads of manure (at thirty

28. Bidwell and Falconer, *History of Agriculture*, 102.

29. Perhaps *required* is an exaggeration. In a multiple regression analysis in which the dependent variable was "number of cattle owned" in 131 towns in the 1771 valuations, Bettye Hobbs Pruitt found that, while "tons of hay" explained 89 percent of the dependent variable, the introduction of the variable "acres of pasture" increased the explanatory power of the regression by a mere 0.3 percent ("Agriculture and Society in the Towns of Massachusetts," 183).

30. Bidwell goes so far as to say that the distinction the valuations made between pasture and woodlands—i.e., between pasture and unimproved—"was probably not of great importance" (Bidwell and Falconer, *History of Agriculture*, 120).

31. Massachusetts Society for Promoting Agriculture, *Papers*, 1807, p. 48.

bushels a load) and an additional load if yarded at night during the sum-mer.[32] At thirty loads to the acre (the rate often cited for manuring tillage and mowing), it would have taken ten cows eating three tons of hay apiece for a year to manure one acre.[33] There were horses, swine, and sheep to help, of course, and there were nonanimal sources of fertiliz-ers, but with over twenty-eight hundred acres of pasture in the average Massachusetts town in 1801, the effort was formidable. Small wonder that one farmer from the hill country replied to the Massachusetts Soci-ety for Promoting Agriculture: "If you have rocky pasture, to subdue it would cost the whole value of the farm. . . . It makes no sense to cul-tivate [rocky pastures] till our country shall count as China does its 270 million souls."[34]

Fortunately, improved animal husbandry in Massachusetts did not need to wait upon the reclamation of depleted pasturelands. The com-bination of summer out-pasturing in the hill country and stall feeding the rest of the year on corn and English hays whose yields *per grazing animal* were rising (see table 26) proved sufficient, even with inferior pastures, to support the very large increase in grazing stock we observe in table 26.

And it did more. Livestock were increasing both in number and in weight, and the "edible weight" of hogs and beef cattle had a direct bearing on the nutrition, health, and standard of living of the human population.[35] The sample of hog weights collected from account books and inventories to test the price elasticity of butchering decisions in chapter 4 shows a dramatic increase in live weights after 1800.[36] The

32. Massachusetts Society for Promoting Agriculture, *Papers*, responses to questions 38–44.

33. In the 1790s, Dr. Nathaniel Ames of Dedham, brother of Fisher Ames, spread four-hundred loads of manure per acre (at thirty bushels, or one yard cubed, to the load) to cover the soil three inches deep! His memorandum book is at the Dedham Historical Society.

34. *The New England Farmer*, 3 August 1801, 22.

35. "Americans achieved an average level of meat consumption by the middle of the eigh-teenth century that was not achieved in Europe until well into the twentieth century . . . . Ameri-cans achieved modern heights by the middle of the eighteenth century [and] reached levels of life expectancy that were not attained by the general population of England or even by the British peerage until the first quarter of the twentieth century" (Fogel, "The Conquest of High Mortality," 36). As his evidence of Americans' meat consumption, Fogel cites Sarah McMahon's study of widows' portions, which is based on Massachusetts wills (see McMahon, "Provisions Laid by for the Family"). It is relevant to the concerns of this book to point out, therefore, that it was *Massa-chusetts farmers* who achieved this high level of meat consumption.

36. In chap. 4 I described how I converted the sample of adult hog weights to live weights. For the convenience of the reader, I will repeat it here. In each case a determination had to be made as to whether the weight given in the farm account books was a live or a dressed weight, and there are few clues in the sources themselves. I compared the per pound price of the hog (usually given) with the per pound price of fresh pork for that region in that year. If the per pound price of the hog

twenty-six observations before 1800 average 164.5 pounds; the next twenty-six observations, from 1800 to 1816, averaged 287.3 pounds. The first four-hundred-pound hogs appeared in 1801.

If it is indeed the case that "grain supplies offer clearer evidence of meat production capacity than do . . . animal inventories,"[37] and if the weight gains in my small sample of hog weights are representative, it suggests that we err in modeling grains and livestock, corn and hay, tillage and mowing, as if they were *substitute* uses of resources. Animal husbandry is a thickly textured web of complementarities made possible only by the increased yields achieved in tillage agriculture, which in turn is made possible only by the continuous improvement of manure achieved in animal husbandry. Corn, small grains, root crops, and legumes grown on richly manured soils were both consumption goods and intermediate products that along with nutritious grasses produced rich manures, fat cattle, dairy products, meats, hides, wool, and the natural increase of animals after their kind. In addition to grasses, animals used every part of the cereal plants: the grains for feed, the straw and the stover for fodder and for bedding, the stubble for forage, and what was not consumed by grazing livestock as "after-feed" was composted into "green manure" to augment animal manure. The process is profoundly circular.

III

A circular process was transformed into a growth process. It took the form of increased yields; of better management of livestock, manures,

---

was less than the price of fresh pork, the weight was called a live weight. If the per pound price of the hog equaled or exceeded the price of fresh pork, the weight was called dressed weight and divided by 0.70 to standardize all weights to live weights. The dressed weight/live weight ratio of 0.70 was chosen because it lies midway between the figure of 0.75 or 0.76 used by some authorities and 0.65 used by others.

At the time these calculations were being done I assumed that dressed weight was the proper measure of the accessible nutriments in meat. Apparently, there is still another correction to be made: to multiply dressed weight by 0.64 to reduce it to "edible weight" (see Fogel, "The Conquest of High Mortality," 53, no. 14).

37. Gallman, "Self-Sufficiency in the Cotton Economy of the Antebellum South," 18. In Massachusetts it was not only grain supplies but also skimmed milk, root crops, and legumes in animal feeds that determined meat production. As a consequence (presumably), Massachusetts hogs, fattened for one month, weighed more in 1800 than southern hogs, fattened for four months, weighed in 1860. The average live weight of Massachusetts hogs, calculated from probate inventory appraisals, was 224 pounds in 1780–1805; the average live weight of southern hogs, as estimated by Gallman, was 192 pounds in 1860 (ibid., 15).

woodlots, fruit orchards, cultivated meadows, seed selection, stall feeding, and dairying. Legumes and root crops were planted that were both nutritious in feeds and nitrogen fixing in rotation. Land clearing, fencing, and connected farm buildings were part of the restructuring of farm space. None of these improvements required more capital, but all called for more labor inputs, more effective labor hours, the application of know-how learned by doing, and the reorganization of farm work.

If, in the course of the development process, agriculture's share of the labor force goes down, then an increase in agricultural output per capita can be achieved only by a very great increase in agricultural output per agricultural worker.[38] Where is that increase to come from if, as late as the 1840s, there was virtually no capital deepening—that is, no technological change—in New England agriculture? From endogenously generated intensification in the use of labor. "Labor is the great thing in farming."[39]

Chapters 6 and 7 examined the farm labor force and the roles that day and monthly labor may have played in labor productivity growth. But in this chapter we seek to distinguish between growth and development. Increments to the quantity and quality of factors of production will produce *growth*, but only structural change effects the transformation we call *development*, and it is structural change, more than mere growth, that distinguished the New England economy from all other regional economies in the United States in the antebellum period. Among the most important structural changes that take place in a developing agricultural economy is the shift of resources to sectors with economies of, and increasing returns to, scale. If these can seldom, if ever, be realized within the confines of a New England farm, we should look for signs of a shift of resources out of farming.

To seek evidence of developmental structural change within the limited categories of taxable property, we will judge those towns to be developing most rapidly where the agricultural sector bears a diminishing

38. Paul David's "conjectural estimating equation" to measure growth in a two-sector economy is $O/P = LF/P \times [S_A(O/LF)_A + S_N \times k(O/LF)_A]$, where O/P is output per capita, LF/P is the labor force participation rate, S_A is the share of the labor force in agriculture, and S_N is the share of the labor force in nonagriculture (both S_A and S_N are weights on sectoral output per worker). "It was also assumed that output per worker in nonagriculture remained equal to a constant multiple of that in agriculture," $(O/LF)_N = k \times (O/LF)_A$ (Weiss, "U.S. Labor Force Estimates," 4; 25, n. 8).

39. Larkin, " 'Labor Is the Great Thing in Farming.' "

proportion, and nonagricultural property an increasing proportion, of the total tax burden.[40]

As early as 1647, the General Court authorized taxation not only on polls and real estate but also on the income from "mils, ships and all smaller vessels, marchantable goods, cranes, wharfes, and all sorts of cattell and all other visible estate."[41] In 1771, the state taxed (and therefore the valuations enumerated) shops, tanneries, slaughter houses, potash and pearl-ash works, warehouses, vessel tonnage, wharf footage, iron works, bake houses, distilleries, sugar houses, grist mills, sawmills, slitting mills, fulling mills, stock in trade, and money at interest (net of debts on interest). In 1786, money on hand (including bank deposits) and debts were added and taxed at 6 percent; in 1801, annual income from holdings of U.S. and state securities, bank stock, and shares in bridges, toll roads, and turnpikes were added and taxed at 6 percent.

The expansion of the nonagriculture sector can be inferred from table 30, where in all counties agricultural property, averaged across towns, paid a decreasing share—and, by inference, nonagricultural property an increasing share—of taxes. (Because the 1771 valuation list does not include tax assessments, we can trace only the changes between 1786 and 1801.) Within counties, the variance among towns in the same years, and for the same towns between years, is striking. Even excluding Salem and Boston, the range in 1786 extended from towns where agriculture paid less than 3 percent of total taxes to towns where agriculture paid more than 90 percent. While the range did not appreciably narrow by 1801, individual towns experienced a dramatic retreat from agriculture. The agricultural sector in Freetown (Bristol County) moved from paying 93 percent of taxes in 1786 to paying just over 50 percent; and in Kingston (Plymouth County) agriculture moved from paying over 90 percent of taxes in 1786 to just over 30 percent fifteen years later.

Stock in trade is only one index of commercialization, but it deserves special attention. It is the measure of inventory investment in the era before GNP accounting, measuring as it does the value of tools and

40. By "agriculture's share of the tax burden" I mean each town's tax rate on taxable agricultural property (acres of tillage, mowing, meadow, marsh, pasture, woodlands, and head of livestock), multiplied by the quantity of each such property taxed by each town, and summed over all towns. Cider was not included because, although it had been enumerated in all three valuations, it was not taxed in 1801 and hence had no tax rate in 1801.

41. Felt, comp. *Statistics of Taxation in Massachusetts*, 237.

Table 30   Taxes on Agriculture as a Percentage of Total Taxes

County and Date	Mean	Range	
		Highest	Lowest
All towns:[a]			
1786	.74		
	(.14)		
1801	.66		
	(.13)		
Hampshire:			
1786	.78	.90 (Heath)	.55 (Springfield)
	(.09)		
1801	.71	.89 (Shelburne)	.50 (Springfield)
	(.07)		
Worcester:			
1786	.75	.85 (Hubbardston)	.57 (Worcester)
	(.09)		
1801	.69	.78 (Hubbardston)	.49 (Worcester)
	(.05)		
Berkshire:			
1786	.82	.92 (New Ashford)	.71 (Windsor)
	(.05)		
1801	.75	.86 (Southfield)	.67 (Pittsfield & Stockbridge)
	(.05)		
Suffolk/Norfolk:			
1786	.71	.91 (Chelsea)	.52 (Hingham)
	(.10)		
1801	.61	.46 (Chelsea)	.44 (Hingham)
	(.10)		
Essex:			
1786	.55	.76 (Lynnfield)	.03 (Newburyport)
	(.22)		
1801	.47	.69 (Lynnfield)	.01 (Newburyport)
	(.24)		
Middlesex:			
1786	.71	.80 (Hopkinton)	.39 (Medford)
	(.17)		
1801	.66	.79 (Boxborough)	.19 (Charlestown)
	(.11)		
Plymouth:			
1786	.70	.91 (Kingston)	.39 (Plymouth)
	(.12)		
1801	.56	.78 (Halifax)	.20 (Plymouth)
	(.15)		

Table 30 *(Continued)*

County and Date	Mean	Range	
		Highest	Lowest
Bristol:			
1786	.78	.93 (Freetown)	.61 (Taunton)
	(.08)		
1801	.61	.52 (Freetown)	.29 (New Bedford)
	(.12)		

Note: Taxes on agriculture is the sum of taxes on tillage, mowing, meadow and marsh, pasture, woodlands, and livestock. Standard deviations are shown in parentheses.
[a] Boston, Salem, Maine, Cape Cod, and Martha's Vineyard, as in all these tables, are excluded from "all towns."

goods in process found in artisanal shops and the magnitude of merchandise stocks in retail and wholesale shops.[42] Shops and stores constitute significant nodes in a dendritic marketing network.[43] When, around 1800, the little inland town of Shrewsbury found a market in Boston—ninety miles away—for its cheese, butter, chickens, veal, pork, and hay and in Brighton for its cattle, it was in large measure because Artemas Ward's general store was a node in a proliferating network of symbiotic enterprises stretching from Worcester County to Boston along the two roads that ran through Shrewsbury. Stores, and peddlers as well, not only expanded the marketing perimeters of farmers qua suppliers but also played an important role in fashioning among farmers a demand for store-bought goods the insatiability of which may very well have been one of the "kicks" that got agriculture moving.[44]

42. A considerable literature is emerging on the transitional role played by artisanal shops in the industrialization of southern New England. Deeply rooted as they were in traditional rural society, they occupied a transitional place on a continuum between farm and factory—part farmers, part craftsmen, part industrial workers. Shadrach Steere, a woodworker who made bobbins for the Slater mills in Rhode Island, continued to farm all his life. His farm protected him from the vicissitudes facing the urban artisan, while his craft protected him from the risks confronting New England farmers in the early nineteenth century (Cooper and Malone, "The Mechanical Woodworker in Early Nineteenth Century New England"; see also Sokoloff, "Was the Transition from the Artisanal Shop to the Non-Mechanized Factory Associated with Gains in Efficiency?" Cooper, "Thomas Blanchard's Woodworking Machines"; Gordon, "Edge Tools in Context"; and Lance, "Upper Quinebaug Mill Survey."

43. On the importance of distribution networks in the growth of consumer demand and the role that proliferating retail shops played in those networks, see Shammas, *The Pre-Industrial Consumer in England and America*, chaps. 8 and 9, pp. 225–90.

44. "Peddlers were central to this process of creating a market structure in ante-bellum America . . . . They inaugurated a commercial revolution which swept away the village culture which

IV

Market-led productivity growth is a harsh process, one that produces both winners and losers. Presumably, the towns in table 30 that lay on the yonder edge of developmental change, the towns that by 1801 still derived 70, 80, or 90 percent of their taxable wealth from farming, were among the losers. Perhaps the most politically significant losers in Massachusetts history were the followers of Daniel Shays, whose rebellion affords an opportunity to explore the economic contours of what is for me one of its most resonant attributes: the fact that it happened in 1786, annus mirabilis in the time path of rural market integration and agricultural productivity growth. Can differential access to the emerging market economy, and to the differential agricultural productivity growth that was its consequence, explain why some Massachusetts towns supported the insurrection, others supported the state militia, and still others produced leaders for both sides?

Table 31 relates proxy measures of agricultural productivity in "Shays Country"[45] to town sympathies in the rebellion.[46] While we are fortunate to have a tax valuation exactly contemporaneous with the event, two serious obstacles inhere in this source. First, because the 1786 valuations are aggregated to the town level, we are compelled to aggregate our two variables—both of which are, after all, decisions made on the individual level—to the town level. We are forced to say that the *town* has or does not have Shaysite sympathies, that the *town* is or is not realizing increases in farm labor productivity. The second major

---

had nourished them leaving us with some of their products and a rich folklore. Rural residents were less concerned with resisting the intrusion of capitalism than with articulating their own mode of indigenous commercialization. Peddlers were a part of this articulation as much as were farmers—their roles were different but they were part of the same world—a world which they were both unintentionally destroying" (Jaffee, "Peddlers of Progress and the Transformation of the Rural North").

45. "Shays Country" consists of 128 towns in what were at the time the three western counties of Massachusetts: Berkshire, Hampshire, and Worcester. There were outbreaks of the insurrection in several eastern towns as well, most conspicuously in Groton, where Job Shattuck led the rebellion before Daniel Shays, but the eastern towns are not included in this analysis.

46. I owe my attribution of town sympathies in the rebellion to Brooke's "A Deacon's Orthodoxy." Brooke determines the allegiance of towns in the three western counties on the basis of warrants, arrests, indictments, imprisonments, the Hampshire County Black List, and lists of militia leaders. See also Marini's "The Religious World of Daniel Shays," which uses church histories, minutes of Baptist and Presbyterian associations, and sermons to characterize the town by characterizing its minister and his relation to his congregation. Marini also extends his analysis to the pockets of Shaysite sympathy in the eastern counties of Bristol and Middlesex.

Table 31   Comparing Towns Supporting and Opposing Shays' Rebellion
with Respect to Selected Agricultural Productivity Proxies

	Shaysite	Militia and Conflicted
No. of polls	206	257
No. of barns	75	103
Tillage acres	673	938
Tillage assessment = acres × tax rate ($)	855	1,243
Mowing tax rate ($)	1.51	1.63
Meadow acres	342	669
Meadow tax rate ($)	.85	.91
Meadow assessment = acres × tax rate ($)	297	611
Pasture acres	1,177	1,611
Barrels of cider	336	700
No. of head of livestock	1,320	1,589
Livestock assessment = no. head × tax rate ($)	592	761
Money on hand ($)	77	135
Debts ($)	438	2,151
Stock in trade ($)	259	1,176
Total tax ($)	4,948	6,934
Aggregate taxes on agriculture ($)	3,380	4,685

Source: 1786 town tax valuations.
Note: The 128 towns in "Shays Country" (the three western counties of Massachusetts in 1786) were partitioned into two groups according to the measures of allegiance cited in n. 46. For each category enumerated in the 1786 valuations, group means were calculated. The categories shown in this table are those for which the difference between the means is significant at the < .05 level (with the exception of number of head of livestock, where the difference between means was significant at the .09 level).

problem is the failure of the 1786 valuations to enumerate any outputs (except cider). This, of course, seriously compromises our efforts to generate productivity estimates. Lacking any alternative, I am compelled to argue that the striking variance in tax rates on land in the same use in different towns and in different uses in the same town can serve as a proxy for the differential income-earning capacities of these lands.

The experimental design consists of testing, with respect to each of the taxable magnitudes in the valuations, the differences between the means and the variances of two groups of towns: those with Shaysite sympathies, on one hand, and, on the other, those opposed, either because they supported the state militia, or because, as "conflicted towns," they produced leaders for both sides. The magnitudes in the 1786 valuation that are not included in table 31 are those for which the means between the two groups of towns were not significantly different from one another at the 5 percent level.

In table 32, two-way contingency tables rank the same two groups

Table 32   Two-Way Contingency Tables Relating Shaysite Sympathy to
                      Productivity Proxies

	Total Tax		Agriculture Taxes		Agriculture/ Total Tax	
	0	1	0	1	0	1
Anti-Shays towns	31	44	33	42	32	43
Pro-Shays towns	26	8	26	8	21	13
Chi-square	11.6		9.9		3.4	
Significance level	.001		.002		.06	

Note: "Anti-Shays towns" are those that supported the state militia and conflicted towns. "Agriculture taxes" are the assessments on tillage, grasslands, and livestock. "Agriculture/total tax" is the share of total taxes paid by taxes on agriculture.

of towns, by the frequency with which each group fell above (1) or below (0) the mean of all 128 western towns with respect to selected items in the 1786 valuation. The chi-square test results allow us to assert that the two groups of towns were "really" (or "significantly") different from one another with respect to these three measures of economic performance.

Shaysite towns lay significantly below the mean (0), and non-Shaysite (militia and conflicted) towns lay significantly above the mean (1) with respect to total taxes assessed, the assessment on agricultural property, and the proportion of the tax paid by agriculture. In other words, the towns that did not throw their lot in with the insurrection had significantly more prosperous agricultural enterprises than did the towns supporting the insurrection.[47] Given the intractabilities in the data referred to earlier, I interpret these results as confirming my surmise that, whatever its significance as an event in anti-Federalist politics or democratic populism, Shays' Rebellion seems now to loom as a deeply conservative impulse, a fist shaken at impending change. The danger to the Shaysites came, not from the "competitive capitalism of merchants,"[48]

47. This does not contradict the discussion in sec. III above measuring economic development by a *decline* in the proportion of total taxes paid by the agricultural sector. Recall that the movement out of agriculture has to do with the shift over time, between 1786 and 1801, whereas this analysis of what we may call "the economic origins of Shaysite sympathies" has to do with the towns' relative status at a point in time, 1786.

48. This is the view of David P. Szatmary (*Shays's Rebellion*) and others, who see the rebellion as a defense of the moral economy in rural Massachusetts. For a sophisticated statement of this position, see Brooke, *The Heart of the Commonwealth*, who writes, "Until [the Massachusetts State constitution-making process], the most powerful insurgent forces . . . drew upon implied or

but from within the farm economy, poised, as it was quite literally in 1786, on the cusp of structural transformation.

Shays' Rebellion serves to illustrate the serious political consequences of uneven rural development, but my purpose in introducing this material at this time is to use the association, confirmed in the chi-square tests and in table 31, between the political polarities in 1786 and agricultural productivity proxies, to reverse the direction of the inquiry. Having run a causal chain from agricultural improvement to partisanship in Shays' Rebellion, I propose now to run the chain backward, from partisanship in Shays' Rebellion to agricultural improvement, in order to suggest which towns may be presumed to have had access to the market in 1786 and which did not. Since the argument sounds circular, let me schematize it. There are three propositions here: A is a proposition about productivity; B is a proposition about market access; and C is a proposition about sympathies in the insurrection. I consider the link between A and C to have been demonstrated by the results in tables 31 and 32. I consider the link between A and B to have been demonstrated many times over in the course of this book, explicitly in figure 13 of chapter 6. If C and B are both linked to A, then they are linked to each other, and allegiance in Shays' Rebellion can be used as presumptive evidence of market access or the lack of it.

I suggest, then, that, of the 128 towns in Shays Country, the thirty-four towns loyal to the Regulators were probably "locked out" of access to markets in 1786 and that the seventy-five conflicted and militia towns, in addition to those that remained hors de combat, were in varying degrees involved in a market economy, had in varying degrees embraced, so to speak, the new dispensation, and were, by 1786, enjoying its consequences for productivity growth.

---

explicit Lockean critiques of the corporate order and the classical tradition. With the framing of the constitution, people of such Lockean, liberal persuasions were no longer at odds with the dominant ideology; the future lay with the principle of voluntary individual association that they had espoused—in varying degrees—since the Land Bank and the emergence of religious dissent in the Great Awakening. Already in the 1780s the new institutional order that would shape a structural transformation of society and economy was rapidly taking shape. After 1780 insurgent forces would emerge out of those social orbits that were now out of step with a liberal framework, among people who still responded to the corporate categories defining the inclusive, unitary world of provincial orthodoxy. Perhaps conservative, even archaic, the people schooled in these traditions became the political conscience of the new society, carrying the classical republican, Harringtonian synthesis of personal independence and collective obligation far into the nineteenth century" (pp. 191–92).

V

I have focused deliberately in this chapter on a very narrow period—what might be called the turning point—a point in time too narrow, I had feared, for the mercurial changes in the behavior of prices to register in the behavior of lumpy aggregates. But I submit that in the analysis in this chapter, which is based on a detailed examination of the town tax valuations of 1771, 1786, 1792, and 1801, the turning point stands confirmed.

We might still ask, Why? Why did the productivity turnaround happen at the end of the eighteenth century? Why did farmers choose that time to respond to market signals in a new way? Questions of that kind, if they have any answer at all, tend to have a great many answers. One was suggested at the beginning of this chapter: the process may have begun as a Smithian feedback loop in which falling real wages, increased output, extended markets, and division of labor worked together to generate more of the same. But if so, that process was embedded in a far more profound one: a change in climate regimes. The market-led transformation of Massachusetts agriculture was set against a major regional climate shift between 1750 and 1850. And the two phenomena, I suggest, may not have been unrelated. Confronted by a long transitional regime of hazardously unpredictable weather, reorganizing the farm to achieve productivity growth may have been perceived as the only way to succeed in farming.

Weather happens both on a scale so large that we can speak of a "global climate" and on a scale so small that places a mile apart can have different "weathers." But that it is important to agriculture, even if not decisively so, goes without saying. (Which may explain why so far in this book it has gone without saying!) Extremely important work on New England's climate history and its relation to agricultural change is being done now, and the results may cast light on dating the transformation of Massachusetts agriculture.[49]

49. In the discussion of climate and weather to follow, I shall be summarizing, to the best of my ability, the following articles by William R. Baron, supervisor of the Historical Climate Records Office, Northern Arizona University, and his colleagues: "The Reconstruction of Eighteenth Century Temperature Records through the Use of Content Analysis," "A Reconstruction of New England Climate Using Historical Materials," "Frost-Free Record Reconstruction for Eastern Massachusetts," "A Comparative Study of Climate Fluctuation and Agricultural Practices in Southern New England," and "Retrieving American Climate History." I am deeply indebted to Professor Baron for generously sharing his extraordinary work with me.

The years 1750–1850, on which all the studies in this volume have focused, are identified by climate historian William R. Baron as a "change-over" period, an interval caught in the shift from one major climatic regime to another. The earlier regime, called the Neoglacial, was "a time of somewhat cooler temperatures, prominent polar anticyclones, southwardly displaced depression tracks, and considerable blocking of upper winds by high pressure cells over Iceland and the northeastern Atlantic." The later regime was a "very different" pattern of warmer and more stable weather. Like all such transitional periods, 1750–1850 was marked by great instability, by heightened variability in all the relevant parameters: in "growing season lengths, storm frequencies, snowfall, droughts, and harsh and unusual weather."[50] From the point of view of the farmer, it is this variability in the weather, far more than the weather itself, that increases his risks and endangers his enterprise. And risk there was: in thirteen out of the twenty-four years— more than half—between 1750 and 1774, there were too few "growing-degree days" in Cambridge, Massachusetts, for the corn to mature at all.[51] The most extreme instance of eccentric weather was 1815, which had the longest growing season by far—240 days between killing frosts—of any year between 1750 and 1970, followed the very next year by 1816—the so-called year without a summer—which had a growing season of only eighty days, by far the shortest. For any one year during the eighteenth century, a Massachusetts farmer could anticipate that the last killing frost before spring planting might happen anytime between 11 March and 14 June and that the first killing frost in the fall (which would destroy at least half his crop) might come anytime between 29 August and 17 November![52]

Risks on this scale—uninsurable, random, devastating—dwarfed the risks of producing for market. Confronted by a nature that must certainly have appeared to play dice with the universe, production for market becomes a *risk-aversive* strategy. And in 1801 it must really have

50. The source of these quotations is Baron, "A Comparative Study of Climate Fluctuation," 1.

51. This is my understanding of Baron, "Retrieving American Climate History," fig. 1, p. 21. As mentioned earlier, the length of the growing season is one of the variables that can be expected to affect yields. Since we relied heavily on the yield data that could be extracted from the tax valuations for 1771, 1786, and 1801, it is of interest to note that 1771, at 212 days, had the longest growing season before the extraordinary summer of 1815, 1786 had 152 days and 1801 had 190 days.

52. Baron et al., "Frost-Free Record Reconstruction," 318.

looked as though the enhanced yields, changes in output mix, intensified use of labor, spatial reorientation of farm functions, shift of capital out of agriculture, and perceptible gains in total factor productivity—all achieved under the aegis of the market—would indeed save Massachusetts agriculture.

9

Conclusion

As Central and Eastern Europe and the Former Soviet Union struggle to reinvent a market economy, their struggle against daunting odds bids fair, finally, to remove from the word *capitalism* the embarrassment, "the whiff of brimstone" that attaches to it.[1] But, given the path dependence of historical processes, will economies long administered by coercion and command be able to "get there from here"? Which among the myriad conditions that somehow conjoined in the seventeenth century will prove to have been necessary, and which merely epiphenomenal, to the genesis of the market: a worldview that defines the individual as the unit of social action? secure rights to the ownership and transfer of property? judicial enforcement of contracts? representative government? a measure of religious heterodoxy? a peasantry torn from its ascriptive rights to the land? a favorable balance of trade? a colonial empire? an adequate supply of monetary metals? Surely there is much to learn from understanding the historical process by which the market was "invented" in the first place.

To locate the emergence of a market economy in the seventeenth century is to distinguish it both from market-place economies (which have probably existed for close to ten thousand years) and from the thin layer of merchants, adventurers, and bankers whose capitalism in the Middle Ages and the Renaissance never penetrated beneath the shallowest surface of society. The market economy "happened" when the economic system became "disembedded" from the political, cultural, and social systems constraining it, becoming itself a homeostatic system and an autonomous agent of change. In penetrating local markets, the market economy became a *vehicle*, carrying what might be called *the culture of capitalism* deep into all but the most stagnant layers of a social structure hitherto resistant to it. In England, this process would appear to have had its beginnings in an extraordinary concatenation of revolutions in the sixteenth and seventeenth centuries—the Price Revolution, the Puritan revolution, the constitutional revolution, and the proletarianization of agricultural labor in the countryside—that worked to unsettle customary land tenures, to legitimize entrepreneurial and property rights institutions, and to delegitimize the feudal, ecclesiastical, and monarchical institutions that had held the economy in thrall.

The working definition of a market economy that I have used throughout this study is an extension of the neoclassical definition of the

1. This memorable phrase is Fernand Braudel's (*The Wheels of Commerce*, 238).

market for a single good: it is a region in space and time within which prices (net of transactions costs) for each good and for each service are arbitraged toward uniformity by the unconstrained mobility of buyers and sellers in pursuit (it is assumed) of their economic advantage. It is the hegemony of such a process over the prices set in local *market-places* that constitutes a *market economy* and defines its spatial and temporal boundaries. The wider the market in space and time, the more likely it is that resources will find their way to their most productive uses, and therein lies the link between a market economy and economic development.

This definition has a singular advantage: it makes it possible to identify and to date the emergence of a market economy from its observable and testable correlates rather than from unverifiable assertions about values, attitudes, motivations, and orientations. The correlates investigated in this study have been the following: the proliferation of market towns and the concentration of central places, the travel patterns and transport costs of farmers, the synchronous movement of rural and big-city prices, the convergence of farm prices, the price elasticity of the slaughter weights of hogs, the extension of credit networks to more remote credit partners, the increasing liquidity of rural portfolio holdings, the enhanced negotiability of financial instruments, free-floating interest rates, the convergence of wage rates for hired farm labor, the growth of labor productivity, a shift in crop mix and land use, more intensive use of inputs (among which may be laborers on monthly contracts), increased outputs, increased yields, and, finally, evidence of the shift of resources out of agriculture that is the sine qua non of economic development.

That with respect to all these indicators there is a break point between 1785 and 1800[2] makes the case, both as strongly and as strongly empirical as I think it can be made, that Massachusetts agriculture, the preindustrial economy that rested upon it, and the farm family it rested upon were all transformed by and under the subtle dominion of regional and interregional markets for labor, farm commodities, and capital that emerged soon after the Revolution.

The dynamism ran *from* agriculture *to* industry. It was market-driven productivity *increases* in agriculture, not stagnation, that permitted the

---

2. It will be recalled, however, that, on the one hand, what we have called a *proto-market* process had emerged by 1750 and that, on the other hand, the onset of price-responsive behavior in the supply of pork appeared, in the regression analysis, to come between 1810 and 1820.

exodus of labor from agriculture to industry[3] and that made it possible, well in advance of improvements in farm technology in the region, for a decreasing share of the labor force to feed an increasingly nonagricultural population. Market-driven alterations in the social relations of the farm family delivered labor from the family farm to manufacturing. The enhanced liquidity and negotiability of financial instruments (also, of course, market driven) delivered savings accumulated in the rural economy to the burgeoning insurance, banking, manufacturing, and infrastructure sectors. The expansion of markets worked here, as it did in early manufacturing, to "unleash powerful forces that acted to raise productivity . . . without major additions to the stock of capital equipment"[4] and to achieve thereby self-sustaining growth.

Decades of experience in the planning of Third World economic development have sharpened our understanding of the role of agriculture in that process. The rising productivity of agriculture is accomplished in the face of implacable income and price inelasticities of demand, falling prices, falling farm incomes, constant returns to scale, and worsening terms of trade, the combination of which drives resources out of agriculture to higher earnings elsewhere. When the market is allowed to preside, agriculture is doomed to grow by shrinking.

The process of rural transformation under the aegis of a market economy—which is to say, the sectoral decline of agriculture—produces losers as well as winners. The costs of being among the losers can be very high,[5] too high for many governments in Europe, Japan, and, to a lesser extent, the United States to contemplate even if the financial burden of impeding the decline is far higher. It is small wonder that eastern Europe, overwhelmingly agrarian, approaches capitalism and the market economy that is at its origin, with apprehension.

3. Thus, my findings controvert the position taken by Field in "Sectoral Shift in Antebellum Massachusetts."

4. Sokoloff, "Productivity Growth in Manufacturing," 725.

5. A particularly vivid story of one such loser is told in Johnson, "The Modernization of Mayo Greenleaf Patch."

Bibliography

Abramovitz, Moses. 1989. *Thinking about Growth and Other Essays on Economic Growth and Welfare.* New York: Cambridge University Press.

Adams, Donald R., Jr. 1986. "Prices and Wages in Maryland, 1750–1850." *Journal of Economic History* 46, no. 3:625–45.

Adams, Thurston M. 1944. *Prices Paid by Vermont Farmers for Goods and Services and Received by Them for Farm Products, 1790–1940: Wages of Vermont Farm Labor, 1780–1940.* Bulletin no. 507. Burlington: Vermont Agricultural Experiment Station.

Aharoni, Yohanan, and Michael Avi-Yonah. 1968. *The Macmillan Bible Atlas.* Jerusalem: Carta; New York: Macmillan.

Albert, William. 1972. *The Turnpike Road System in England. 1663–1840.* Cambridge: Cambridge University Press.

Allen, David Grayson. 1981. *In English Ways: The Movement of Societies and the Transferral of English Local Law and Customs to Massachusetts Bay in the Seventeenth Century.* Chapel Hill: University of North Carolina Press.

Allen, Robert C. 1988. "The Growth of Labor Productivity in Early Modern English Agriculture." *Explorations in Economic History.* 25, no. 2:117–46.

———. 1988. "Inferring Yields from Probate Inventories." *Journal of Economic History.* 48, no. 1:117–25.

Anderson, B. L. 1970. "Money and the Structure of Credit in the Eighteenth Century." *Business History* 12, no. 2:85–101.

Anderson, Ralph V., and Robert E. Gallman. 1977. "Slaves as Fixed Capital: Slave Labor and Southern Economic Development." *Journal of American History* 64, no. 2:24–46.

Appleby, Andrew. 1979. "Grain Prices and Subsistence Crises in England and France, 1590–1740." *Journal of Economic History* 39, no. 4:865–87.

Appleby, Joyce O. 1978. *Economic Thought and Ideology in Seventeenth Century England.* Princeton, N.J.: Princeton University Press.

———. 1978. "The Social Origins of American Revolutionary Ideology." *Journal of American History* 64, no. 4:935–58.

Arensberg, Conrad. 1955. "American Communities." *American Anthropologist* 57 (December):1143–62.

Ashley, William J. 1894. *Introduction to English Economic History and Theory.* 3d ed. London: Longmans, Green.

Ashton, T. H., and C. H. E. Philpin, eds. 1985. *The Brenner Debate: Agrarian Class Structure and Economic Development in Pre-Industrial Europe.* Cambridge: Cambridge University Press.

Atack, Jeremy. 1988. "The Agricultural Ladder Revisited: A New Look at an Old Question with Some Data for 1860." University of Illinois and Harvard University. Typescript.

———. 1988. "Tenants and Yeomen in the Nineteenth Century." *Agricultural History* 62, no. 3:6–32.

————. 1989. "The Agricultural Ladder Revisited: A New Look at an Old Question with Some Data for 1860." *Agricultural History* 63, no. 1:1–25. (This is an abridged version of the unpublished paper.)

Atack, Jeremy, and Fred Bateman. 1981. "The 'Egalitarian Ideal' and the Distribution of Wealth in the Northern Agricultural Community: A Backward Look." *Review of Economics and Statistics* 63, no. 1:124–29.

————. 1984. "Mid-Nineteenth Century Crop Yields and Labor Productivity Growth in American Agriculture: A New Look at Parker & Klein." In *Technique, Spirit and Form in the Making of Modern Economies: Essays in Honor of William Parker.* ed. Gavin Wright and Gary Saxonhouse, 215–42. *Research in Economic History.* suppl. 3.

————. 1987. *To Their Own Soil: Agriculture in the Antebellum North.* Ames: Iowa State University Press.

Atack, Jeremy, Fred Bateman, and Thomas Weiss. n.d. *Risk, the Rate of Return, and the Pattern of Investment in Nineteenth-Century American Manufacturing.* Reprint no. 464. Urbana: Bureau of Economics and Business Research, University of Illinois.

Bailyn, Bernard. 1964. *The New England Merchants in the Seventeenth Century.* New York: Harper & Row.

Bardhan, Pranab K. 1980. "Interlocking Factor Markets and Agrarian Development: A Review of Issues." *Oxford Economic Papers.* 32, no. 1:82–98.

Baron, William R. 1982. "Eighteenth-Century New England Climate Variation and Its Suggested Impact on Society." *Maine Historical Society Quarterly.* 21, no. 4:201–18.

————. 1982. "The Reconstruction of Eighteenth Century Temperature Records through the Use of Content Analysis." *Climatic Change* 4:385–98.

————. 1984. "Frost-Free Record Reconstruction for Eastern Massachusetts, 1733–1980." *Journal of Climate and Applied Meteorology* 23, no. 2:317–19.

————. 1985. "A Reconstruction of New England Climate Using Historical Materials, 1620–1980." *Climatic Change in Canada* 5:229–45.

————. 1989. "Retrieving American Climate History: A Bibliographic Essay." *Agricultural History* 63, no. 2:7–35.

————. 1990. "A Comparative Study of Climate Fluctuation and Agricultural Practices in Southern New England, 1790–1850: Research Proposal and Final Report" Northern Arizona University. Typescript.

Barzel, Yoram. 1989. *Economic Analysis of Property Rights.* New York: Cambridge University Press.

Bateman, Fred. 1969. "Labor Inputs and Productivity in American Dairy Agriculture, 1850–1910." *Journal of Economic History.* 29, no. 2:206–29.

Bateman, Fred, and Jeremy Atack. 1979. "The Profitability of Northern Agriculture in 1860." *Research in Economic History* 4:87–125.

Battalio, Raymond C., and John Kagel. 1970. "The Structure of Antebellum Slave Agriculture: South Carolina: A Case Study." *Agricultural History.* 44 no. 1:25–37.

Battis, J. Emery. 1962. *Saints and Sectaries: Anne Hutchinson and the Antinomian Controversy in the Massachusetts Bay Colony.* Chapel Hill: University of North Carolina Press.

Beales, Ross W. 1989. "The Reverend Ebenezer Parkman's Farm Workers, Westborough, Massachusetts, 1726–82." *Proceedings of the American Antiquarian Society,* 99, no. 1:121–49.

Becker, Gary S. 1965. "A Theory of the Allocation of Time." *Economic Journal* 75, no. 299 (September):493–517.

———. 1981. *A Treatise on the Family.* Cambridge, Mass.: Harvard University Press.

Bell, Daniel. 1976. *The Cultural Contradictions of Capitalism.* New York: Basic.

Belshaw, Cyril S. 1965. *Traditional Exchange and Modern Markets.* Englewood Cliffs, N.J.: Prentice-Hall.

Belz, Herman J. 1967. "Currency Reform in Colonial Massachusetts, 1749–1750." *Essex Institute Historical Collections* 103, no. 1:66–84.

Bender, Thomas. 1978. *Community and Social Change in America.* New Brunswick, N.J.: Rutgers University Press.

Berlin, Isaiah. 1963. *Karl Marx: His Life and Environment.* 3d ed. Oxford: Oxford University Press.

Berry, Thomas S. 1942. *Western Prices before 1861: A Study of the Cincinnati Market.* Harvard Economic Studies no. 74. Cambridge, Mass.: Harvard University Press.

———. 1968. *Estimated Annual Variations in Gross National Product. 1789–1909.* Richmond, Va.: Bostwick.

Biddick, Kathleen. 1985. "Medieval English Peasants and Market Involvement." *Journal of Economic History* 45, no. 4:823–31.

———. 1987. "Missing Links: Taxable Wealth, Markets and Stratification among Medieval English Peasants." *Journal of Interdisciplinary History* 18 (Autumn): 277–98.

Bidwell, Percy W. 1916. "Rural Economy in New England at the Beginning of the Nineteenth Century." *Transactions of the Connecticut Academy of Arts and Sciences.* 20 (April):241–399.

———. 1921. "The Agricultural Revolution in New England." *American Historical Review* 26 (July):683–702.

Bidwell, Percy W., and John I. Falconer. [1925] 1941. *History of Agriculture in the Northern United States, 1620–1860.* Reprint. New York. Peter Smith.

Binswanger, Hans P., and Mark R. Rosenzweig, eds. 1984. *Contractual Arrangements, Employment, and Wages in Rural Labor Markets in Asia.* New Haven, Conn.: Yale University Press.

Bloch, Marc. 1961. *The Feudal Society.* Vol. 1, *The Growth of Ties of Dependence.* Chicago: University of Chicago Press.

Blodget, Samuel, Jr. [1806] 1964. *Economica: A Statistical Manual for the U.S. of A.* Reprint. New York: A. M. Kelley.

Bois, Guy. 1985. "Against the Neo-Malthusian Orthodoxy." In *The Brenner Debate: Agrarian Class Structure and Economic Development in Pre-Industrial Europe,* ed. T. H. Ashton and C. H. E. Philbin. Cambridge: Cambridge University Press.

Bonomi, Patricia U. 1986. *Under the Cope of Heaven: Religion, Society and Politics in Colonial America.* New York: Oxford University Press.

Boserup, Ester. 1965. *The Conditions of Agricultural Growth: The Economics of Agrarian Change under Population Pressure.* Chicago: Aldine.

Boyer, Paul, and Stephen Nissenbaum. 1974. *Salem Possessed: The Social Origins of Witchcraft.* Cambridge, Mass.: Harvard University Press.

Braudel, Fernand. 1982. *Civilization and Capitalism, 15th to 18th Century.* Vol. 1, *The*

Structures of Everyday Life. Vol. 2, *The Wheels of Commerce*. New York: Harper & Row.

Braudel, Fernand, and Frank Spooner. 1967. "Prices in Europe from 1450 to 1750." In *The Cambridge Economic History of Europe*, vol. 4, *The Economy of Expanding Europe in the 16th and 17th Centuries*, ed. E. E. Rich and C. H. Wilson. Cambridge: Cambridge University Press.

Brooke, John L. 1989. *The Heart of the Commonwealth: Society and Political Culture in Worcester County, Massachusetts, 1713–1861*. New York: Cambridge University Press.

———. 1992. "A Deacon's Orthodoxy: Religion, Class, and the Moral Economy of Shays's Rebellion." In *In Debt to Shays: The Bicentennial of an Agrarian Insurrection*, ed. Robert A. Gross. Charlottesville: University of Virginia Press.

Brown, Abram English. 1900. *Faneuil Hall and the Faneuil Hall Market: Or, Peter Faneuil and His Gift*. Boston: Lee & Shepard.

Brown, Richard D. 1989. *Knowledge Is Power: The Diffusion of Information in Early America, 1700–1865*. New York: Oxford University Press.

Bruchey, Stuart. 1956. *Robert Oliver, Merchant of Baltimore, 1783–1819*. Baltimore: Johns Hopkins University Press.

Burbank, Harold Hitchings. 1915. "The General Property Tax in Massachusetts, 1771–1792." Ph.D. diss., Harvard University.

Bureau of Labor Statistics. U.S. Department of Labor. 1929. *The History of Wages in the United States from Colonial Times to 1928*. Bulletin no. 499. Washington, D.C.

Bushman, Richard L. 1967. *From Puritan to Yankee: Character and the Social Order in Connecticut, 1690–1765*. Cambridge, Mass.: Harvard University Press.

Cain, Glen G. 1976. "The Challenge of Segmented Labor Market Theories to Orthodox Theory: A Survey." *Journal of Economic Literature* 14, no. 4:1215–57.

Caldwell, J. C. 1981. "The Mechanisms of Demographic Change in Historical Perspective." *Population Studies* 35 (March):5–27.

Calomiris, Charles W. 1988. "Institutional Failure, Monetary Scarcity, and the Depreciation of the Continental." *Journal of Economic History* 48, no. 1:47–68.

Carman, Harry J., and Rexford G. Tugwell, eds. 1934. *Jared Eliot's Essays upon Field Husbandry in New England and Other Papers, 1748–1762*. New York: Columbia University Press.

Cassedy, James H. 1969. *Demography in Early America: Beginnings of the Statistical Mind, 1600–1800*. Cambridge, Mass.: Harvard University Press.

Chickering, Jesse. 1846. *A Statistical View of the Population of Massachusetts from 1765 to 1840*. Boston: C. C. Little & J. Brown.

Clark, Christopher. 1979. "Household Economy, Market Exchange, and the Rise of Capitalism in the Connecticut Valley, 1800–1860." *Journal of Social History* 13, no. 2:169–89.

———. 1990. *The Roots of Rural Capitalism: Western Massachusetts, 1780–1860*. Ithaca, N.Y.: Cornell University Press.

Clark, Colin. 1967. *Population Growth and Land Use*. New York: St. Martin's.

Clark, Elaine. 1983. "Medieval Labor Law and English Local Courts." *American Journal of Legal History* 27 (October):330–53.

Coelho, Philip R. P., and James F. Shepherd. 1979. "The Impact of Regional Differences in Prices and Wages on Economic Growth: The United States in 1890." *Journal of Economic History* 39, no. 1:69–85.

Cohen, Charles L. 1987. "Onward Christian Politicos." *Reviews in American History* 15, no. 4:550–56.

Cohen, Mark Nathan, and George J. Armelagos, eds. 1984. *Paleopathology at the Origins of Agriculture*. Orlando, Fla.: Academic.

Cohen, Patricia Cline. 1982. *A Calculating People: The Spread of Numeracy in Early America*. Chicago: University of Chicago Press.

Cole, Arthur Harrison. 1938. *Wholesale Commodity Prices in the United States, 1700–1861*. Cambridge, Mass.: Harvard University Press.

Colles, Christopher. 1789. *Survey of the Roads of the United States of America*. New York: C. Colles.

Commonwealth of Massachusetts. 1856. *State of Industry in Massachusetts, 1855*. Boston: William White.

Conrad, Alfred, and John Meyer. 1964. "Statistical Inference and Historical Explanation." In *The Economics of Slavery and Other Studies in Econometric History*. Chicago: University of Chicago Press.

Cooper, Carolyn C. 1985. "The Roles of Thomas Blanchard's Woodworking Inventions in 19th-Century American Manufacturing Technology." Ph.D. diss., Yale University.

Cooper, Carolyn C. 1987. "Thomas Blanchard's Woodworking Machines: Tracking 19th Century Technological Diffusion." *Journal of the Society of Industrial Archaeology* 13:52–54.

Cooper, Carolyn C., and Patrick Malone. 1990. "The Mechanical Woodworker in Early Nineteenth Century New England as a Spin-off from Textile Industrialization." Yale University. Typescript.

Cooper, J. P. 1985. "In Search of Agrarian Capitalism." In *The Brenner Debate: Agrarian Class Structure and Economic Development in Pre-Industrial Europe*, ed. T. H. Ashton and C. H. E. Philpin. Cambridge: Cambridge University Press.

Corbin, Donald A. 1964. *Accounting and Economic Decisions*. New York: Dodd, Mead.

Cremin, Lawrence A. 1977. *Traditions of American Education*. New York: Basic.

Critchfield, Richard. 1981. *Villages*. Garden City, N.Y.: Anchor/Doubleday.

Cronon, William. 1983. *Changes in the Land: Indians, Colonists and the Ecology of New England*. New York: Hill & Wang.

Cropsey, Joseph. 1957. *Polity and Economy: An Interpretation of the Principles of Adam Smith*. The Hague: M. Nijhoff.

Crowley, Jack. 1974. *This Sheba, Self: The Conceptualization of Economic Life in Eighteenth Century America*. Baltimore: Johns Hopkins University Press.

Curtin, Philip. 1975. *Economic Change in Precolonial Africa: Senegambia in the Era of the Slave Trade*. Madison: University of Wisconsin Press.

Danhof, Clarence. 1969. *Change in Agriculture: The Northern United States, 1820–1870*. Cambridge, Mass.: Harvard University Press.

———. 1979. "The Farm Enterprise: The Northern United States, 1820–1860." *Research in Economic History* 4:127–91.

David, Paul A. 1967. "The Growth of Real Product in the United States before 1840: New Evidence, Controlled Conjectures." *Journal of Economic History* 27, no. 2: 151–97.

David, Paul A., and Peter Solar. 1977. "A Bicentenary Contribution to the History of the Cost of Living in America." *Research in Economic History* 2:1–80.

David, Paul A., and William A. Sundstrom. 1984. "Bargains, Bequests and Births." Working Paper no. 12. Stanford Project on the History of Fertility Control.

David, Paul A., and Peter Temin. 1974. "Slavery, the Progressive Institution?" *Journal of Economic History,* 34:739–83.

Davis, Lance E. 1963–64. "Capital Immobilities and Finance Capitalism: A Study of Economic Evolution in the United States, 1820–1920." *Explorations in Entrepreneurial History,* ser. 2, no. 1, pp. 88–105.

———. 1971. "Capital Mobility and American Growth." In *The Reinterpretation of American Economic History,* ed. Robert W. Fogel and Stanley L. Engerman. New York: Harper & Row.

Davis, Lance E., Robert E. Gallman, and Teresa D. Hutchins. 1989. "Productivity in Whaling: The New Bedford Fleet in the Nineteenth Century." In *Markets in History: Economic Studies of the Past,* ed. David W. Galenson 97–147. New York: Cambridge University Press.

Day, John. 1987. *The Medieval Market Economy.* Oxford: Oxford University Press.

Deane, Samuel. 1790. *The New England Farmer: or, Georgical Dictionary.* Worcester: Isaiah Thomas.

Demos, John. 1970. *A Little Commonwealth: Family Life in Plymouth Colony.* New York: Oxford University Press.

de Roover, Raymond. 1974. *Business, Banking and Economic Thought in Late Medieval and Early Modern Europe,* ed. J. Kirshner. Chicago: Univ. of Chicago Press.

DeVries, Jan. 1973. "On the Modernity of the Dutch Republic." *Journal of Economic History* 33, no. 1:191–202.

———. 1974. *The Dutch Rural Economy in the Golden Age, 1500–1700.* New Haven, Conn.: Yale University Press.

Doeringer, Peter B., and Michael J. Piore. 1971. *Internal Labor Markets and Manpower Analysis.* Lexington, Mass.: D. C. Heath.

Dwight, Timothy. [1822] 1969. *Travels in New England and New York.* Edited by Barbara Miller Solomon. Cambridge, Mass.: Belknap.

Earle, Carville V., and Ronald Hoffman. 1980. "The Foundation of the Modern Economy: Agriculture and the Costs of Labor in the United States and England, 1800–1860." *American Historical Review* 85, no. 5:1055–94.

Eatwell, John, Murray Milgate, and Peter Newman, eds. 1987. *The New Palgrave: A Dictionary of Economics.* New York: Stockton.

Ellis, Frank. 1988. *Peasant Economics: Farm Households and Agrarian Development.* Cambridge: Cambridge University Press.

Elster, Jon. 1985. *Making Sense of Marx.* Cambridge: Cambridge University Press.

Elton, G. R. 1983. "Two Kinds of History." In *Which Road to the Past?* by Robert William Fogel and G. R. Elton. New Haven, Conn.: Yale University Press.

Engerman, Stanley L., and Robert E. Gallman. n.d. "Economic Growth, 1783–1860." University of Rochester and University of North Carolina, Chapel Hill. Typescript.

Engerman, Stanley L., and Claudia Goldin. 1991. "Seasonality in Nineteenth Century Labor Markets." NBER Historical Factors in Long-Run Growth Working Paper no. 20. Cambridge, Mass.: National Bureau of Economic Research.

Faith, R. J. 1966. "Peasant Families and Inheritance Customs in Medieval England." *Agricultural History Review* 14:77–95.

Feeny, David. 1983. "The Moral or the Rational Peasant? Competing Hypotheses of Collective Action." *Journal of Asian Studies* 42, no. 4:769–89.

Feer, Robert A. 1958. "Shays's Rebellion." Ph.D. diss., Harvard University.

———. 1961. "Imprisonment for Debt in Massachusetts before 1800." *Mississippi Valley Historical Review* 48 (September):252–69.

Feige, Edgar L. 1990. "Perestroika and Socialist Privatization: What Is to Be Done: and How?" and "Socialist Privatization: A Rejoinder." *Comparative Economic Studies* 32 (Fall):1–81.

Felt, Joseph B. 1847. *Statistics of Taxation in Massachusetts Including Valuation and Population.* Boston: American Statistical Association.

Field, Alexander James. 1978. "Sectoral Shift in Antebellum Massachusetts: A Reconsideration." *Explorations in Economic History* 15 (April):146–71.

Field, Barry C. 1985. "The Evolution of Property-Rights Institutions: Common Lands in Early Massachusetts Agriculture." Department of Agriculture and Resource Economics, University of Massachusetts, Amherst. Typescript.

Field, Barry C., and Martha A. Kimball. 1984. "Agricultural Land Institutions in Colonial New England." University of Massachusetts, Amherst. Typescript.

Firth, Raymond. 1964. "A Viewpoint from Economic Anthropology." In *Capital, Saving and Credit in Peasant Societies: Studies from Asia, Oceania, the Caribbean and Middle America.* Chicago: Aldine.

Firth, Raymond, and B. S. Yamey, eds. 1964. *Capital, Saving and Credit in Peasant Societies: Studies from Asia, Oceania, the Caribbean and Middle America.* Chicago: Aldine.

Fisher, Douglas. 1989. "The Price Revolution: A Monetary Interpretation." *Journal of Economic History* 49, no. 4:883–902

Fishlow, Albert. 1965. *American Railroads and the Transformation of the Antebellum Economy.* Cambridge, Mass.: Harvard University Press.

Flaherty, David H., ed. 1969. *Essays in the History of Early American Law.* Chapel Hill: University of North Carolina Press.

Fogel, Robert W. 1964. *Railroads and American Economic Growth: Essays in Econometric History.* Baltimore: Johns Hopkins University Press.

———. 1989. "Second Thoughts on the European Escape from Hunger: Famines, Price Elasticities, Entitlements, Chronic Malnutrition, and Mortality Rates." NBER Historical Factors in Long-Run Growth Working Paper no. 1. Cambridge, Mass.: National Bureau of Economic Research.

———. 1990. "The Conquest of High Mortality and Hunger in Europe and America: Timing and Mechanisms." NBER Historical Factors in Long-Run Growth Working Paper no. 16. Cambridge, Mass.: National Bureau of Economic Research.

Fogel, Robert W., and G. R. Elton. 1983. *Which Road to the Past?* New Haven, Conn.: Yale University Press.

Fogel, Robert W., and Stanley L. Engerman. 1974. *Time on the Cross.* Vol. 1, *The Economics of American Negro Slavery.* Boston: Little, Brown.

Freyer, Tony A. 1976. "Negotiable Instruments and the Federal Courts in Antebellum American Business." *Business History Review* 50, no. 4:435–55.

Fussell, G. E., ed. 1936. *Robert Loder's Farm Accounts, 1610–1620.* London: Royal Historical Society.

Galenson, David W. 1989. "Labor Market Behavior in Colonial America: Servitude, Slavery, and Free Labor." In *Markets in History: Economic Studies of the Past,* ed. David W. Galenson, 52–96. New York: Cambridge University Press.

Gallman, Robert E. 1970. "Self-Sufficiency in the Cotton Economy of the Antebellum South." *Agricultural History* 44, no. 1:5–23.

———. 1972. "The Pace and Pattern of American Economic Growth." In *American Economic Growth: An Economist's History of the United States,* ed. Lance E. Davis, Richard A. Easterlin, William N. Parker, et al., 15–60. New York: Harper & Row.

———. 1988. "Changes in the Level of Literacy in a New Community of Early America." *Journal of Economic History* 48, no. 3:567–82.

———. 1992. "American Economic Growth before the Civil War: The Testimony of the Capital Stock Estimates." In *American Economic Growth and Standards of Living before the Civil War,* ed. Robert E. Gallman and John Wallis. Chicago: University of Chicago Press.

Gallman, Robert E., and John Wallis, eds. 1992. *American Economic Growth and Standards of Living before the Civil War.* Chicago: University of Chicago Press.

Gardner, Martin. 1987. "Count-Up." *New York Review of Books* (3 December), 34–36.

Garrison, J. Ritchie. 1985. "Surviving Strategies: The Commercialization of Life in Rural Massachusetts, 1790–1860." Ph.D. diss., University of Pennsylvania.

———. 1987. "Farm Dynamics and Regional Exchange: The Connecticut Valley Beef Trade, 1670–1850." *Agricultural History* 61, no. 3:1–17.

Geertz, Clifford. 1963. *Peddlers and Princes: Social Change and Economic Modernization in Two Indonesian Towns.* Chicago: University of Chicago Press.

Gerschenkron, Alexander. 1968. *Continuity in History and Other Essays.* Cambridge, Mass.: Belknap.

Goldin, Claudia, and Robert A. Margo. 1989. "The Poor at Birth: Birth Weights and Infant Mortality at Philadelphia's Almshouse Hospital, 1848–1873." *Explorations in Economic History* 26, no. 3:360–79.

Goldthwaite, Richard A. 1980. *The Building of Renaissance Florence: An Economic and Social History.* Baltimore: Johns Hopkins University Press.

Gordon, Robert B. 1990. "Edge Tools in Context." Paper presented at Old Sturbridge Village, Sturbridge, Mass.

Goubert, Pierre. 1960. *Beauvais et les Beauvaisis de 1600 à 1730: Contribution à l'histoire sociale de la France du XVII siècle.* 2 vols. Paris: S.E.V.P.E.N.

Grant, Charles S. 1961. *Democracy in the Connecticut Frontier Town of Kent.* New York: AMS.

Greenhut, Melvin L. 1970. *A Theory of the Firm in Economic Space.* New York: Appleton-Century-Crofts.

Gregory, C. A. 1982. *Gifts and Commodities.* New York: Academic.

Greven, Philip J. 1970. *Four Generations: Population, Land, and Family in Colonial Andover, Massachusetts.* Ithaca, N.Y.: Cornell University Press.

Griliches, Zvi. 1968. "Agriculture: Productivity and Technology." In *The International Encyclopedia of the Social Sciences,* 1:241–45. Chicago: University of Chicago Press.

Gross, Robert A. 1982. "Culture and Cultivation: Agriculture and Society in Thoreau's Concord." *Journal of American History* 69 (June):42–61.

Gujarati, Damodar N. 1988. *Basic Econometrics.* 2d ed. New York: McGraw-Hill.

Gwyn, Julian. 1971. "Money Lending in New England: The Case of Admiral Sir Peter Warren and His Heirs." *New England Quarterly* 44, no. 1:117–34.

Habakkuk, H. J. 1962. *American and British Technology in the Nineteenth Century: The Search for Labour-Saving Inventions.* Cambridge: Cambridge University Press.

Hahn, Steven. 1983. *The Roots of Southern Populism: Yeoman Farmers and the Transformation of the Georgia Upcountry, 1850–1890.* New York: Oxford University Press.

Hahn, Steven, and Jonathan Prude, eds. 1985. *The Countryside in the Age of Capitalist Transformation: Essays in the Social History of Rural America.* Chapel Hill: University of North Carolina Press.

Hallagan, William S. 1980. "Labor Contracting in Turn-of-the-Century California Agriculture." *Journal of Economic History* 40, no. 4:757–76.

Hamilton, Earl J. 1934. *American Treasure and the Price Revolution in Spain, 1501–1650.* Cambridge, Mass.: Harvard University Press.

Hart, Albert Bushnell. 1928. *Commonwealth History of Massachusetts,* vol. 2. New York: States History Co.

Hart, Oliver, and Bengt Holmstrom. 1987. "The Theory of Contracts. In *Advances in Economic Theory,* ed. Truman F. Bewley. New York: Cambridge University Press.

Hartz, Louis. 1955. *The Liberal Tradition in America: An Interpretation of American Political Thought since the Revolution.* New York: Harcourt, Brace.

Harvey, Barbara. 1977. *Westminster Abbey and Its Estates in the Middle Ages.* Oxford: Oxford University Press.

Haskins, George L. 1969. "The Beginnings of Partible Inheritance in the American Colonies." In *Essays in the History of Early American Law,* ed. David H. Flaherty. Chapel Hill: University of North Carolina Press.

Henretta, James. 1978. "Families and Farms: Mentalité in Pre-Industrial America." *William and Mary Quarterly,* 3d ser., 35 (January):3–32.

Heyrman, Christine L. 1984. *Commerce and Culture: The Maritime Communities of Colonial Massachusetts, 1690–1750.* New York: Norton.

Hickey, Daniel. 1987. "Innovation and Obstacles to Growth in the Agriculture of Early Modern France: The Example of Dauphine." *French Historical Studies* 15, no. 2: 208–40.

Hirschman, Albert O. 1970. *Exit, Voice, and Loyalty: Responses to Decline in Firms, Organizations, and States.* Cambridge, Mass.: Harvard University Press.

———. 1986. *Rival Views of Market Society and Other Recent Essays.* New York: Viking.

Hoffman, Richard C. 1975. "Medieval Origins of the Common Fields." In *European Peasants and Their Markets: Essays in Agrarian History,* ed. William N. Parker and Eric L. Jones. Princeton, N.J.: Princeton University Press.

Hofstadter, Richard. 1948. *The American Political Tradition.* New York: Knopf.
———. 1970. *The Progressive Historians: Turner, Beard, Parrington.* New York: Knopf.
Holderness, B. A. 1973. "Elizabeth Parkin and Her Investments, 1733–66: Aspects of the Sheffield Money Market in the Eighteenth Century." *Transactions of the Hunter Archeological Society* 10:81–87.
———. 1975. "Credit in a Rural Community, 1660–1800." *Midland History* 3 (Autumn):94–115.
———. 1976. "Credit in English Rural Society before the Nineteenth Century, with Special Reference to the Period 1650–1720." *Agricultural History Review* 24, pt. 2:97–109.
Homer, Sidney. 1963. *A History of Interest Rates.* New Brunswick, N.J.: Rutgers University Press.
Horwitz, Morton J. 1977. *The Transformation of American Law, 1780–1860.* Cambridge, Mass.: Harvard University Press.
Hosmer, James Kendall, ed. 1908. [*John*] *Winthrop's Journal: "History of New England," 1630–1649.* 2 vols. New York: Scribner's.
Hubka, Thomas C. 1984. *Big House, Little House, Back House, Barn: The Connected Farm Buildings of New England.* Hanover, N.H.: University Press of New England.
Hughes, J. R. T. 1976. *Social Control in the Colonial Economy.* Charlottesville: University of Virginia Press.
———. 1976. "Transference and Development of Institutional Constraints upon Economic Activity." *Research in Economic History* 1:45–68.
Hutchinson, Terence W. 1988. *Before Adam Smith: The Emergence of Political Economy, 1662–1776.* Oxford: Basil Blackwell.
Innes, Stephen. 1983. *Labor in a New Land: Economy and Society in Seventeenth-Century Springfield.* Princeton, N.J.: Princeton University Press.
Jacobs, Jane. 1984. "Why the TVA Failed." *New York Review of Books* (10 May), pp. 41–48.
Jacobson, David L., ed. 1965. *The English Libertarian Heritage: From the Writings of John Trenchard and Thomas Gordon in "The Independent Whig" and "Cato's Letters."* Indianapolis: Bobbs-Merrill.
Jaffee, David. 1990. "Peddlers of Progress and the Transformation of the Rural North, 1760–1860." City College of New York. Typescript.
Johnson, Paul E. 1982. "The Modernization of Mayo Greenleaf Patch: Land, Family, and Marginality in New England, 1766–1818." *New England Quarterly* 55 (December):488–516.
Jones, Alice Hanson. 1972. "Wealth Estimates for the New England Colonies about 1770." *Journal of Economic History* 32, no. 1:98–127.
———. 1977. *American Colonial Wealth: Documents and Methods.* 3 vols. 2d ed. New York: Arno.
———. 1980. *Wealth of a Nation to Be: The American Colonies on the Eve of the Revolution.* New York: Columbia University Press.
———. 1982. "Estimating Wealth of the Living from a Probate Sample." *Journal of Interdisciplinary History* 13, no. 2:273–300.

Jones, Eric L., and E. J. T. Collins. 1965. "The Collection and Analysis of Farm Record Books." *Journal of the Society of Archivists* 3:86–89.

Kantor, Shawn E., and J. Morgan Kousser. 1989. "Common Sense or Commonwealth? The Fence Law and Institutional Change in the Postbellum South." Social Science Working Paper no. 703. California Institute of Technology.

Karsten, Peter. 1990. " 'Bottomed on Justice': A Reappraisal of Critical Legal Studies Scholarship Concerning Breaches of Labor Contracts by Quitting or Firing in Britain and the U.S., 1630–1880," *Journal of American Legal History* 34:213–261.

Kelsey, Darwin, ed. 1972. *Farming in the New Nation: Interpreting American Agriculture, 1790–1840*. Washington, D.C.: Agricultural History Society.

Kindleberger, Charles P. 1989. *Spenders and Hoarders: The World Distribution of Spanish American Silver, 1550–1750*. Singapore: Institute of Southeast Asian Studies.

King, Mervyn A., and Jonathan I. Leape. 1984. "Wealth and Portfolio Composition: Theory and Evidence." NBER Working Paper no. 1468. Cambridge, Mass.: National Bureau of Economic Research.

Kirshner, Julius, and Jacob Klerman. 1991. "The Seven Percent Fund of Renaissance Florence." Genoa: Banchi pubblici, banchi privati e monti di Pietà, Nell'Europa preindustriale.

Klingaman, David C. 1972. "The Coastwise Trade of Colonial Massachusetts." *Essex Institute Historical Collections* 108, no. 3:217–34.

Kloppenburg, Jack Ralph, Jr. 1988. *First the Seed: The Political Economy of Plant Biotechnology, 1492–2000*. New York: Cambridge University Press.

Komlos, John. 1987. "The Height and Weight of West Point Cadets: Dietary Change in Antebellum America." *Journal of Economic History* 47, no. 4:897–927.

Konig, David Thomas. 1979. *Law and Society in Puritan Massachusetts: Essex County, 1629–1692*. Chapel Hill: University of North Carolina Press.

Kulikoff, Allan. 1989. "The Transition to Capitalism in Rural America." *William and Mary Quarterly*, 3d ser., 46, no. 1:120–44.

Kussmaul, Ann. 1981. *Servants in Husbandry in Early Modern England*. Cambridge: Cambridge University Press.

Kuznets, Simon. 1952. *Income and Wealth of the United States. Trends and Structures*. International Association for Research in Income and Wealth, ser. 2. Baltimore: Johns Hopkins University Press.

Lamar, Howard. 1985. "From Bondage to Contract: Ethnic Labor in the American West, 1600–1890." In *The Countryside in the Age of Capitalist Transformation: Essays in the Social History of Rural America*, ed. Steven Hahn and Jonathan Prude. Chapel Hill: University of North Carolina Press.

Lance, Martha. 1987. "Upper Quinebaug Mill Survey: Testing the Waters of Industrial Development." Paper presented at Old Sturbridge Village, Sturbridge, Mass.

Landels, J. G. 1978. *Engineering in the Ancient World*. Berkeley and Los Angeles: University of California Press.

Larkin, Jack. 1984. "The World of the Account Book: Some Perspectives on Economic Life in Rural New England in the Nineteenth Century." Paper presented at the Symposium on Social History, Keene State College, Keene, N.H.

————. 1989. "'Labor Is the Great Thing in Farming': The Farm Laborers of the Ward Family of Shrewsbury, Massachusetts, 1787–1860." *Proceedings of the American Antiquarian Society* 99, no. 1:189–226.

————. 1991. "From 'Country Mediocrity' to 'Rural Improvement': Transforming the Slovenly Countryside in Central Massachusetts, 1771–1840." Old Sturbridge Village, Sturbridge, Mass. Typescript.

Lebergott, Stanley. 1964. *Manpower in Economic Growth: The American Record since 1800*. New York: McGraw-Hill.

————. 1972. "Comments on Measuring Agricultural Change." In *Farming in the New Nation: Interpreting American Agriculture, 1790–1840*, ed. Darwin Kelsey, 227–33. Washington, D.C.: Agricultural History Society.

Lee, G. A. 1975. "The Concept of Profit in British Accounting, 1760–1900." *Business History Review* 49, no. 1:6–36.

Lemon, James T. 1967. "Household Consumption in the Eighteenth Century and Its Relationship to Production and Trade: The Situation among Farmers in Southeastern Pennsylvania." *Agricultural History* 41, no. 1:59–70.

————. 1980. "Early Americans and Their Social Environment." *Journal of Historical Geography* 6, no. 2:115–31.

Letwin, William. 1963. *The Origins of Scientific Economics: English Economic Thought, 1660–1776*. London: Methuen.

Libecap, Gary D. 1989. *Contracting for Property Rights*. New York: Cambridge University Press.

Lipton, Michael. 1968. "The Theory of the Optimising Peasant." *Journal of Development Studies* 4, no. 3:327–51.

Lockridge, Kenneth. 1970. *A New England Town: The First Hundred Years: Dedham, Massachusetts, 1636–1736*. New York: Norton.

Loehr, Rodney C. 1952. "Self-Sufficiency on the Farm." *Agricultural History* 26 (April):37–41.

Lyman, Richard B., Jr. 1989. "'What Is Done in My Absence?': Levi Lincoln's Oakham, Massachusetts, Farm Workers, 1807–20." *Proceedings of the American Antiquarian Society* 99:151–87.

McAlpin, Michelle. 1974. "Railroads, Prices and Peasant Rationality." *Journal of Economic History* 34, no. 3:662–84.

McCallum, Bennett T. 1990. "Money and Prices in Colonial America: A New Test of Competing Theories." NBER Working Paper no. 3383. Cambridge, Mass.: National Bureau of Economic Research.

McClelland, Peter. 1968. "Railroads, American Growth and the New Economic History: A Critique." *Journal of Economic History* 28, no. 1:102–23.

McCloskey, Donald N. 1985. "The Loss Function Has Been Mislaid: The Rhetoric of Significance Tests." *American Economic Review: Papers and Proceedings* 75 (May):201–5.

————. 1989. "The Open Fields of England: Rent, Risk, and the Rate of Interest, 1300–1815." In *Markets in History: Economic Studies of the Past*, ed. David W. Galenson, 5–51. New York: Cambridge University Press.

————. 1990. "New Findings on Open Fields." Paper presented to the Economic History Association.

McCusker, John J. 1978. *Money and Exchange in Europe and America, 1600–1775: A Handbook.* Chapel Hill: University of North Carolina Press.

McCusker, John J., and Russell R. Menard. 1985. *The Economy of British America, 1607–1789.* Chapel Hill: University of North Carolina Press.

McKibben, Bill. 1990. "What Are People For?" *New York Review of Books* (14 June), 30–34. (A review of books by Wendell Berry.)

McKinnon, Ronald. 1973. *Money and Capital in Economic Development.* Washington, D.C.: Brookings.

McMahon, Sarah F. 1981. "Provisions Laid by for the Family." *Historical Methods* 14:4–21.

———. 1985. "A Comfortable Subsistence: The Changing Composition of Diet in Rural New England, 1620–1840." *William and Mary Quarterly,* 3d ser. 42, no. 1:28–65.

———. 1989. "'All Things in Their Proper Season': Seasonal Rhythms of Diet in Nineteenth Century New England." *Agricultural History* 63, no. 2:130–51.

———. 1989. "Laying Foods By: Gender, Dietary Decisions, and the Technology of Food Preservation in New England Households, 1750–1850." Bowdoin College. Typescript.

Main, Gloria L. 1974. "The Correction of Biases in Colonial American Probate Records." *Historical Methods Newsletter* 8, no. 1:10–28.

Maine, Henry Sumner. 1861. *Ancient Law: Its Connection with the Early History of Society, and Its Relation to Modern Ideas.* London: J. Murray.

Mann, Bruce H. 1987. *Neighbors and Strangers: Law and Community in Early Connecticut.* Chapel Hill: University of North Carolina Press.

Manzoni, Alesssandro. [1827] 1961. *The Betrothed.* Reprint. New York: Dutton.

Margo, Robert A. 1992. "Wages and Prices during the Antebellum period: A Survey and New Evidence." In *American Economic Growth and Standards of Living before the Civil War,* ed. Robert E. Gallman and John Wallis. Chicago: University of Chicago Press.

Margo, Robert A., and Georgia C. Villaflor. 1987. "The Growth of Wages in Antebellum America: New Evidence." *Journal of Economic History* 47, no. 4:873–95.

Marini, Stephen A. 1986. "The Religious World of Daniel Shays." Wellesley College. Typescript.

Marshall, Alfred. [1890] 1946. *Principles of Economics.* 8th ed. Reprint. London: Macmillan.

Martin, Robert. 1939. *National Income in the United States, 1799–1938.* New York: National Industrial Conference Board.

Massachusetts Agricultural Repository and Journal. 1793–1832. Boston.

Massachusetts Society for Promoting Agriculture. 1799–1816. *Papers.* Boston.

Mayr, Otto. 1970. *The Origins of Feedback Control.* Cambridge, Mass.: MIT Press.

———. 1986. *Authority, Liberty and Automatic Machinery in Early Modern Europe.* Baltimore: Johns Hopkins University Press.

Merrill, Michael. 1977. "Cash Is Good to Eat: Self-Sufficiency and Exchange in the Rural Economy of the United States." *Radical History Review* 3, no. 4:42–71.

———. 1983. "The Ghost of Karl Polanyi: Another View of Early American Farmers and Their Markets." Princeton, N.J. Typescript.

Metzer, Jacob. 1972. "Some Aspects of Railroad Development in Tsarist Russia."
    Ph.D. diss., University of Chicago.
Miskimin, Harry A. 1971. "Agenda for Early Modern Economic History." *Journal of
    Economic History* 31, no. 1:172–83.
Mokyr, Joel. 1977. "Demand vs. Supply in the Industrial Revolution." *Journal of Eco-
    nomic History* 37, no. 4:981–1008.
————, ed. 1985. *The Economics of the Industrial Revolution.* Totowa, N.J.: Rowman
    & Allanheld.
————. 1988. "Was There a British Industrial Evolution?" Evanston, Ill.: Northwestern
    University. Typescript.
————. 1990. "Comments on McCloskey. . . ." Paper presented at the meeting of the
    Economic History Association, 13 September.
Morison, Samuel Eliot. 1921. *The Maritime History of Massachusetts, 1783–1860.*
    Boston: Houghton, Mifflin.
Morse, Jedidiah. 1810. *The American Gazeteer.* Boston: Thomas & Andrews.
————. 1812. *The American Universal Geography.* Boston: Thomas & Andrews.
Mosher, A. T. 1966. *Getting Agriculture Moving: Essentials for Development and Mod-
    ernization.* New York: Praeger.
Mun, Thomas. 1641. *England's Treasure by Forraign Trade.* Abridged in Leonard Dal-
    ton Abbott, ed. *Masterworks of Economics,* vol. 1, pp. 1–27. New York: McGraw-
    Hill, 1946.
Murrin, John. 1972. "Review Essay." *History and Theory* 11:226–75. (Review of De-
    mos, Greven, Zuckerman, and Lockridge.)
Mutch, Robert E. 1977. "Yeoman and Merchant in Pre-Industrial America: Eighteenth-
    Century Massachusetts as a Case Study." *Societas* 7, no. 4:279–302.
Nash, Manning, 1966. *Primitive and Peasant Economic Systems.* San Francisco: Chan-
    dler.
Nelson, Benjamin. 1969. *The Idea of Usury: From Tribal Brotherhood to Universal
    Otherhood.* 2d ed. Chicago: University of Chicago Press.
Nelson, William E. 1975. *The Americanization of the Common Law: The Impact of
    Legal Change on Massachusetts Society, 1760–1830.* Cambridge, Mass.: Harvard
    University Press.
Nerlove, Marc. 1958. *The Dynamics of Supply: Estimation of Farmers' Response to
    Price.* Baltimore: Johns Hopkins University Press.
North, Douglass C. 1990. *Institutions, Institutional Change and Economic Perform-
    ance.* New York: Cambridge University Press.
North, Douglass C., and Barry R. Weingast. 1989. "Constitutions and Commitment:
    Evolution of Institutions Governing Public Choice in Seventeenth-Century En-
    gland." *Journal of Economic History* 49, no. 4:803–32.
Ommer, Rosemary E., ed. 1990. *Merchant Credit and Labour Strategies in Historical
    Perspective.* Fredericton, New Brunswick: Acadiensis.
Overton, Mark. 1979. "Estimating Crop Yields from Probate Inventories: An Example
    from East Anglia, 1585–1735." *Journal of Economic History* 39, no. 2:363–78.
Parker, William N. 1972. "Agriculture." In *American Economic Growth: An Econo-
    mist's History of the United States,* ed. Lance E. Davis, Richard A. Easterlin,
    William N. Parker, et al., 369–417. New York: Harper & Row.

Parker, William N., and Eric L. Jones, eds. 1975. *European Peasants and Their Markets: Essays in Agrarian History.* Princeton, N.J.: Princeton University Press.

Parker, William N., and Judith L. V. Klein. 1966. "Productivity Growth in Grain Production in the United States, 1840–60 and 1900–10." In *Output, Employment and Productivity in the United States after 1800*, Studies in Income and Wealth, vol. 30, pp. 523–82. Princeton, N.J.: Princeton University Press.

Parker, William N., and Franklee G. Whartenby. 1960. "The Growth of Output before 1840." In *Trends in the American Economy in the Nineteenth Century*, Studies in Income and Wealth, vol. 24. Princeton, N.J.: Princeton University Press.

Parks, Roger Neal. 1966. "The Roads of New England, 1790–1840." Ph.D. diss., Michigan State University.

Paskoff, Paul F. 1980. "Labor Productivity and Managerial Efficiency against a Static Technology: The Pennsylvania Iron Industry, 1750–1800." *Journal of Economic History* 40, no. 1:129–35.

———. 1983. *Industrial Evolution: Organization, Structure and Growth of the Pennsylvania Iron Industry, 1750–1850.* Baltimore: Johns Hopkins University Press.

Phelps Brown, E. H., and Sheila V. Hopkins. 1955. "Seven Centuries of Building Wages." *Economica* 22 (August):195–206.

———. 1956. "Seven Centuries of the Prices of Consumables, Compared with Builders' Wage-Rates." *Economica* 23 (November):296–314.

———. 1957. "Wage Rates and Prices: Evidence for Population Pressure in the Sixteenth Century." *Economica* 24 (November):289–306.

Platteau, Jean-Philippe. 1989. "Traditional Systems of Social Security and Hunger Insurance: Some Lessons from the Evidence Pertaining to Third World Village Societies." In *Social Security in Developing Countries*, ed. E. Ahmad, J. P. Drèze, J. Hills, and A. K. Sen. Oxford: Oxford University Press.

Polanyi, Karl. 1957. *The Great Transformation: The Political and Economic Origins of Our Time.* Boston: Beacon.

———. 1957. *Trade and Markets in the Early Empires: Economies in History and Theory.* Glencoe, Ill.: Free Press.

———. 1968. *Primitive, Archaic and Modern Economies: Essays of Karl Polanyi.* Edited by George Dalton. Garden City, N.Y.: Anchor.

Pollard, Sidney. 1965. *The Genesis of Modern Management: A Study of the Industrial Revolution in Great Britain.* Cambridge, Mass.: Harvard University Press.

Pollock, Sir Frederick, and Frederic William Maitland. [1895] 1968. *The History of English Law before the Time of Edward I.* 2 vols. Cambridge: Cambridge University Press.

Postan, M. M. 1972. *The Medieval Economy and Society.* Berkeley: University of California Press.

Poulson, B. W. 1975. *Value Added in Manufacturing, Mining, and Agriculture in the American Economy from 1809 to 1839.* New York: Arno.

Powell, Sumner Chilton. 1963. *Puritan Village: The Formation of a New England Town.* Middletown, Conn.: Wesleyan University Press.

Pred, Allan. 1973. *Urban Growth and the Circulation of Information: The U.S. System of Cities, 1790–1840.* Cambridge, Mass.: Harvard University Press.

Prest, W. R. 1976. "Stability and Change in Old and New England: Clayworth and Dedham." *Journal of Interdisciplinary History* 6 (Winter):359–74.

Pruitt, Bettye Hobbs. 1981. "Agriculture and Society in the Towns of Massachusetts, 1771: A Statistical Analysis." Ph.D. diss., Boston University.

———. 1984. "Self-Sufficiency and the Agricultural Economy of Eighteenth-Century Massachusetts." *William and Mary Quarterly,* 3d ser., 41 (January):333–64.

Raftis, J. Ambrose. 1957. *The Estates of Ramsey Abbey: A Study in Economic Growth and Organization.* Toronto: Pontifical Institute of Mediaeval Studies.

Ransom, Roger L., and Richard Sutch. 1977. *One Kind of Freedom: The Economic Consequences of Emancipation.* New York: Cambridge University Press.

Reddy, William M. 1984. *The Rise of Market Culture: The Textile Trade and French Society, 1750–1900.* New York: Cambridge University Press.

Redlich, Fritz. 1969. "On the Origin of Created Deposits in the Commonwealth of Massachusetts." *Business History Review* 43, no. 2:204–8.

Reed, Clyde G. 1973. "Transactions Costs and Differential Growth in Seventeenth Century Western Europe." *Journal of Economic History* 33, no. 1:177–90.

Reyerson, Kathryn L. 1985. *Business, Banking and Finance in Medieval Montpellier.* Toronto: Pontifical Institute of Mediaeval Studies.

Rich, E. E., and C. H. Wilson, eds. 1967. *The Cambridge Economic History of Europe.* Vol. 4, *The Economy of Expanding Europe in the Sixteenth and Seventeenth Centuries.* Cambridge: Cambridge University Press.

Richardson, John G. 1987. "Town versus Countryside and Systems of Common Schooling." *Social Science History* 11, no. 4:401–32.

Rikoon, J. Sanford. 1988. *Threshing in the Midwest, 1820–1940: A Study of Traditional Culture and Technological Change.* Bloomington: Indiana University Press.

Roberts, Christopher. 1938. *The Middlesex Canal, 1793–1860.* Harvard Economic Studies, vol. 41. Cambridge, Mass.: Harvard University Press.

Rogin, Leo. 1931. *The Introduction of Farm Machinery and Its Relation to the Productivity of Labor in the Agriculture of the United States during the Nineteenth Century.* University of California Publications in Economics no. 9. Berkeley: University of California Press.

Rosen, Sherwin. 1985. "Implicit Contracts: A Survey." *Journal of Economic Literature* 23, no. 3:1144–75.

Rosenbloom, Joshua L. 1987. "The Integration of U.S. Labor Markets, 1870–1898: An Examination of the Evidence." Stanford University. Typescript.

———. 1990. "One Market or Many? Labor Market Integration in the Late Nineteenth-Century United States." *Journal of Economic History* 50, no. 1:85–107.

———. 1991. "Occupational Differences in Labor Market Integration: The United States in 1890." *Journal of Economic History* 51, no. 2:427–439.

Rostow, W. W. 1985. "No Random Walk: A Comment on 'Why Was England First?' " In *The Economics of the Industrial Revolution,* ed. Joel Mokyr. Totowa, N.J.: Rowman & Allenheld.

Rothenberg, Winifred B. 1979. "A Price Index for Rural Massachusetts, 1750–1855." *Journal of Economic History* 39, no. 4:975–1001.

———. 1981. "The Market and Massachusetts Farmers, 1750–1855." *Journal of Economic History* 41, no. 2:283–314.

———. 1985. "The Emergence of a Capital Market in Rural Massachusetts, 1730–1838." *Journal of Economic History* 45, no. 4:781–808.

———. 1987. "The Bound Prometheus: A Review of Steven Hahn and Jonathan Prude, eds., *The Countryside in the Age of Capitalist Transformation*." *Reviews in American History* 15, no. 4:628–37.

———. 1988. "The Emergence of Farm Labor Markets and the Transformation of the Rural Economy: Massachusetts, 1750–1855." *Journal of Economic History* 48, no. 3:537–66.

———. 1992. "The Productivity Consequences of Market Integration: Agriculture in Massachusetts, 1771–1801." In *American Economic Growth and Standards of Living before the Civil War*, ed. Robert E. Gallman and John Wallis. Chicago: University of Chicago Press.

———. 1992. "Structural Change in the Farm Labor Force: Contract Labor in Massachusetts Agriculture, 1765–1865." In *Strategic Factors in Nineteenth Century American Economic History: A Volume to Honor Robert W. Fogel*, ed. Claudia Goldin and Hugh Rockoff. Chicago: University of Chicago Press.

Rotstein, Abraham. 1970. "Karl Polanyi's Concept of Non-Market Trade." *Journal of Economic History* 30, no. 1:117–26.

Russell, Howard S. 1976. *A Long, Deep Furrow: Three Centuries of Farming in New England*. Hanover, N.H.: University Press of New England.

Rutman, Darrett B. 1965. *Winthrop's Boston: Portrait of a Puritan Town, 1630–1649*. Chapel Hill: University of North Carolina Press.

Sahlins, Marshall. 1972. *Stone Age Economics*. Chicago: Aldine-Atherton.

Salsbury, Stephen. 1967. *The State, the Investor, and the Railroad: The Boston & Albany, 1825–1867*. Cambridge, Mass.: Harvard University Press.

Schaefer, Donald F. 1987. "A Model of Migration and Wealth Accumulation: Farmers at the Antebellum Southern Frontier." *Explorations in Economic History* 24, no. 2:130–57.

Schama, Simon. 1987. *Embarrassment of Riches: An Interpretation of Dutch Culture in the Golden Age*. New York: Knopf.

Schlebeker, John T. 1976. "Agricultural Markets and Marketing in the North, 1774–1777." *Agricultural History* 50 (January):21–36.

Schob, David E. 1975. *Hired Hands and Plowboys: Farm Labor in the Midwest, 1815–60*. Urbana: University of Illinois Press.

Schumacher, Max George. 1975. *The Northern Farmer and His Markets during the Late Colonial Period*. New York: Arno. (Ph.D. diss. University of California, Berkeley, 1948.)

Scott, James. 1976. *The Moral Economy of the Peasant*. New Haven, Conn.: Yale University Press.

Seaman, Ezra C. 1846. *Essays on the Progress of Nations in Productive Industry, Civilization, Population, and Wealth*. Detroit: M. Geiger.

Searle, Eleanor. 1974. *Lordship and Community: Battle Abbey and Its Banlieu, 1066–1538*. Toronto: Pontifical Institute of Mediaeval Studies.

Shammas, Carole. 1990. *The Pre-Industrial Consumer in England and America*. Oxford: Oxford University Press.

Shammas, Carole, Marylynn Salmon, and Michel Dahlin. 1987. *Inheritance in Amer-*

ica: From Colonial Times to the Present. New Brunswick, N.J.: Rutgers University Press.

Silver, Morris. 1983. *Prophets and Markets: The Political Economy of Ancient Israel*. Boston: Kluwer-Nijhoff.

Simler, Lucy. 1990. "The Landless Worker: An Index of Economic and Social Change in Chester County, Pennsylvania, 1750–1820." *Pennsylvania Magazine of History and Biography* 114, no. 2:163–99.

Smith, Bruce D. 1984. "Money and Inflation in Colonial Massachusetts." *Federal Reserve Bank of Minneapolis Quarterly Review* 8, no. 1:1–14.

Smith, Carol A. 1974. "Economics of Marketing Systems." *Annual Review of Anthropology* 3:167–96.

Smith, Daniel Scott. 1973. "Population, Family and Society in Hingham, Massachusetts, 1635–1880." Ph.D. diss. University of California, Berkeley.

———. 1977. "Child-Naming Patterns and Family Structure Change: Hingham, Massachusetts, 1640–1880." Paper no. 76–5. *Newberry Papers in Family and Community History*.

———. 1984. "A Mean and Random Past: The Implications of Variance for History." *Historical Methods* 17, no. 3:141–48.

Smith, David C., William R. Baron, et al. 1982. "Climate Fluctuation and Agricultural Change in Southern and Central New England, 1765–1880." *Maine Historical Society Quarterly* 21, no. 4:179–200.

Smith, David C., Victor Konrad, et al. 1989. "Salt Marshes as a Factor in the Agriculture of Northeastern North America." *Agricultural History* 63, no. 2:270–94.

Sokoloff, Kenneth L. 1984. "Was the Transition from the Artisanal Shop to the Non-Mechanized Factory Associated with Gains in Efficiency? Evidence from the U.S. Manufacturing Censuses of 1820 and 1850." *Explorations in Economic History* 21, no. 4:351–82.

———. 1986. "Productivity Growth in Manufacturing during Early Industrialization: Evidence from the American Northeast, 1820–1860." In *Long-Term Factors in American Economic Growth*, ed. Stanley L. Engerman and Robert E. Gallman. NBER Studies in Income and Wealth, vol. 51. Chicago: University of Chicago Press.

———. 1986. "The Puzzling Record of Real Wage Growth in Early Industrial America: 1820–1860." University of California, Los Angeles. Typescript.

———. 1988. "Inventive Activity in Early Industrial America: Evidence from Patent Records, 1790–1846." *Journal of Economic History* 48, no. 4:813–50.

Sokoloff, Kenneth L., and David Dollar. 1991. "Agricultural Seasonality and the Organization of Manufacturing during Early Industrialization: The Contrast between Britain and the United States." University of California, Los Angeles, and the World Bank. Typescript.

Stabler, Lois K., ed. 1986. *Very Poor and of a Lo Make: The Journal of Abner Sanger*. Portsmouth, N.H.: Peter E. Randall for the Historical Society of Cheshire County.

Stephen, Sir Leslie. 1902. *History of English Thought in the Eighteenth Century*. 3d ed. London: Smith, Elder.

Stilgoe, John R. 1982. *Common Landscape of America, 1580–1845*. New Haven, Conn.: Yale University Press.

Strauss, Frederick, and Louis H. Bean. 1940. "Gross Farm Income and Indices of Farm

Production and Prices in the United States, 1869–1937." Technical Bulletin no. 703. Washington, D.C.: U.S. Department of Agriculture.

Strickland, William. 1801. *Observations on the Agriculture of the United States of America*. London: W. Bulmer.

Sturm, James L. 1969. "Investing in the United States, 1798–1893: Upper Wealth-Holders in a Market Economy." Ph.D. diss. University of Wisconsin.

Sundstrom, William A., and Paul A. David. 1988. "Old Age Security Motives, Labor Markets, and Farm Family Fertility in Antebellum America." *Explorations in Economic History* 25, no. 2:164–97.

Supple, Barry E. 1959. *Commercial Crisis and Change in England, 1600–1642: A Study in the Instability of a Mercantile Economy*. Cambridge: Cambridge University Press.

Sylla, Richard. 1971–72. "American Banking and Growth in the Nineteenth Century: A Partial View of the Terrain." *Explorations in Economic History* 9, no. 2:197–227.

Synenki, Alan, ed. 1990. *Archeological Investigations of Minute Man National Historical Park*. Vol. 1, *Farmers and Artisans of the Historical Period*. Cultural Resources Management Study no. 22. Boston: National Park Service, U.S. Department of the Interior.

Szatmary, David P. 1980. *Shays's Rebellion: The Making of an Agrarian Insurrection*. Amherst: University of Massachusetts Press.

Tax, Sol. 1963. *Penny Capitalism: A Guatemalan Indian Economy*. Chicago: University of Chicago Press.

Taylor, Alan. 1987. " 'A Struggle of Finesse': Creditors and Debtors on the Northeastern Frontier, 1780–1820." Boston University. Typescript.

Taylor, George R. 1951. *The Transportation Revolution. 1815–1860*. New York: Harper & Row.

———. 1964. "American Economic Growth before 1840: An Exploratory Essay." *Journal of Economic History* 24, no. 4:427–44.

Taylor, P. E. 1934. "The Turnpike Era in New England." Ph.D. diss. Yale University.

Temin, Peter. 1971. "Labor Scarcity in America." *Journal of Interdisciplinary History* 1 (Winter):251–64.

Thomas, Isaiah, Jr. 1803. *Massachusetts, Connecticut, Rhode Island, New Hampshire and Vermont Almanack for the Year of Our Lord 1804*. Worcester: Isaiah Thomas.

Thompson, E. P. 1963. *The Making of the English Working Class*. London: Vintage.

Timmer, C. Peter. 1988. "The Agricultural Transformation." In *Handbook of Development Economics*, vol. 1, ed. Hollis Chenery and T. N. Srinivasan, 276–331. Amsterdam: North Holland.

Towne, Marvin, and Wayne Rasmussen. 1960. "Farm Gross Product and Gross Investment in the Nineteenth Century." In *Trends in the American Economy in the Nineteenth Century*, Studies in Income and Wealth, vol. 24. Princeton, N.J.: Princeton University Press.

U.S. Census Office. 1850. *Seventh Census (1850), Manuscript Census of Population: Massachusetts*. Washington, D.C.

Vickers, Daniel. 1988. "Working the Fields in a Developing Economy: Essex County, Massachusetts, 1630–1675." In *Work and Labor in Early America*, ed. Stephen Innes. Chapel Hill: University of North Carolina Press.

Walett, Francis G., ed. 1974. *The Diary of Ebenezer Parkman, 1703–1782.* Worcester, Mass.: American Antiquarian Society.

Weiss, Thomas J. 1989. "Economic Growth before 1860." NBER Development of the American Economy Working Paper no. 7. Cambridge, Mass.: National Bureau of Economic Research.

———. 1992. "U.S. Labor Force Estimates and Economic Growth, 1800 to 1860." In *American Economic Growth and Standards of Living before the Civil War,* ed. Robert E. Gallman and John Wallis. Chicago: University of Chicago Press.

Weitzman, Martin L. 1974. "Prices vs. Quantities." *Review of Economic Studies* 41, no. 4:477–91.

Weld, Isaac, Jr. 1807. *Travels through the States of North America . . . during the Years 1795, 1796, and 1797.* London: J. Stockdale.

Whatley, Warren C. 1987. "Southern Agrarian Labor Contracts as Impediments to Mechanization." *Journal of Economic History* 47, no. 1:45–70.

Wilber, Clifford C., ed. 1924–27. *The Repertory.* 2 vols. Keene, N.H.

Wilson, Robert J., III. 1984. *The Benevolent Deity: Ebenezer Gay and the Rise of Rational Religion in New England, 1696–1787.* Philadelphia: University of Pennsylvania Press.

Wilson, Thomas. [1572] 1965. *A Discourse upon Usury.* With an introduction by R. H. Tawney. Reprint. New York: Augustus M. Kelley.

Wolf, Eric. 1957. "Closed, Corporate Peasant Communities in Mesoamerica and Central Java." *Southwestern Journal of Anthropology* 13 (Spring):1–18.

———. 1966. *Peasants.* Englewood Cliffs, N.J.: Prentice-Hall.

Wolfson, Robert. 1958. "An Econometric Investigation of Regional Differentials in American Agricultural Wages." *Econometrica* 26 (April):225–57.

World Bank. 1982. *World Development Report.* New York: Oxford University Press.

Wright, Carroll D. 1885. *History of Wages and Prices in Massachusetts, 1752–1883.* Boston: Wright & Potter.

Wright, Gavin, and Howard Kunreuther. 1975. "Cotton, Corn and Risk in the Nineteenth Century." *Journal of Economic History* 35, no. 3:526–51.

Wrigley, E. A. 1985. "Urban Growth and Agricultural Change: England and the Continent in the Early Modern Period." *Journal of Interdisciplinary History* 15:683–727.

Wrigley, E. A., and R. S. Schofield. 1981. *The Population History of England, 1541–1871.* Cambridge: Cambridge University Press.

Ziff, Larzer. 1974. *Puritanism in America: New Culture in a New World.* New York: Viking.

Zuckerman, Michael. 1970. *Peaceable Kingdoms: New England Towns in the Eighteenth Century.* New York: Knopf.

CREDITS

For those photographs reproduced on the title page and at the openings of chapters in this book, the captions and credit lines are given below. For all other illustrations, the appropriate captions and credit lines occur where the photos are reproduced in the book.

Title page: Painting of Deacon J. Richards's house (neg. B17015). © Old Sturbridge Village.

Chapters 1, 2, 4–9: Reproduced courtesy of the Society for the Preservation of New England Antiquities.

Ch. 1: Back of the Frary House, Deerfield, Massachusetts. Photograph by Emma L. Coleman, mid-1890s (neg. 15548-B).

Ch. 2: Garfield Place, Shrewsbury, Massachusetts. Photograph by William Parker, 1892–1895 (neg. 10301a-B).

Ch. 4: Ox team in orchard, Ground Nut Hill, Cape Neddick, Maine. Photograph by Frederick B. Quimby, 1892 (neg. 4426-B).

Ch. 5: Garfield barn floor, Shrewsbury, Massachusetts. Photograph by William Parker, 1892–1895 (neg. 10302a-B).

Ch. 6: Harvest time, Shrewsbury, Massachusetts (?) (neg. HH28721-A).

Ch. 7: Gathering onions, Deerfield, Massachusetts. Photograph by Emma L. Coleman, circa 1890 (neg. 7854-A).

Ch. 8: Ploughing, Ground Nut Hill, Cape Neddick, Maine. Photograph by Frederick B. Quimby, 1893 (neg. 4390-B).

Ch. 9: Road to York Village, Maine. Photograph by Frederick B. Quimby (neg. 4347-B).

Chapter 3: Account book of Henry Eames of Framingham. Reproduced courtesy of the Manuscripts Division, Baker Library, Harvard Business School, Cambridge, Massachusetts.

Author Index

Subject Index